VENETIAN LIFE

BY

W. D. HOWELLS

W. D. HOWELLS
VENETIAN LIFE

WITH ILLUSTRATIONS BY JOSEPH PENNELL

THE MARLBORO PRESS
MARLBORO, VERMONT
1989

First published in 1866.

The present reprint of VENETIAN LIFE is
based upon the 1885 edition.

Publication of this volume is made possible
in part by a grant from the National
Endowment for the Arts.

Manufactured in the United States of America

Library of Congress Catalog Card Number 88-64142

ISBN 0-910395-47-0

CONTENTS

LIST OF ILLUSTRATIONS

VENETIAN LIFE

CHAPTER I

VENICE IN VENICE

ONE night at the little theatre in Padua, the ticket-seller gave us the stage-box (of which he made a great merit), and so we saw the play and the by-play. The prompter, as noted from our point of view, bore a chief part in the drama (as indeed the prompter always does in the Italian theatre), and the scene-shifters appeared as prominent characters. We could not help seeing the virtuous wife, when hotly pursued by the villain of the

1

piece, pause calmly in the wings, before rushing, all tears and desperation, upon the stage; and we were dismayed to behold the injured husband and his abandoned foe playfully scuffling behind the scenes. All the shabbiness of the theatre was perfectly apparent to us; we saw the grossness of the painting and the unreality of the properties. And yet I cannot say that the play lost one whit of its charm for me, or that the working of the machinery and its inevitable clumsiness disturbed my enjoyment in the least. There was so much truth and beauty in the playing that I did not care for the sham of the ropes and gilding, and presently ceased to take any note of them. The illusion which I had thought an essential in the dramatic spectacle turned out to be a condition of small importance.

It has sometimes seemed to me as if fortune had given me a stage-box at another and grander spectacle, and I had been suffered to see this VENICE, which is to other cities like the pleasant improbability of the theatre to every-day, commonplace life, to much the same effect as that melodrama in Padua. I could not, indeed, dwell three years in the place without learning to know it differently from those writers who have described it in romances, poems, and hurried books of travel, nor help seeing from my point of observation the sham and cheapness with which Venice is usually brought out, if I may so speak, in literature. At the same time, it has never lost for me its claim upon constant surprise and regard, nor the fascination of its excellent beauty, its peerless picturesqueness, its sole and wondrous grandeur. It is true that the streets in Venice are canals; and yet you can walk to any part of the city, and need not take boat whenever you go out-of-doors, as I once fondly thought you must. But after all, though I find dry land enough in it, I do not find the place less unique, less a mystery, or less a charm. By day, the canals are still the main thoroughfares; and if these avenues are not so full of light and color as some would have us believe, they at least do not smell so offensively as others pretend. And by night they are still as dark and silent as when the secret vengeance of the Republic plunged its victims into the ungossiping depths of the Canalazzo!

Did the vengeance of the Republic ever do any such thing?

Possibly. In Venice one learns not quite to question that reputation for vindictive and gloomy cruelty alien historians have given to a government which endured so many centuries in the willing obedience of its subjects; but to think that the careful student of the old Republican system will condemn it for faults far different from those for which it is chiefly blamed. At all events, I find it hard to understand why, if the Republic was an oligarchy utterly selfish and despotic, it has left to all classes of Venetians so much regret and sorrow for its fall.

So, if the reader care to follow me to my stage-box, I imagine he will hardly see the curtain rise upon just the Venice of his dreams,—the Venice of Byron, of Rogers, and Cooper; or upon the Venice of his prejudices,—the merciless Venice of Darù, and of the historians who follow him. But I still hope that he will be pleased with the Venice he sees, and will think with me that the place loses little in the illusion removed; and—to take leave of our theatrical metaphor—I promise to fatigue him with no affairs of my own, except as allusion to them may go to illustrate Life in Venice; and positively he shall suffer no annoyance from the fleas and bugs which, in Latin countries, so often get from travellers' beds into their books.

Let us mention here at the beginning some of the sentimental errors concerning the place, with which we need not trouble ourselves hereafter, but which no doubt form a large part of every one's associations with the name of Venice. Let us take, for example, that pathetic swindle, the Bridge of Sighs. There are few, I fancy, who will hear it mentioned without connecting its mystery and secrecy with the taciturn justice of the Three, or some other cruel machinery of the Serenest Republic's policy. When I entered it the first time I was at the pains to call about me the sad company of those who had passed its corridors from imprisonment to death; and, I doubt not, many excellent tourists have done the same. I was somewhat ashamed to learn afterward that I had, on this occasion, been in very low society, and that the melancholy assemblage which I then conjured up was composed entirely of honest rogues, who might indeed have given as graceful and ingenious excuses for being in misfortune as the galley-slaves rescued by Don Quixote,—who might even have been very picturesque,—but who were not at all the material with which a well-regulated imagination would deal. The Bridge of Sighs was not built till the end of the sixteenth century, and no romantic episode of political imprisonment and punishment (except that of Antonio Foscarini) occurs in Venetian history later than that period. But the Bridge of Sighs could have nowise a savor of sentiment from any such episode, being, as it was, merely a means of communication between the Criminal Courts sitting in the Ducal Palace and the Criminal Prison across the little canal. Housebreakers, cut-purse knaves, and murderers do not commonly impart a poetic interest to places which have known them; and yet these are the only sufferers on whose Bridge of Sighs the whole sentimental world has looked with pathetic sensation ever since Byron drew attention to it. The name of the bridge was given by the people from that opulence of compassion which enables the Italians to pity even rascality in difficulties.[1]

Political offenders were not confined in the "prison on each hand" of the poet, but in the famous *pozzi* (literally, wells) or dungeons under the Ducal Palace. And what fables concerning these cells have not been uttered and believed! For my part, I prepared my coldest chills for their exploration, and I am not sure that before I entered their gloom some foolish and lying literature

---

[1] The reader will remember that Mr. Ruskin has said in a few words, much better than I have said in many, the same thing of sentimental errors about Venice:—

"The Venice of modern fiction and drama is a thing of yesterday, a mere efflorescence of decay, a stage-dream, which the first ray of daylight must dissipate into dust. No prisoner whose name is worth remembering, or whose sorrows deserved sympathy, ever crossed the Bridge of Sighs which is the centre of the Byronic ideal of Venice; no great merchant of Venice ever saw that Rialto under which the traveller now pauses with breathless interest; the statue which Byron makes Faliero address as one of his great ancestors was erected to a soldier of fortune a hundred and fifty years after Faliero's death."—*Stones of Venice.*

was not shaping itself in my mind, to be afterward written out as my Emotions on looking at them. I do not say now that they are calculated to enamor the unimpounded spectator with prison-life; but they are certainly far from being as bad as I hoped. They are not joyously light nor particularly airy, but their occupants could have suffered no extreme physical discomfort; and the thick wooden casing of the interior walls evidences at least the intention of the state to inflict no wanton hardships of cold and damp.

But on whose account had I to be interested in the *pozzi*? It was difficult to learn, unless I took the word of sentimental hearsay. I began with Marin Falier, but history would not permit the doge to languish in these dungeons for a moment. He was imprisoned in the apartments of state, and during one night only. His fellow-conspirators were hanged nearly as fast as taken.

Failing so signally with Falier, I tried several other political prisoners of sad and famous memory with scarcely better effect. To a man, they struggled to shun the illustrious captivity designed them, and escaped from the *pozzi* by every artifice of fact and figure.

The Carraras of Padua were put to death in the city of Venice, and their story is the most pathetic and romantic in Venetian history. But it was not the cells under the Ducal Palace which witnessed their cruel taking-off: they were strangled in the prison formerly existing at the top of the palace, called the Torresella.[2] It is possible, however, that Jacopo Foscari may have been confined in the *pozzi* at different times about the middle of the fifteenth century. With his fate alone, then, can the horror of these cells be satisfactorily associated by those who relish the dark romance of Venetian annals; for it is not to be expected that the less tragic fortunes of Carlo Zeno and Vitore Pisani, who may also have been imprisoned in the *pozzi,* can move the true sentimentalizer. Certainly, there has been anguish enough in the prisons of the Ducal Palace, but we know little of it by name, and cannot confidently relate it to any great historic presence.

---

[2] Galliciolli, *Memorie Venete.*

Touching the Giant's Stairs in the court of the palace, the inexorable dates would not permit me to rest in the delusion that the head of Marin Falier had once bloodily stained them as it rolled to the ground—at the end of Lord Byron's tragedy. Nor could I keep unimpaired my vision of the Chief of the Ten brandishing the sword of justice, as he proclaimed the traitor's death to the people from between the two red columns in the southern gallery of the palace;—that façade was not built till nearly a century later.

I suppose—always judging by my own average experience—that, besides these gloomy associations, the name of Venice will conjure up scenes of brilliant and wanton gayety, and that in the foreground of the brightest picture will be the Carnival of Venice, full of antic delight, romantic adventure, and lawless prank. But the carnival, with all the old merry-making life of the city, is now utterly obsolete, and, in this way, the conventional, masquerading, pleasure-loving Venice is become as gross a fiction as if, like that other conventional Venice of which I have but spoken, it had never existed. There is no greater social dullness and sadness, on land or sea, than in contemporary Venice.

The causes of this change lie partly in the altered character of the whole world's civilization, partly in the increasing poverty of the city, doomed four hundred years ago to commercial decay, and chiefly (the Venetians would be apt to tell you wholly) in the implacable anger, the inconsolable discontent, with which the people regard their present political condition.

If there be more than one opinion among men elsewhere concerning the means by which Austria acquired Venetia and the tenure by which she holds the province, there would certainly seem to be no division on the question of Venice. To the stranger first inquiring into public feeling, there is something almost sublime in the unanimity with which the Venetians appear to believe that these means were iniquitous, and that this tenure is abominable; and though shrewder study and carefuller observation will develop some interested attachment to the present government, and some interested opposition to it; though after-

knowledge will discover, in the hatred of Austria, enough meanness, lukewarmness, and selfish ignorance to take off its sublimity,
the hatred is still found marvellously unanimous and bitter. I
speak advisedly, and with no disposition to discuss the question or
exaggerate the fact. Exercising at Venice official functions by
permission and trust of the Austrian government, I cannot regard
the cessation of those functions as release from obligations both to
that government and my own, which render it improper for me, so
long as the Austrians remain in Venice, to criticise their rule, or
contribute, by comment on existing things, to embitter the feeling
against them elsewhere. I may, nevertheless, speak dispassionately
of facts of the abnormal social and political state of the place; and
I can certainly do this, for the present situation is so disagreeable
in many ways to the stranger forced to live there, the inappeasable
hatred of the Austrians by the Italians is so illiberal in application
to those in any wise consorting with them, and so stupid and
puerile in many respects, that I think the annoyance which it gives
the foreigner might well damp any passion with which he was
disposed to speak of its cause.

This hatred of the Austrians dates in its intensity from the defeat
of patriotic hopes of union with Italy, in 1859, when Napoleon
found the Adriatic at Peschiera, and the peace of Villafranca was
concluded. But it is not to be supposed that a feeling so general,
and so thoroughly interwoven with Venetian character, is altogether recent. Consigned to the Austrians by Napoleon I., confirmed in the subjection into which she fell a second time after
Napoleon's ruin by the treaties of the Holy Alliance, defeated in
several attempts to throw off her yoke, and loaded with heavier
servitude after the fall of the short-lived Republic of 1849, Venice
has always hated her masters with an exasperation deepened by
each remove from the hope of independence, and she now detests
them with a rancor which no concession short of absolute
relinquishment of dominion would appease.

Instead, therefore, of finding that public gayety and private
hospitality in Venice for which the city was once famous, the
stranger finds himself planted between two hostile camps, with

merely the choice of sides open to him. Neutrality is solitude and friendship with neither party; society is exclusive association with the Austrians or with the Italians. The latter do not spare one of their own number if he consorts with their masters, and though a foreigner might expect greater allowance, it is seldom shown to him. To be seen in the company of officers is enmity to Venetian freedom, and in the case of Italians it is treason to country and to race. Of course, in a city where there is a large garrison and a great many officers who have nothing else to do, there is inevitably some international love-making, although the Austrian officers are rigidly excluded from association with the citizens. But the Italian who marries an Austrian severs the dearest ties that bind her to life, and remains an exile in the heart of her country. Her friends mercilessly cast her off, as they cast off everybody who associates with the dominant race. In rare cases I have known Italians to receive foreigners who had Austrian friends, but this with the explicit understanding that there was to be no sign of recognition if they met them in the company of these detested acquaintance.

There are all degrees of intensity in Venetian hatred, and after hearing certain persons pour out the gall of bitterness upon the Austrians you may chance to hear these persons spoken of as tepid in their patriotism by yet more fiery haters. Yet it must not be supposed that the Italians hate the Austrians as individuals. On the contrary, they have rather a liking for them,—rather a contemptuous liking, for they think them somewhat slow and dull-witted,—and individually the Austrians are amiable people, and try not to give offence. The government is also very strict in its control of the military. I have never seen the slightest affront offered by a soldier to a citizen; and there is evidently no personal ill-will engendered. The Austrians are simply hated as the means by which an alien and despotic government is imposed upon a people believing themselves born for freedom and independence. This hatred, then, is a feeling purely political, and there is political machinery by which it is kept in a state of perpetual tension.

The Comitato Veneto is a body of Venetians residing within the province and abroad, who have charge of the Italian interests, and who work in every way to promote union with the dominions of Victor Emanuel. They live for the most part in Venice, where they have a secret press for the publication of their addresses and proclamations, and where they remain unknown to the police, upon whose spies they maintain an espionage. On every occasion of interest, the Committee is sure to make its presence felt; and from time to time persons find themselves in the possession of its printed circulars, stamped with the Committee's seal; but no one knows how or whence they came. Constant arrests of suspected persons are made, but no member of the Committee has yet been identified; and it is said that the mysterious body has its agents in every department of the government, who keep it informed of inimical action. The functions of the Committee are multiplied and various. It takes care that on all patriotic anniversaries (such as that of the establishment of the Republic in 1848, and that of the union of the Italian States under Victor Emanuel in 1860) salutes shall be fired in Venice, and a proper number of red, white, and green lights displayed. It inscribes revolutionary sentiments on the walls; and all attempts on the part of the Austrians to revive popular festivities are frustrated by the Committee, which causes petards to be exploded in the Place of St. Mark and on the different promenades. Even the churches are not exempt from these demonstrations: I was present at the Te Deum performed on the Emperor's birthday, in St. Mark's, when the moment of elevating the host was signalized by the bursting of a petard in the centre of the cathedral. All this, which seems of questionable utility, and worse than questionable taste, is approved by the fiercer of the Italianissimi; and though possibly the strictness of the patriotic discipline in which the members of the Committee keep their fellow-citizens may gall some of them, yet any public demonstration of content, such as going to the opera, or to the Piazza while the Austrian band plays, is promptly discontinued at a warning from the Committee. It is, of course, the Committee's business to keep the world informed of public feeling in Venice, and of each new act of Austrian severity. Its members are inflexible men, whose ability has been as frequently manifested as their patriotism.

The Venetians are now, therefore, a nation in mourning, and have, as I said, disused all their former pleasures and merry-makings. Every class, except a small part of the resident *titled* nobility (a great part of the nobility is in either forced or voluntary exile), seems to be comprehended by this feeling of despondency and suspense. The poor of the city formerly found their respite and diversion in the numerous holidays which fell in different parts of the year, and which, though religious in their general character, were still inseparably bound up in their origin with ideas of patriotism and national glory. Such of these holidays as related to the victories and pride of the Republic naturally ended with her fall. Many others, however, survived this event in all their splendor, but there is not one celebrated now as in other days. It is true that the churches still parade their pomps in the Piazza on the day of Corpus Christi; it is true that the bridges of boats are still built across the Canalazzo to the church of Our Lady of Salvation, and across the canal of the Giudecca to the temple of the Redeemer, on the respective festivals of these churches; but the concourse is always meagre, and the mirth is forced and ghastly. The Italianissimi have so far imbued the people with their own ideas and feelings that the recurrence of the famous holidays now merely awakens them to lamentations over the past and vague longings for the future.

As for the carnival, which once lasted six months of the year, charming hither all the idlers of the world by its peculiar splendor and variety of pleasure, it does not, as I said, any longer exist. It is dead, and its shabby, wretched ghost is a party of beggars, hideously dressed out with masks and horns and women's habits, who go from shop to shop droning forth a stupid song, and levying tribute upon the shopkeepers. The crowd through which these melancholy jesters pass regards them with a pensive scorn, and goes about its business untempted by the delights of carnival.

All other social amusements have shared in greater or less degree the fate of the carnival. At some houses *conversazioni* are still held, and it is impossible that balls and parties should not now and then be given. But the greater number of the nobles and the richer of the professional classes lead for the most part a life of listless seclusion, and attempts to lighten the general gloom and heaviness in any way are not looked upon with favor. By no sort of chance are Austrians, or Austriacanti, ever invited to participate in the pleasures of Venetian society.

As the social life of Italy, and especially of Venice, was, in great part, to be once enjoyed at the theatres, at the *caffè*, and at the other places of public resort, so is its absence now to be chiefly noted in those places. No lady of perfect standing among her people goes to the opera, and the men never go in the boxes, but if they frequent the theatre at all, they take places in the pit, in order that the house may wear as empty and dispirited a look as possible. Occasionally a bomb is exploded in the theatre, as a note of reminder, and as means of keeping away such of the nobles as are not enemies of the government. As it is less easy for the Austrians to participate in the diversion of comedy, it is less offence to attend the comedy, though even this is not good Italianissimism. In regard to the *caffè*, there is a perfectly understood system by which the Austrians go to one, and the Italians to another; and Florian's, in the Piazza, seems to be the only common ground in the city on which the hostile forces consent to meet. This is because it is thronged with foreigners of all nations, and to go there is not thought a demonstration of any kind. But the other *caffè* in the Piazza do not enjoy Florian's cosmopolitan immunity, and nothing would create more wonder in Venice than to see an Austrian officer at the Specchi, unless, indeed, it were the presence of a good Italian at the Quadri.

It is in the Piazza that the tacit demonstration of hatred and discontent chiefly takes place. Here, thrice a week, in winter and summer, the military band plays that exquisite music for which the Austrians are famous. The selections are usually from Italian operas, and the attraction is the hardest of all others for the music-loving Italian to resist. But he does resist it. There are some noble ladies who have not entered the Piazza, while the band was playing there, since the fall of the Republic of 1849; and one of good standing for patriotism has attended the concerts since the treaty of Villafranca in '59. Until very lately, the promenaders in the Piazza were exclusively foreigners, or else the families of such goverment officials as were obliged to show themselves there. Last summer, however, before the Franco-Italian convention for the evacuation of Rome revived the drooping hopes of the Venetians, they had begun visibly to falter in their long endurance. But this was, after all, only a slight and transient weakness. As a general thing, now, they pass from the Piazza when the music begins, and walk upon the long quay at the sea-side of the Ducal Palace; or if they remain in the Piazza they pace up and down under the arcades on either side; for Venetian patriotism makes a delicate distinction between listening to the Austrian band in the Piazza and hearing it under the Procuratie, forbidding the first and permitting the last. As soon as the music ceases the Austrians disappear, and the Italians return to the Piazza.

But since the catalogue of demonstrations cannot be made full, it need not be made any longer. The political feeling in Venice affects her prosperity in a far greater degree than may appear to those who do not understand how large an income the city formerly derived from making merry. The poor have to lament not merely the loss of their holidays, but also of the fat employments and bountiful largess which these occasions threw into their hands. With the exile or the seclusion of the richer families, and the reluctance of foreigners to make a residence of the gloomy and dejected city, the trade of the shopkeepers has fallen off; the larger commerce of the place has also languished and dwindled year by year; while the cost of living has constantly increased, and heavier burdens of taxation have been laid upon the impoverished and despondent people. And in all this, Venice is but a type of the whole province of Venetia.

The alien life to be found in the city is scarcely worth noting. The Austrians have a *casino*, and they give balls and parties, and now and then make some public manifestation of gayety. But they detest Venice as a place of residence, being naturally averse to living in the midst of a people who shun them like a pestilence. Other foreigners, as I said, are obliged to take sides for or against the Venetians, and it is amusing enough to find the few English residents divided into Austriacanti and Italianissimi.[3] Even the consuls of the different nations, who are in every way bound to neutrality and indifference, are popularly reputed to be of one party or the other; and my predecessor, whose unhappy knowledge of German threw him on his arrival among people of that race, was always regarded as the enemy of Venetian freedom, though I believe his principles were of the most vivid republican tint in the United States.

The present situation has now endured five years, with only slight modifications by time, and only faint murmurs from some of the more impatient, that *bisogna, una volta o l' altra, romper il chiodo* (sooner or later the nail must be broken). As the Venetians are a people of indomitable perseverance, long schooled to obstinacy by oppression, I suppose they will hold out till their union with the kingdom of Italy. They can do nothing of themselves, but they seem content to wait forever in their present gloom. How deeply their attitude affects their national character I shall inquire hereafter, when I come to look somewhat more closely at the spirit of their demonstration.

For the present, it is certain that the discontent of the people has its peculiar effect upon the city as the stranger sees its life, casting a glamour over it all, making it more and more ghostly and sad, and giving it a pathetic charm which I would fain transfer to my pages; but failing that, would pray the reader to remember as a fact to which I must be faithful in all my descriptions of Venice.

---

[3] Austriacanti are people of Austrian politics, though not of Austrian birth. Italianissimi are those who favor union with Italy at any cost.

CHAPTER II

ARRIVAL AND FIRST DAYS IN VENICE

I THINK it does not matter just when I first came to Venice. Yesterday and to-day are the same here. I arrived one winter morning about five o'clock, and was not so full of Soul as I might have been in warmer weather. Yet I was resolved not to go to my hotel in the omnibus (the large, many-seated boat so called), but to have a gondola solely for myself and my luggage. The porter who seized my valise in the station inferred from some very polyglottic Italian of mine the nature of my wish, and ran out and threw that slender piece of luggage into a gondola. I followed, lighted to my seat by a beggar in picturesque and desultory costume. He was one of a class of mendicants whom I came, for my sins, to know better in Venice, and whom I dare say every traveller recollects,—the merciless tribe who hold your gondola to shore, and affect to do you a service and not a displeasure, and pretend not to be abandoned swindlers. The Venetians call them *gransieri,* or crab-catchers; but as yet I did not know the name or

15

the purpose of this *poverino*[1] at the station, but merely saw that he had the Venetian eye for color: in the distribution and arrangement of his fragments of dress he had produced some miraculous effects of red, and he was altogether as infamous a figure as any friend of brigands would like to meet in a lonely place. He did not offer to stab me and sink my body in the Grand Canal, as, in all Venetian keeping, I felt that he ought to have done; but he implored an alms, and I hardly know now whether to exult or regret that I did not understand him, and left him empty-handed. I suppose that he withdrew again the blessings which he had advanced me, as we pushed out into the canal; but I heard nothing, for the wonder of the city was already upon me. All my nether-spirit, so to speak, was dulled and jaded by the long, cold railway journey from Vienna, while every surface-sense was taken and tangled in the bewildering brilliancy and novelty of Venice. For I think there can be nothing else in the world so full of glittering and exquisite surprise as that first glimpse of Venice which the traveller catches as he issues from the railway station by night, and looks upon her peerless strangeness. There is something in the blessed breath of Italy (how quickly, coming south, you know it, and how bland it is, after the harsh, transalpine air!) which prepares you for your nocturnal advent into the place; and O you! whoever you are, that journey toward this enchanted city for the first time, let me tell you how happy I count you! There lies before you for your pleasure the spectacle of such singular beauty as no picture can ever show you nor book tell you,—beauty which you shall feel perfectly but once, and regret forever.

For my own part, as the gondola slipped away from the blaze and bustle of the station down the gloom and silence of the broad canal, I forgot that I had been freezing two days and nights; that I was at that moment very cold and a little homesick. I could at first feel nothing but that beautiful silence, broken only by the star-silvered dip of the oars. Then on either hand I saw stately

---

[1] *Poverino* is the compassionate generic for all unhappy persons who work for a living in Venice, as well as many who decline to do so.

palaces rise gray and lofty from the dark waters, holding here and there a lamp against their faces, which brought balconies and columns and carven arches into momentary relief, and threw long streams of crimson into the canal. I could see by that uncertain glimmer how fair was all, but not how sad and old; and so, unhaunted by any pang for the decay that afterward saddened me amid the forlorn beauty of Venice, I glided on. I have no doubt it was a proper time to think all the fantastic things in the world, and I thought them; but they passed vaguely through my mind, without at all interrupting the sensations of sight and sound. Indeed, the past and present mixed there, and the moral and material were blent in the sentiment of utter novelty and surprise. The quick boat slid through old troubles of mine, and unlooked-for events gave it the impulse that carried it beyond, and safely around sharp corners of life. And all the while I knew that this was a progress through narrow and crooked canals, and past marble angles of palaces. But I did not know then that this fine confusion of sense and spirit was the first faint impression of the charm of life in Venice.

Dark, funereal barges like my own had flitted by, and the gondoliers had warned each other at every turning with hoarse, lugubrious cries; the lines of balconied palaces had never ended;— here and there at their doors larger craft were moored, with dim figures of men moving uncertainly about on them. At last we had passed abruptly out of the Grand Canal into one of the smaller channels, and from comparative light into a darkness only remotely affected by some far-streaming corner lamp. But always the pallid, stately palaces; always the dark heaven with its trembling stars above, and the dark water with its trembling stars below; but now innumerable bridges, and an utter lonesomeness, and ceaseless sudden turns and windings. One could not resist a vague feeling of anxiety, in these strait and solitary passages, which was part of the strange enjoyment of the time, and which was referable to the novelty, the hush, the darkness, and the piratical appearance and unaccountable pauses of the gondoliers. Was not this Venice, and is not Venice forever associated with bravoes and unexpected dagger-thrusts? That valise of mine might represent fabulous wealth to the uncultivated imagination. Who, if I made an outcry, could understand the Facts of the Situation (as we say in the journals)? To move on was relief; to pause was regret for past transgressions mingled with good resolutions for the future. But I felt the liveliest mixture of all these emotions, when, slipping from the cover of a bridge, the gondola suddenly rested at the foot of a stairway before a closely-barred door. The gondoliers rang and rang again, while their passenger

"Divided the swift mind,"

in the wonder whether a door so grimly bolted and austerely barred could possibly open into a hotel, with cheerful overcharges for candles and service. But as soon as the door opened, and he beheld the honest swindling countenance of a hotel *portier,* he felt secure against everything but imposture, and all wild absurdities of doubt and conjecture at once faded from his thought when the *portier* suffered the gondoliers to make him pay a florin too much.

So, I had arrived in Venice, and I had felt the influence of that complex spell which she lays upon the stranger. I had caught the most alluring glimpses of the beauty which cannot wholly perish while any fragment of her sculptured walls nods to its shadow in the canal; I had been penetrated by a deep sense of the mystery of the place, and I had been touched already by the anomaly of modern life amid scenes where its presence offers, according to the humor in which it is studied, constant occasion for annoyance or delight, enthusiasm or sadness.

I fancy that the ignorant impressions of the earlier days after my arrival need scarcely be set down even in this perishable record; but I would not wholly forget how, though isolated from all acquaintance and alien to the place, I yet felt curiously at home in Venice from the first. I believe it was because I had, after my own fashion, loved the beautiful that I here found the beautiful, where it is supreme, full of society and friendship, speaking a language which, even in its unfamiliar forms, I could partly understand, and at once making me citizen of that Venice from which I shall never be exiled. It was not in the presence of the great and famous monuments of art alone that I felt at home,—indeed, I could as yet understand their excellence and grandeur only very imperfectly,— but wherever I wandered through the quaint and marvellous city, I found the good company of

"The fair, the old;"

and to tell the truth, I think it is the best society in Venice, and I learned to turn to it later from other companionship with a kind of relief.

My first rambles, moreover, had a peculiar charm which knowledge of locality has since taken away. They began commonly with some purpose or destination, and ended by losing me in the intricacies of the narrowest, crookedest, and most inconsequent little streets in the world, or left me cast-away upon the unfamiliar waters of some canal as far as possible from the point aimed at. Dark and secret little courts lay in wait for my blundering steps, and I was incessantly surprised and brought to surrender by paths that beguiled me up to dead walls, or the sudden brinks of canals. The wide and open squares before the innumerable churches of the city were equally victorious, and continually took me prisoner. But all places had something rare and worthy to be seen: if not loveliness of sculpture or architecture, at least interesting squalor and picturesque wretchedness; and I believe I had less delight in proper Objects of Interest than in the dirty neighborhoods that reeked with unwholesome winter damps below, and peered curiously out with frowzy heads and beautiful eyes from the high, heavy-shuttered casements above. Every court had its carven well to show me, in the noisy keeping of the water-carriers and the slatternly, statuesque gossips of the place. The remote and noisome canals were pathetic with empty old palaces peopled by herds of poor, that decorated the sculptured balconies with the tatters of epicene linen, and patched the lofty windows with obsolete hats.

I found the night as full of beauty as the day, when caprice led me from the brilliancy of St. Mark's and the glittering streets of shops that branch away from the Piazza, and lost me in the quaint recesses of the courts or the tangles of the distant alleys, where the dull little oil-lamps vied with the tapers burning before the street-corner shrines of the Virgin[2] in making the way obscure, and deepening the shadows about the doorways and under the frequent arches. I remember distinctly, among the beautiful nights of that time, the soft night of late winter, which first showed me the scene you may behold from the Public Gardens at the end of the long concave line of the Riva degli Schiavoni. Lounging there upon the southern parapet of the Gardens, I turned from the dim bell-towers of the evanescent islands in the east (a solitary gondola gliding across the calm of the water and striking its moonlight silver into multitudinous ripples), and glanced athwart the vague shipping in the basin of St. Mark, and saw all the lights from the Piazzetta to the Giudecca, making a crescent of flame in the air, and casting deep into the water under them a crimson glory that sank also down and down in my own heart, and illumined all its memories of beauty and delight. Behind these lamps rose the shadowy masses of church and palace; the moon stood bright and full in the heavens; the gondola drifted away to the northward; the islands of the lagoons seemed to rise and sink with the light palpitations of the waves like pictures on the undulating fields of banners; the stark rigging of a ship showed black against the sky; the Lido sank from sight upon the east, as if the shore had composed itself to sleep by the side of its beloved sea, to the music of the surge that gently beat its sands; the yet leafless boughs of the trees above me stirred themselves together, and out of one of those trembling towers in the lagoons one rich, full sob burst from the heart of a bell, too deeply stricken with the glory of the scene, and suffused the languid night with the murmur of luxurious, ineffable sadness.

But there is a perfect democracy in the realm of the beautiful, and whatsoever pleases is equal to any other thing there, no

---

[2] In the early times these tapers were the sole means of street illumination in Venice.

matter how low its origin or humble its composition; and the magnificence of that moonlight scene gave me no deeper joy than I won from the fine spectacle of an old man whom I saw burning coffee one night in the little court behind my lodgings, and whom I recollect now as one of the most interesting people I saw in my first days at Venice. All day long the air of that neighborhood had reeked with the odors of the fragrant berry, and all day long this patient old man—sage, let me call him—had turned the sheet-iron cylinder in which it was roasting over an open fire, after the picturesque fashion of roasting coffee in Venice. Now that the night had fallen, and the stars shone down upon him, and the red flame luridly illumined him, he showed more grand and venerable than ever. Simple, abstract humanity has its own grandeur in Italy, and it is not hard here for the artist to find the primitive types with which genius loves best to deal. As for this old man, he had the beard of a saint and the dignity of a senator, harmonized with the squalor of a beggar, superior to which shone his abstract, unconscious grandeur of humanity. A vast and calm melancholy, which had nothing to do with burning coffee, dwelt in his aspect and attitude; and if he had been some dread supernatural agency, turning the wheel of fortune, and doing men, instead of coffee, brown, he could not have looked more sadly and weirdly impressive. When, presently, he rose from his seat, and lifted the cylinder from its place, and the clinging flames leaped after it, and he shook it, and a volume of luminous smoke enveloped him and glorified him, then I felt with secret anguish that he was beyond art, and turned sadly from the spectacle of that sublime and hopeless magnificence.

At other times (but this was in broad daylight) I was troubled by the æsthetic perfection of a certain ruffian boy, who sold cakes of baked Indian meal to the soldiers in the military station near the Piazza, and whom I often noted from the windows of the little *caffè* there, where you get an excellent *caffè bianco* (coffee with milk) for ten soldi and one to the waiter. I have reason to fear that this boy dealt over-shrewdly with the Austrians, for a pitiless war raged between him and one of the sergeants. His hair was dark,

his cheek was of a bronze better than olive, and he wore a brave
cap of red flannel, drawn down to eyes of lustrous black. For the
rest, he gave unity and coherence to a jacket and pantaloons of
heterogeneous elements, and, such was the elasticity of his spirit,
a buoyant grace to feet encased in wooden shoes. Habitually came
a barrel-organist, and ground before the barracks, and

> "Took the soul
> Of that waste place with joy;"

and ever, when this organist came to a certain lively waltz, and
threw his whole soul, as it were, into the crank of his instrument,
my beloved ragamuffin failed not to seize another cake-boy in his
arms, and, thus embraced, to whirl through a wild inspiration of
figures, in which there was something grotesquely rhythmic,
something of indescribable barbaric magnificence, spiritualized
into a grace of movement superior to the energy of the North and
the extravagant fervor of the East. It was coffee, and not wine,
that I drank, but I fable all the same that I saw reflected in this
superb and artistic superation of the difficulties of dancing in that
unfriendly foot-gear something of the same genius that combated
and vanquished the elements, to build its home upon sea-washed
sands in marble structures of airy and stately splendor, and gave
to architecture new glories full of eternal surprise.

So, I say, I grew early into sympathy and friendship with
Venice, and, being newly from a land where everything, morally
and materially, was in good repair, I rioted sentimentally on the
picturesque ruin, the pleasant discomfort and hopelessness of
everything about me here. It was not yet the season to behold all
the delight of the lazy, out-door life of the place; but nevertheless
I could not help seeing that a great part of the people, both rich
and poor, seemed to have nothing to do, and that nobody seemed
driven by any inward or outward impulse. When, however, I
ceased (as I must in time) to be merely a spectator of this idleness,
and learned that I too must assume my share of the common
indolence, I found it a grievous burden. Old habits of work, old
habits of hope, made my endless leisure irksome to me, and almost

intolerable when I ascertained fairly and finally that, in my desire to fulfil long-cherished but, after all, merely general designs of literary study, I had forsaken wholesome struggle in the currents where I felt the motion of the age, only to drift into a lifeless eddy of the world, remote from incentive and sensation.

For such is Venice, and the will must be strong and the faith indomitable in him who can long retain, amid the influences of her stagnant quiet, a practical belief in God's purpose of a great moving, anxious, toiling, aspiring world outside. When you have yielded, as after a while I yielded, to these influences, a gentle incredulity possesses you; and if you consent that such a thing is as earnest and useful life, you cannot help wondering why it need be. The charm of the place sweetens your temper, but corrupts you; and I found it a sad condition of my perception of the beauty of Venice and friendship with it that I came in some unconscious way to regard her fate as my own; and when I began to write the sketches which go to form this book, it was as hard to speak of any ugliness in her, or of the doom written against her in the hieroglyphic seams and fissures of her crumbling masonry, as if the fault and penalty were mine. I do not so greatly blame, therefore, the writers who have committed so many sins of omission concerning her, and made her all light, color, canals, and palaces. One's conscience, more or less uncomfortably vigilant elsewhere, drowses here, and it is difficult to remember that fact is more virtuous than fiction. In other years, when there was life in the city, and this sad ebb of prosperity was full tide in her canals, there might have been some incentive to keep one's thoughts and words from lapsing into habits of luxurious dishonesty, some reason for telling the whole hard truth of things, some policy to serve, some end to gain. But now, what matter?

CHAPTER III

THE WINTER IN VENICE

I T was winter, as I said, when I first came to Venice, and my experiences of the city were not all purely æsthetic. There was, indeed, an every-day roughness and discomfort in the weather, which travellers passing their first winter in Italy find it hard to reconcile with the habitual ideas of the season's clemency in the South. But winter is apt to be very severe in mild climates. People do not acknowledge it, making a wretched pretence that it is summer only a little out of humor.

The Germans have introduced stoves at Venice, but they are not in much favor with the Italians, who think their heat unwholesome, and endure a degree of cold in their wish to dispense with fire, which we of the winter-lands know nothing of in our houses. They pay for their absurd prejudice with terrible chilblains; and their hands, which suffer equally with their feet, are, in the case of those most exposed to the cold, objects pitiable and revolting to behold when the itching and the effort to allay it has turned them into bloated masses of sores. It is not a pleasant thing to speak of; and the constant sight of the affliction among people who bring you bread, cut you cheese, and weigh you out sugar by no means reconciles the Northern stomach to its prevalence. I have observed that priests and those who have much to do in the frigid churches are the worst sufferers in this way; and I think no one can help noting in the harsh, raw winter-complexion (for in summer the tone is quite different) of the women of all classes the protest of systems cruelly starved of the warmth which health demands.

The houses are, naturally enough in this climate, where there are eight months of summer in the year, all built with a view to coolness in summer, and the rooms which are not upon the ground-floor are very large, lofty, and cold. In the palaces, indeed, there are two suites of apartments,—the smaller and cozier suite upon the first floor for the winter, and the grander and airier chambers and saloons above, for defence against the insidious heats of the sirocco. But, for the most part, people must occupy the same room summer and winter, the sole change being in the strip of carpet laid meagrely before the sofa during the latter season. In the comparatively few houses where carpets are the rule, and not the exception, they are always removed during the summer,—for the triple purpose of sparing them some month's wear, banishing fleas and other domestic insects, and showing off the beauty of the oiled and shining pavement, which in the meanest houses is tasteful, and in many of the better sort is often inwrought with figures and designs of mosaic work. All the floors in Venice are of stone; and whether of marble flags, or of that species of composition formed of dark cement, with fragments of colored marble imbedded, and smoothed and polished to the most glassy and even surface, and the general effect and complexion of petrified plum-pudding, all the floors are death-cold in winter. People sit with their feet upon cushions, and their bodies muffled in furs and wadded gowns. When one goes out into the sun, one often finds an overcoat too heavy, but it never gives warmth enough in the house, where the Venetian sometimes wears it.

Indeed, the sun is recognized by Venetians as the only legitimate source of heat, and they sell his favor at fabulous prices to such foreigners as take the lodgings into which he shines.

It is those who remain in-doors, therefore, who are exposed to the utmost rigor of the winter, and people spend as much of their time as possible in the open air. The Riva degli Schiavoni catches the warm afternoon sun in its whole extent, and is then thronged with promenaders of every class, condition, age, and sex; and whenever the sun shines in the Piazza, shivering fashion eagerly courts its favor. At night men crowd the close little *caffè*, where they reciprocate smoke, respiration, and animal heat, and thus temper the inclemency of the weather, and beguile the time with solemn loafing[1] and the perusal of dingy little journals, drinking small cups of black coffee, and playing long games of chess,—an evening that seemed to me as torpid and lifeless as a Lap's and intolerable when I remembered the bright, social winter evenings of another and happier land and civilization.

Sometimes you find a heated stove—that is to say, one in which there has been a fire during the day—in a Venetian house; but the stove seems usually to be placed in the room for ornament, or else to be engaged only in diffusing a very acrid smoke,—as if the Venetian preferred to take warmth, as other people do snuff, by inhalation. The stove itself is a curious structure, and built commonly of bricks and plastering,—white-washed and painted outside. It is a great consumer of fuel, and radiates but little heat. By dint of constant wooding I contrived to warm mine; but my Italian friends always avoided its vicinity when they came to see me, and most amusingly regarded my determination to be comfortable as part of the eccentricity inseparable from the Anglo-Saxon character.

I dare say they would not trifle with winter thus, if they knew him in his northern moods. But the only voluntary concession they

---

[1] I permit myself, throughout this book, the use of the expressive American words *loaf* and *loafer,* as the only terms adequate to the description of professional idling in Venice.

make to his severity is the *scaldino,* and this is made chiefly by the yielding sex, who are denied the warmth of the *caffè.* The use of the *scaldino* is known to all ranks, but it is the women of the poorer orders who are most addicted to it. The *scaldino* is a small pot of glazed earthenware, having an earthen bale: and with this handle passed over the arm, and the pot full of bristling charcoal, the Veneziana's defence against cold is complete. She carries her *scaldino* with her in the house from room to room, and takes it with her into the street; and it has often been my fortune in the churches to divide my admiration between the painting over the altar and the poor old crone kneeling before it, who, while she sniffed and whispered a gelid prayer, and warmed her heart with religion, baked her dirty palms in the carbonic fumes of the *scaldino.* In one of the public bath-houses in Venice there are four prints upon the walls, intended to convey to the minds of the bathers a poetical idea of the four seasons. there is nothing remarkable in the symbolization of Spring, Summer, and Autumn; but Winter is nationally represented by a fine lady dressed in furred robes, with her feet upon a cushioned footstool and a *scaldino* in her lap! When we talk of being invaded in the north, we poetize the idea of defence by the figure of defending our hearthstones. Alas! *could* we fight for our sacred *scaldini?*

Happy are the men who bake chestnuts, and sell hot pumpkins and pears, for they can unite pleasure and profit. There are some degrees of poverty below the standard of the *scaldino,* and the beggars and the wretcheder poor keep themselves warm, I think, by sultry recollections of summer, as Don Quixote proposed to subsist upon savory remembrances, during one of his periods of fast. One mendicant whom I know, and who always sits upon the steps of a certain bridge, succeeds, I believe, as the season advances, in heating the marble beneath him by firm and unswerving adhesion, and establishes a reciprocity of warmth with it. I have no reason to suppose that he ever deserts his seat for a moment during the whole winter; and indeed, it would be a vicious waste of comfort to do so.

In the winter, the whole city *sniffs,* and if the Pipchin theory of
the effect of sniffing upon the eternal interests of the soul be true,
few people go to heaven in Venice. I sometimes wildly wondered
if Desdemona, in *her* time, sniffed, and found little comfort in the
reflection that Shylock must have had a cold in his head. There is
comparative warmth in the broad squares before the churches, but
the narrow streets are bitter thorough-draughts, and fell influenza
lies in wait for its prey in all those picturesque, seducing little
courts of which I have spoken.

It is, however, in the churches, whose cool twilight and airy
height one finds so grateful in summer, that the sharpest malice of
the winter is felt; and having visited a score of them soon after my
arrival, I deferred the remaining seventy-five or eighty, together
with the gallery of the Academy, until advancing spring should in
some degree have mitigated the severity of their temperature. As
far as my imagination affected me, I thought the Gothic churches
much more tolerable than the temples of Renaissance art. The
empty bareness of these, with their huge marbles and their soulless
splendors of theatrical sculpture, their frescoed roofs and broken
arches, was insufferable. The arid grace of Palladio's architecture
was especially grievous to the sense in cold weather; and I warn
the traveller who goes to see the lovely Madonnas of Bellini to
beware how he trusts himself in winter to the gusty, arctic
magnificence of the church of the Redentore. But by all means the
coldest church in the city is that of the Jesuits, which those who
have seen it will remember for its famous marble drapery. This
base, mechanical surprise (for it is a trick, and not art) is effected
by inlaying the white marble of columns and pulpits and altars
with a certain pattern of verd-antique. The workmanship is
marvellously skilful and the material costly, but it only gives the
church the effect of being draped in damask linen; and even where
the marble is carven in vast and heavy folds over a pulpit to
simulate a curtain, or wrought in figures on the steps of the high
altar to represent a carpet, it has no richness of effect, but a
poverty, a coldness, a harshness, indescribably table-clothy. I
think all this has tended to chill the soul of the sacristan, who is

the feeblest and thinnest sacristan conceivable, with a frost of white hair on his temples quite incapable of thawing. In this dreary sanctuary is one of Titian's great paintings, The Martyrdom of St. Lawrence, to which (though it is so cunningly disposed as to light that no one ever yet saw the whole picture at once) you turn involuntarily, envious of the Saint toasting so comfortably on his grid-iron amid all that frigidity.

The Venetians pretend that many of the late winters have been much severer than those of former years, but I think this pretence has less support in fact than in the custom of mankind everywhere to claim that such weather as the present, whatever it happens to be, was never seen before. In fine, the winter climate of North Italy is really very harsh, and though the season is not so severe in Venice as in Milan, or even Florence, it is still so sharp as to make foreigners regret the generous fires and warmly-built houses of the north. There was snow but once during my first Venetian winter, 1861–62; the second there was none at all; but the third, which was last winter, it fell repeatedly to considerable depth, and lay unmelted for many weeks in the shade. The lagoons were frozen for miles in every direction; and under our windows on the Grand Canal great sheets of ice went up and down with the rising and the falling tide for nearly a whole month. The visible misery throughout the fireless city was great; and it was a problem I never could solve, whether people in-doors were greater sufferers from the cold than those who weathered the cruel winds sweeping the squares and the canals, and whistling through the streets of stone and brine. The boys had an unwonted season of sliding on the frozen lagoons, though a good deal persecuted by the police, who must have looked upon such a tremendous innovation as little better than revolution; and it was said that there were card-parties on the ice; but the only creatures which seemed really to enjoy the weather were the seagulls. These birds, which flock into the city in vast numbers at the first approach of cold, and, sailing up and down the canals between the palaces, bring to the dwellers in the city a full sense of mid-ocean forlornness and desolation, now rioted on the savage winds with harsh cries, and danced upon the waves of the bitter brine with a clamorous joy that had something eldritch and unearthly in it.

A place so much given to gossip as Venice did not fail to produce many memorable incidents of the cold; but the most singular adventure was that of the old man employed at the Armenian Convent to bring milk from the island of San Lazzaro to the city. One night, shortly after the coldest weather set in, he lost his oar as he was returning to the island. The wind, which is particularly furious in that part of the lagoon, blew his boat away into the night, and the good brothers at the convent naturally gave up their milkman for lost. The winds and waters drifted him eight miles from the city into the northern lagoon, and there lodged his boat in the marshes, where it froze fast in the stiffening mud. The luckless occupant had nothing to eat or drink in his boat, where he remained five days and nights, exposed to the inclemency of cold many degrees below friendship in severity. He made continual signs of distress, but no boat came near enough to discover him. At last, when the whole marsh was frozen solid, he was taken off by some fishermen, and carried to the convent, where he remains in perfectly recovered health, and where no doubt he will be preserved alive many years in an atmosphere which renders dying at San Lazzaro a matter of no small difficulty. During the whole time of his imprisonment, he sustained life against hunger and cold by smoking. I suppose no one will be surprised to learn that he was rescued by the fishermen through the miraculous interposition of the Madonna,—as any one might have seen by the votive picture hung up at her shrine on a bridge of the Riva degli Schiavoni, wherein the Virgin was represented breaking through the clouds in one corner of the sky, and unmistakably directing the operations of the fishermen.

It is said that no such winter as that of 1863–64 has been known in Venice since the famous *Anno del Ghiaccio* (Year of the Ice), which fell about the beginning of the last century. This year is celebrated in the local literature; the play which commemorates it always draws full houses at the people's theatre, Malibran; and the often-copied picture, by a painter of the time, representing

Lustrissime and Lustrissimi in hoops and bag-wigs on the ice, never fails to block up the street before the shop-window in which it is exposed. The King of Denmark was then the guest of the Republic, and as the unprecedented cold defeated all the plans arranged for his diversion, the pleasure-loving government turned the cold itself to account, and made the ice occasion of novel brilliancy in its festivities. The duties on commerce between the city and the mainland were suspended for as long time as the lagoon should remain frozen, and the ice became a scene of the liveliest traffic, and was everywhere covered with sledges, bringing the produce of the country to the capital, and carrying away its stuffs in return. The Venetians of every class amused themselves in visiting this free mart, and the gentler and more delicate sex pressed eagerly forward to traverse with their feet a space hitherto passable only in gondolas.[1] The lagoon remained frozen, and these pleasures lasted eighteen days, a period of cold unequalled till last winter. A popular song now declares that the present generation has known a winter quite as marvellous as that of the Year of the Ice, and celebrates the wonder of walking on the water:—

> Che bell' affar!
> Che patetico affar!
> Che immenso affar!
> Sora l'acqua camminar!

But after all, the disagreeable winter, which hardly commences before Christmas, and which ends about the middle of March, is but a small part of the glorious Venetian year; and even this ungracious season has a loveliness, at times, which it can have nowhere but in Venice. What summer-delight of other lands could match the beauty of the first Venetian snow-fall which I saw? It had snowed overnight, and in the morning when I woke it was still snowing. The flakes fell softly and vertically through the motionless air, and all the senses were full of languor and repose. It was rapture to lie still, and after a faint glimpse of the golden-winged angel on the bell-tower of St. Mark's to give indolent eyes solely

---

[1] *Origine delle Feste Veneziane,* di Giustina Renier-Michiel.

to the contemplation of the roof opposite, where the snow lay half an inch deep upon the brown tiles. The little scene—a few square yards of roof, a chimney-pot, and a dormer-window—was all that the most covetous spirit could demand; and I lazily lorded it over that domain of pleasure, while the lingering mists of a dream of new-world events blent themselves with the luxurious humor of the moment and the calm of the snow-fall, and made my reverie one of the perfectest things in the world. When I was lost the deepest in it, I was inexpressibly touched and gratified by the appearance of a black cat at the dormer-window. In Venice, roofs commanding pleasant exposures seem to be chiefly devoted to the cultivation of this animal, and there are many cats in Venice. My black cat looked wondering upon the snow for a moment, and then ran across the roof. Nothing could have been better. Any creature less silent, or in point of movement less soothing to the eye, than a cat would have been torture of the spirit. As it was, this little piece of action contented me so well that I left everything else out of my reverie, and could only think how deliciously the cat harmonized with the snow-covered tiles, the chimney-pot, and the dormer-window. I began to long for her reappearance, but when she did come forth, and repeat her manœuver, I ceased to have the slightest interest in the matter, and experienced only the disgust of satiety. I had felt *ennui,*—nothing remained but to get up and change my relations with the world.

In Venetian streets they give the fallen snow no rest. It is at once shovelled into the canals by hundreds of half-naked *facchini;*[2] and now in St. Mark's Place the music of innumerable shovels smote upon my ear, and I saw the shivering legion of poverty as it engaged the elements in a struggle for the possession of the Piazza. But the snow continued to fall, and through the twilight of the descending flakes all this toil and encounter looked like that weary kind of effort in dreams, when the most determined industry seems only to renew the task. The lofty crest of the bell-tower was

---

[2] The term for those idle people in Italian cities who relieve long seasons of repose by occasionally acting as messengers, porters, and day-laborers.

hidden in the folds of falling snow, and I could no longer see the golden angel upon its summit. But looked at across the Piazza, the beautiful outline of St. Mark's Church was perfectly pencilled in the air, and the shifting threads of the snow-fall were woven into a spell of novel enchantment around a structure that always seemed to me too exquisite in its fantastic loveliness to be anything but the creation of magic. The tender snow had compassionated the beautiful edifice for all the wrongs of time, and so hid the stains and ugliness of decay that it looked as if just from the hand of the builder,—or, better said, just from the brain of the architect. There was marvellous freshness in the colors of the mosaics in the great arches of the façade, and all that gracious harmony into which the temple rises, of marble scrolls and leafy exuberance airily supporting the statues of the saints, was a hundred times etherealized by the purity and whiteness of the drifting flakes. The snow lay lightly on the golden globes that tremble like peacock-crests above the vast domes, and plumed them with softest white; it robed the saints in ermine, and it danced over all its work, as if exulting in its beauty—beauty which filled me with subtle, selfish yearning to keep such evanescent loveliness for the little-while-longer of my whole life, and with despair to think that even the poor lifeless shadow of it could never be fairly reflected in picture or poem.

Through the wavering snow-fall, the St. Theodore upon one of the granite pillars of the Piazzetta did not show so grim as his wont is, and the winged lion on the other might have been a winged lamb, so mild and gentle he looked by the tender light of the storm.[3] The towers of the island churches loomed faint and far

---

[3] St. Theodore was the first patron of Venice, but he was deposed and St. Mark adopted, when the bones of the latter were brought from Alexandria. The Venetians seem to have felt some compunctions for this desertion of an early friend, and they have given St. Theodore a place on one of the granite pillars, while the other is surmounted by the Lion, representing St. Mark. *Fra Marco e Todaro* is a Venetian proverb expressing the state of perplexity which we indicate by the figure of an ass between two bundles of hay.

away in the dimness; the sailors in the rigging of the ships that lay in the Basin wrought like phantoms among the shrouds; the gondolas stole in and out of the opaque distance more noiselessly and dreamily than ever; and a silence, almost palpable, lay upon the mutest city in the world.

CHAPTER IV

COMINCIA FAR CALDO

THE Place of St. Mark is the heart of Venice, and from this beats her life in every direction through an intricate system of streets and canals that bring it back again to the same centre. So, if the slightest uneasiness had attended the frequency with which I lost my way in the city at first, there would always havebeen this comfort: that the place was very small in actual extent, and that if I continued walking I must reach the Piazza

37

sooner or later. There is a crowd constantly tending to and from it, and you have but to take this tide, and be drifted to St. Mark's,—or to the Rialto Bridge, whence it is directly accessible.

Of all the open spaces in the city, that before the church of St. Mark alone bears the name of Piazza, and the rest are called merely *campi,* or fields. But if the company of the noblest architecture can give honor, the Piazza San Marco merits its distinction, not in Venice only but in the whole world; for I fancy that no other place in the world is set in such goodly bounds. Its westward length is terminated by the Imperial Palace; its lateral borders are formed by lines of palace called the New Procuratie on the right, and the Old Procuratie on the left;[1] and the church of St. Mark fills up almost its whole width upon the east, leaving space enough, however, for a glimpse of the Gothic perfection of the Ducal Palace. The place then opens southward with the name of Piazzetta, between the eastern façade of the Ducal Palace and the classic front of the Libreria Vecchia, and expands and ends at last on the mole, where stand the pillars of St. Mark and St. Theodore; and then this mole passing the southern façade of the Doge's Palace, stretches away to the Public Gardens at the eastern extremity of the city, over half a score of bridges, between lines of houses and shipping—stone and wooden walls—in the long, crescent-shaped quay called Riva degli Schiavoni. Looking northward up the Piazzetta from the Molo, the vision traverses the eastern breadth of the Piazza, and rests upon the Clock Tower, gleaming with blue and gold, on which the bronze Giants beat the hours; or it climbs the great mass of the Campanile San Marco, standing apart from the church at the corner of the New Procuratie, and rising four hundred feet toward the sky,—the sky where the Venetian might well place his heaven, as the Moors bounded Paradise in the celestial expanse that roofed Granada.

My first lodging was but a step out of the Piazza, and this vicinity brought me early into familiar acquaintance with its beauty. But I never, during three years, passed through it in my

---

[1] In Republican days the palaces of the *Procuratori di San Marco.*

daily walks without feeling as freshly as at first the greatness of this beauty. The church, which the mighty bell-tower and the lofty height of the palace-lines make to look low, is in no wise humbled by the contrast, but is like a queen enthroned amid upright reverence. The religious sentiment is deeply appealed to, I think, in the interior of St. Mark's; but if its interior is heaven's, its exterior, like a good man's daily life, is earth's; and it is this winning loveliness of earth that first attracts you to it, and when you emerge from its portals you enter upon spaces of such sunny length and breadth, set round with such exquisite architecture, that it makes you glad to be living in this world. Before you expands the great Piazza, peopled with its various life; on your left, between the Pillars of the Piazzetta, swims the blue lagoon, and overhead climb the arches, one above another, in excesses of fantastic grace.

Whatever could please, the Venetian seems to have brought hither and made part of his Piazza, that it might remain forever the city's supreme grace; and so, though there are public gardens and several pleasant walks in the city, the great resort in summer and winter, by day and by night, is the Piazza San Marco. Its ground-level, under the Procuratie, is belted with a glittering line of shops and *caffè,* the most tasteful and brilliant in the world, and the arcades that pass round three of its sides are filled with loungers and shoppers, even when there is music by the Austrian bands; for, as we have seen, the purest patriot may then walk under the Procuratie, without stain to the principles which would be hopelessly blackened if he set foot in the Piazza. The absence of dust and noisy hoofs and wheels tempts social life out-of-doors in Venice more than in any other Italian city, though the tendency to this sort of expansion is common throughout Italy. Beginning with the warm days of early May, and continuing till the *villeggiatura* (the period spent at the country-seat) interrupts it late in September, all Venice goes by a single impulse of *dolce far niente,* and sits gossiping at the doors of the innumerable *caffè* on the Riva degli Schiavoni, in the Piazza San Marco, and in the different squares in every part of the city. But, of course, the most

brilliant scene of this kind is in St. Mark's Place, which has a
night-time glory indescribable, won from the light of uncounted
lamps upon its architectural groups. The superb Imperial Palace,
the sculptured, arcaded, and pillared Procuratie, the Byzantine
magic and splendor of the church,—will it all be there when you
come again tomorrow night? The unfathomable heaven above
seems part of the place, for I think it is never so tenderly blue over
any other spot of earth. And when the sky is blurred with clouds,
shall not the Piazza vanish with the azure?—People, I say, come to
drink coffee, and eat ices here in the summer evenings, and then,
what with the promenades in the arcades and in the Piazza, the
music, the sound of feet, and the hum of voices, unbroken by the
ruder uproar of cities where there are horses and wheels—the
effect is that of a large evening party, and in this aspect the Piazza
is like a vast drawing-room.

I liked well to see that strange life, which even the stout,
dead-in-earnest little Bohemian musicians, piping in the centre of
the Piazza, could not altogether substantialize, and which constantly took immateriality from the loveliness of its environment.
In the winter the scene was the most purely Venetian, and in my
first winter, when I had abandoned all thought of churches till
spring, I settled down to steady habits of idleness and coffee, and
contemplated the life of the Piazza.

By all odds the loungers at Florian's were the most interesting,
because they were the most various. People of all shades of politics
met in the dainty little saloons, though there were shades of
division even there, and they did not mingle. The Italians carefully
assorted themselves in a room furnished with green velvet, and the
Austrians and the Austriacanti frequented a red-velvet room. They
were curious to look at, those tranquil, indolent, Italian loafers,
and I had an uncommon relish for them. They seldom spoke
together, and when they did speak, they burst from silence into
tumultuous controversy, and then lapsed again into perfect silence. The elder among them sat with their hands carefully folded
on the heads of their sticks, gazing upon the ground, or else buried
themselves in the perusal of the French journals. The younger

stood a good deal about the doorways, and now and then passed a gentle, gentle jest with the elegant waiters in black coats and white cravats, who hurried to and fro with the orders, and called them out in strident tones to the accountant at his little table; or sometimes these young idlers made a journey to the room devoted to ladies and forbidden to smokers, looked long and deliberately in upon its loveliness, and then returned to the bosom of their taciturn companions. By chance I found them playing chess, but very rarely. They were all well-dressed, handsome men, with beards carefully cut, brilliant hats and boots, and conspicuously clean linen. I used to wonder who they were, to what order of society they belonged, and whether they, like my worthless self, had never anything else but lounging at Florian's to do; but I really know none of these things to this day. Some men in Venice spend their noble, useful lives in this way, and it was the proud reply of a Venetian father, when asked of what profession his son was, "*E in Piazza!*" That was, he bore a cane, wore light gloves, and stared from Florian's windows at the ladies who went by.

At the Caffè Quadri, immediately across the Piazza, there was a scene of equal hopefulness. But there all was a glitter of uniforms, and the idling was carried on with a great noise of conversation in Austrian-German. Heaven knows what it was all about, but I presume the talk was upon topics of mutual improvement, calculated to advance the interests of self-government and mankind. These officers were very comely, intelligent-looking people, with the most good-natured faces. They came and went restlessly, sitting down and knocking their steel scabbards against the tables, or rising and straddling off with their long swords kicking against their legs. They are the most stylish soldiers in the world, and one has no notion how ill they can dress when left to themselves, till one sees them in civil clothes.

Further up toward the Fabbrica Nuova (as the Imperial Palace is called), under the Procuratie Vecchie, is the Caffè Specchi, frequented only by young Italians, of an order less wealthy than those who go to Florian's. Across from the *caffè* is that of the Emperor of Austria, resorted to chiefly by non-commissioned officers, and civilian officials of lower grade. You know the latter, at a glance, by their beard, which in Venice is an index to every man's politics: no Austriacante wears the imperial, no Italianissimo shaves it. Next is the Caffè Suttil, rather Austrian, and frequented by Italian *codini,* or old fogies, in politics: gray old fellows, who caress their sticks with more constant zeal than even the elders at Florian's. Quite at the other end of the Procuratie Nuove is the Caffè of the Greeks, a nation which I have commonly seen represented there by two or three Albanians with an Albanian boy, who, being dressed exactly like his father, curiously impressed me, as if he were the young of some Oriental animal— say a boy-elephant, or infant camel.

I hope that the reader adds to this sketch, even in the winter time, occasional tourists under the Procuratie, at the *caffè,* and in the shops where the shop-keepers are devouring them with the keenness of an appetite unsated by the hordes of summer visitors. I hope that the reader also groups me fishermen, gondoliers, beggars, and loutish boys about the base of St. Mark's and at the feet of the three flag-staffs before the church; that he passes me a slatternly woman and a frowzy girl or two through the Piazza occasionally; and that he calls down the flocks of pigeons hovering near. I fancy the latter half ashamed to show themselves, as being aware that they are a great humbug, and unrightfully in the guide-books.

Meantime, while I sit at Florian's, sharing and studying the universal worthlessness about me, the brief winter passes, and the spring of the south—so unlike the ardent season of the north, where it burns full summer before the snows are dried upon the fields—descends upon the city and the sea. But except in the little gardens of the palaces, and where here and there a fig-tree lifts its head to peer over a lofty stone wall, the spring finds no response of swelling bud and unfolding leaf, and it is human nature alone which welcomes it. Perhaps it is for this reason that the welcome is more visible in Venice than elsewhere, and that here, where the effect of the season is narrowed and limited to men's hearts, the joy it brings is all the keener and deeper. It is certain at least that the rapture is more demonstrative. The city, at all times voiceful, seems to burst into song with the advent of these golden days and silver nights. Bands of young men go singing through the moonlit streets, and the Grand Canal reëchoes the music of the parties of young girls as they drift along in the scarcely moving boats, and sing the glories of the lagoons and the loves of fishermen and gondoliers. In the Public Gardens they walk and sing; and wandering minstrels come forth before the *caffè,* and it is hard to get beyond the tinkling of guitars and the scraping of fiddles. It is as if the city had put off its winter humor with its winter dress; and as Venice in winter is the dreariest and gloomiest place in the world, so in spring it is the fullest of joy and light. There is a plea-sant bustle in the streets, a ceaseless clatter of feet over the stones of the squares, and a constant movement of boats upon the canals.

We say, in a cheap and careless way, that the southern peoples have no *homes.* But this is true only in a restricted sense, for the Italian, and the Venetian especially, makes the whole city his home in pleasant weather. No one remains under a roof who can help it; and now, as I said before, the fascinating out-door life begins. All day long the people sit and drink coffee and eat ices, and gossip together before the *caffè,* and the soft midnight sees the same diligent idlers in their places. The promenade is at all seasons the favorite Italian amusement; it has its rigidly fixed hours, and its limits are also fixed: but now, in spring, even the promenade is a little lawless, and the crowds upon the Riva sometimes walk as far as the Public Gardens, and throng all the wider avenues and the Piazza; while young Venice comes to take the sun at St. Mark's in the arms of its high-breasted nurses,—mighty country-women, who, in their bright costumes, their dangling chains, and head-dresses of gold and silver baubles, stride through the Piazza with the high, free-stepping movement of blood-horses, and look like the women of some elder race of barbaric vigor and splendor, which, but for them, had passed away from our puny, dull-clad times.

"È la stagion che ognuno s' innamora;"

and now young girls steal to their balconies, and linger there for hours, subtly conscious of the young men sauntering to and fro, and looking up at them from beneath. Now, in the shady little courts, the Venetian housewives, who must perforce remain indoors, put out their heads and gossip from window to window; while the pretty water-carriers, filling their buckets from the wells below, chatter and laugh at their work. Every street down which you look is likewise vocal with gossip; and if the picturesque projection of balconies, shutters, and chimneys, of which the vista is full, hide the heads of the gossipers, be sure there is a face looking out of every window for all that, and the social, expansive presence of the season is felt there.

The poor, whose sole luxury the summer is, lavish the spring upon themselves unsparingly. They come forth from their dark dens in crumbling palaces and damp basements, and live in the sunlight and the welcome air. They work, they eat, they sleep out of doors. Mothers of families sit about their doors and spin, or walk volubly up and down with other slatternly matrons, armed with spindle and distaff; while their raven-haired daughters, lounging near the threshold, chase the covert insects that haunt the tangles of the children's locks. Within doors shines the bare bald head of the grandmother, who never ceases talking for an instant.

Before the winter passed, I had changed my habitation from rooms near the Piazza to quarters on the Campo San Bartolomeo, through which the busiest street in Venice passes, from St. Mark's to the Rialto Bridge. It is one of the smallest squares of the city, and the very noisiest, and here the spring came with intolerable uproar. I had taken my rooms early in March, when the tumult under my windows amounted only to a cheerful stir, and made company for me; but when the winter broke, and the windows were opened, I found that I had too much society.

Each campo in Venice is a little city, self-contained and independent. Each has its church, of which it was in the earliest times the burial-ground; and each within its limits compasses an apothecary's shop, a mercer's and draper's shop, a blacksmith's and shoemaker's shop, a *caffè,* more or less brilliant, a green-grocer's and fruiterer's, a family grocery,—nay, there is also a second-hand merchant's shop where you buy and sell every kind of worn-out thing at the lowest rates. Of course there is a coppersmith's and a watchmaker's, and pretty certainly a wood-carver's and gilder's while without a barber's shop no campo could preserve its integrity or inform itself of the social and political news of the day. In addition to all these elements of bustle and disturbance, San Bartolomeo swarmed with the traffic and rang with the bargains of the Rialto market.

Here the small dealer makes up in boastful clamor for the absence of quantity and assortment in his wares; and it often happens that an almost imperceptible boy, with a card of shirt-buttons and a paper of hair-pins, is much worse than the Anvil Chorus with real anvils. Fishermen, with baskets of fish upon their heads; peddlers, with trays of housewife wares; louts who dragged baskets of lemons and oranges back and forth by long cords; men who sold water by the glass; charlatans who advertised cement for mending broken dishes, and drops for the cure of toothache; jugglers who spread their carpets and arranged their temples of magic upon the ground; organists who ground their organs; and poets of the people who brought out new songs, and sang and sold them to the crowd;—these were the children of confusion, whom the pleasant sun and friendly air woke to frantic and interminable uproar in San Bartolomeo.

Yet there was a charm about all this at first, and I spent much time in the study of the vociferous life under my windows, trying to make out the meaning of the different cries, and to trace them back to their sources. There was one which puzzled me for a long time—a sharp, pealing cry that ended in a wail of angry despair, and, rising high above all other sounds, impressed the spirit like the cry of that bird in the tropic forests which the terrified Spaniards called the *alma perdida*. After many days of listening and trembling, I found that it proceeded from a wretched, sun-burnt girl, who carried about some dozens of knotty pears, and whose hair hung disheveled round her eyes, bloodshot with the strain of her incessant shrieks.

In San Bartolomeo, as in other squares, the buildings are palaces above and shops below. The ground-floor is devoted to the small commerce of various kinds already mentioned; the first story above is occupied by tradesmen's families; and on the third or fourth floor is the *appartamento signorile*. From the balconies of these stores hung the cages of innumerable finches, canaries, blackbirds and savage parrots, which sang and screamed with delight in the noise that rose from the crowd. All the human life, therefore, which the spring drew to the casements was perceptible only in dumb show. One of the palaces opposite was used as a hotel, and faces continually appeared at the windows. By all odds the most interesting figure there was that of a stout peasant serving-girl, dressed in a white knitted jacket, a crimson necker-chief, and a bright-colored gown, and wearing long dangling ear-rings of yellowest gold. For hours this idle maiden balanced herself half over the balcony-rail in perusal of the people under her, and I suspect made love at that distance, and in that constrained position, to some one in the crowd. On another balcony, a lady sat and knitted with crimson yarn; and at the window of still another house, a damsel now looked out upon the square, and now gave a glance into the room, in the evident direction of a mirror. Venetian neighbors have the amiable custom of studying one another's features through opera-glasses; but I could not persuade myself to use this means of learning the mirror's response to the damsel's constant "Fair or not?" being a believer in every woman's right to look well a little way off. I shunned whatever trifling temptation there was in the case, and turned again to the campo beneath—to the placid dandies about the door of the *caffè,* to the tide of passers from the Merceria; the smooth-shaven Venetians of other days, and the bearded Vene-tians of these; the dark-eyed, white-faced Venetian girls, hooped in cruel disproportion to the narrow streets, but richly clad, and moving with southern grace; the files of heavily burdened soldiers; the little policemen loitering lazily about with their swords at their sides, and in their spotless Austrian uniforms.

As the spring advances in Venice, and the heat increases, the expansive delight with which the city hails its coming passes into a tranquiller humor, as if the joy of the beautiful season had sunk too deeply into the city's heart for utterance. I, too, felt this longing for quiet, and as San Bartolomeo continued untouched by it, and all day roared and thundered under my windows, and all night long gave itself up to sleepless youths who there melodiously bayed the moon in chorus, I was obliged to abandon San Bartolomeo, and seek calmer quarters, where I might enjoy the last luxurious sensations of the spring-time in peace.

Now, with the city's lapse into this tranquiller humor, the promenades cease. The *facchino* gives all his leisure to sleeping in the sun; and in the mellow afternoons there is scarcely a space of six feet square on the Riva degli Schiavoni which does not bear its brown-cloaked peasant basking face-downward in the warmth. The broad steps of the bridges are by right the berths of the beggars; the sailors and fishermen slumber in their boats; and the gondoliers, if they do not sleep, are yet placated by the season and forbear to quarrel, and only break into brief clamors at the sight of inaccessible Inglesi passing near them under the guard of *valets de place*. Even the play of the children ceases, except in the Public Gardens, where the children of the poor have indolent games, and sport as noiselessly as the lizards that slide from shadow to shadow and glitter in the sun asleep. This vernal silence of the city possesses you,—the stranger in it,—not with sadness, not with melancholy, but with a deep sense of the sweetness of doing nothing, and an indifference to all purposes and chances. If ever you cared to have your name on men's tongues, behold! that old yearning for applause is dead. Praise would strike like pain through this delicious calm. And blame? It is a wild and frantic thing to dare it by any effort. Repose takes you to her inmost heart, and you learn her secrets—arcana unintelligible to you in the new-world life of bustle and struggle. Old lines of lazy rhyme win new color and meaning. The mystical, indolent poems whose music once charmed away all will to understand them are revealed now without your motion. Now, at last, you know *why*

"It was an Abyssinian maid"

who played upon the dulcimer. And Xanadu? It is the land in which you were born!

The slumbrous bells murmur to each other in the lagoons; the white sail faints into the white distance; the gondola slides athwart the sheeted silver of the bay; the blind beggar, who seemed sleepless as fate, dozes at his post.

CHAPTER V

OPERA AND THEATRES

WITH the winter came to an end the amusement which, in spite of the existing political demonstration, I had drawn from the theatres. The Fenice, the great theatre of the city, being the property of private persons, has not been opened since the discontents of the Venetians were intensified in 1859; and it will not be opened, they say, till Victor Emanuel comes to honor the ceremony. Though not large, and certainly not so magnificent as the Venetians think, the Fenice is a superb and tasteful theatre. The best opera was formerly given in it, and now that it is closed the musical drama, of course, suffers. The Italians seldom go to it, and as there is not a sufficient number of foreign residents to support it in good style the opera commonly conforms to the character of the theatre San Benedetto, in which it is given, and is second-rate. It is nearly always subsidized by the city to the amount of several thousand florins; but nobody need fall into the error, on this account, of supposing that it is cheap to the opera-goer, as it is in the little German cities. A box does not cost a great deal; but as the theatre is carried on in Italy by two different managements,—one of which receives the money for the boxes and seats, and the other the fee of admission to the theatre,—there is always the demand of the latter to be satisfied with nearly the same outlay as that for the box, before you can reach your place. The pit is fitted up with seats, of course, but you do not sit down there without paying. So, most Italians (who if they go at all go without ladies) and the poorer sort of government officials stand; the orchestra seats are reserved for the officers of the garrison. The first row of boxes, which is on a level with the heads of people in the pit, is well enough, but rank and fashion take a loftier flight, and sit in the second tier.

You look about in vain, however, for that old life of the theatre which once formed so great a part of Venetian gayety,—the visits from box to box, the gossiping between the acts, and the half-occult flirtations. The people in the boxes are few, the dressing not splendid, and the beauty is the blonde, unfrequent beauty of the German aliens. Last winter being the fourth season the Italians had defied the temptation of the opera, some of the Venetian ladies yielded to it, but went plainly dressed, and sat far back in boxes of the third tier, and when they issued forth after the opera were veiled beyond recognition. The audience usually takes its enjoyment quietly; hissing now and then for silence in the house, and clapping hands for applause, without calling *bravo,*—an Italian custom which I have noted to be chiefly habitual with foreigners: with Germans, for instance, who spell it with a *p* and *f.*

I fancy that to find good Italian opera you must seek it somewhere out of Italy,—at London, or Paris, or New York,— though possibly it might be chanced upon at La Scala in Milan, or San Carlo in Naples. The cause of the decay of the musical art in

Venice must be looked for among the events which seem to have doomed her to decay in everything; certainly it cannot be discerned in any indifference of the people to music. The *dimostrazione* keeps the better class of citizens from the opera, but the passion for it still exists in every order; and God's gift of beautiful voice cannot be smothered in the race by any Situation. You hear the airs of opera sung as commonly upon the streets in Venice as our own colored melodies at home; and the street-boy when he sings has an inborn sense of music and a power of execution which put to shame the cultivated tenuity of sound that issues from the northern mouth,—

"That frozen, passive, palsied breathing-hole."

In the days of the Fenice there was a school for the ballet at that theatre, but this last and least worthy part of dramatic art is now an imported element of the opera in Venice. No novices appear on her stages, and the musical conservatories of the place, which were once so famous, have long ceased to exist. The musical theatre was very popular in Venice as early as the middle of the seventeenth century; and the care of the state for the drama existed from the first. The government, which always piously forbade the representation of Mysteries, and, as the theatre advanced, even prohibited plays containing characters of the Old or New Testament, began about the close of the century to protect and encourage the instruction of music in the different foundling hospitals and public refuges in the city. The young girls in these institutions were taught to play on instruments, and to sing,—at first for the alleviation of their own dull and solitary life, and afterward for the delight of the public. In the merry days that passed just before the fall of the Republic, the Latin oratorios which they performed in the churches attached to the hospitals were among the most fashionable diversions in Venice. The singers were instructed by the best masters of the time; and at the close of the last century the conservatories of the Incurables, the Foundlings, and the Mendicants were famous throughout Europe for their dramatic concerts, and for those pupils who found the transition from sacred to profane opera natural and easy.

With increasing knowledge of the language, I learned to enjoy best the unmusical theatre, and went oftener to the comedy than the opera. It is hardly by any chance that the Italians play ill, and I have seen excellent acting at the Venetian theatres, both in the modern Italian comedy, which is very rich and good, and in the elder plays of Goldoni,—compositions deliciously racy when seen in Venice, where alone their admirable fidelity of drawing and coloring can be perfectly appreciated. The best comedy is usually given to the educated classes at the pretty Teatro Apollo, while a bloodier and louder drama is offered to the populace at Teatro Malibran, where on a Sunday night you may see the plebeian life of the city in one of its most entertaining and characteristic phases. The sparings of the whole week which have not been laid out for chances in the lottery are spent for this evening's amusement; and in the vast pit you see, besides the families of comfortable artisans who can evidently afford it, a multitude of the ragged poor, whose presence, even at the low rate of eight or ten soldi[1] apiece, it is hard to account for. It is very peremptory, this audience, in its likes and dislikes, and applauds and hisses with great vehemence. It likes best the sanguinary local spectacular drama; it cheers and cheers again every allusion to Venice; and when the curtain rises on some well-known Venetian scene, it has out the scene-painter by name three times,—which is all the police permits. The auditors wear their hats in the pit, but deny that privilege to the people in the boxes, and raise stormy and wrathful cries of *cappello!* till these uncover. Between acts they indulge in excesses of water flavored with anise, and even go to the extent of candied nuts and fruits, which are hawked about the theatre, and sold for two soldi the stick,—with the tooth-pick on which they are spitted thrown into the bargain.

The Malibran Theatre is well attended on Sunday night, but the

---

[1] The soldo is the hundredth part of the Austrian florin, which is worth about forty-nine cents of American money.

one entertainment which never fails of drawing and delighting full houses is the theatre of the puppets or the Marionette, and thither I like best to go. The Marionette prevail with me, for I find in the performances of these puppets no new conditions demanded of the spectator, but rather a frank admission of unreality that makes every shadow of verisimilitude delightful, and gives a marvellous relish to the immemorial effects and traditionary tricks of the stage.

The little theatre of the puppets is at the corner of a narrow street opening from the Calle del Ridotto, and is of the tiniest dimensions and simplest appointments. There are no boxes,—the whole theatre is scarcely larger than a stage-box,—and you pay ten soldi to go into the pit, where you are much more comfortable than the aristocrats who have paid fifteen for places in the dress-circle above. The stage is very small, and the scenery a kind of coarse miniature painting. But it is very complete, and everything is contrived to give relief to the puppets and to produce an illusion of magnitude in their figures. They are very artlessly introduced, and are manœuvred, according to the exigencies of the scene, by means of cords running from their heads, arms, and legs to the top of the stage. To the management of the cords they owe all the vehemence of their passions and the grace of their oratory, not to mention a certain gliding, ungradual locomotion, altogether spectral.

The drama of the Marionette is of a more elevated and ambitious tone than that of the Burattini, which exhibit their vulgar loves and coarse assassinations in little punch-shows on the Riva and in the larger squares; but the standard characters are nearly the same with both, and are all descended from the *commedia a braccio*[2] which flourished on the Italian stage before the time of Goldoni. And I am very far from disparaging the Burattini, which have great and peculiar merits, not the least of which is the art of drawing the most delighted, dirty, and picturesque audiences. Like most of the Marionette, they converse vicariously in the Venetian dialect, and have such a rapidity of utterance that it is difficult to follow them. I only remember to

---

[2] Comedy by the yard.

have made out one of their comedies,—a play in which an
ingenious lover procured his rich and successful rival to be
arrested for lunacy, and married the disputed young person while
the other was raging in the mad-house. This play is performed to
enthusiastic audiences; but for the most part the favorite drama of
the Burattini appears to be a sardonic farce, in which the chief
character—a puppet ten inches high, with a fixed and staring
expression of Mephistophelean good-nature and wickedness—
deludes other and weak-minded puppets into trusting him, and
then beats them with a club upon the back of the head until they
die. The murders of this famous creature, which are always
executed in a spirit of jocose *sang-froid,* and accompanied by
humorous remarks, are received with the keenest relish by the
spectators; and, indeed, the action is every way worthy of
applause. The dramatic spirit of the Italian race seems to commu-
nicate itself to the puppets, and they perform their parts with a
fidelity to theatrical unnaturalness which is wonderful. I have
witnessed death agonies on the little stages which the great
American tragedian himself (whoever he may happen to be) could
not surpass in degree of energy. And then the Burattini deserve the
greater credit because they are agitated by the legs from below the
scene, and not managed by cords from above, as at the Marionette
Theatre. Their audiences, as I said, are always interesting, and
comprise: first, boys ragged and dirty in inverse ratio to their size;
then, weaker little girls, supporting immense weight of babies;
then, Austrian soldiers, with long coats and short pipes; lumbering
Dalmat sailors; a transient Greek or Turk; Venetian loafers,
pale-faced, statuesque, with the drapery of their cloaks thrown
over their shoulders; young women, with bare heads of thick
black hair; old women, all fluff and fangs; wooden-shod peasants,
with hooded cloaks of coarse brown; then, boys—and boys. They
all enjoy the spectacle with approval, and take the drama *au grand
sérieux,* uttering none of the gibes which sometimes attend efforts
to please in our own country. Even when the hat, or other
instrument of extortion, is passed round, and they give nothing,
and when the manager, in an excess of fury and disappointment,

calls out, "Ah! sons of dogs! I play no more to you!" and closes the theatre, they quietly and unresentfully disperse. Though, indeed, *fioi de cani* means no great reproach in Venetian parlance; and parents of the lower classes caressingly address their children in these terms. Whereas to call one Figure of a Pig is to wreak upon him the deadliest insult which can be put into words.

In the *commedia a braccio,* before mentioned as the inheritance of the Marionette, the dramatist furnished merely the plot and the outline of the action; the players filled in the character and dialogue. With any people less quick-witted than the Italians this sort of comedy must have been insufferable, but it formed the delight of that people till the middle of the last century, and even after Goldoni went to Paris he furnished his Italian players with the *commedia a braccio.* I have heard some very passable *gags* at the Marionette, but the real *commedia a braccio* no longer exists, and its familiar and invariable characters perform written plays.

Facanapa is a modern addition to the old stock of *dramatis personæ,* and he is now without doubt the popular favorite in Venice. He is always, like Pantalon, a Venetian; but whereas the latter is always a merchant, Facanapa is anything that the exigency of the play demands. He is a dwarf, even among puppets, and his dress invariably consists of black knee-breeches and white stockings, a very long, full-skirted black coat, and a three-cornered hat. His individual traits are displayed in all his characters, and he is ever a coward, a boaster, and a liar; a glutton and avaricious, but withal of an agreeable *bonhomie* that wins the heart. To tell the truth, I care little for the plays in which he has no part, and I have learned to think a certain trick of his—lifting his leg rigidly to a horizontal line, by way of emphasis, and saying, "Capisse la?" or "Sa la?" (You understand? You know?)—one of the finest things in the world.

In nearly all of Goldoni's Venetian comedies, and in many which he wrote in Italian, appear the standard associates of Facanapa,—Arlecchino, il Dottore, Pantalon dei Bisognosi, and Brighella. The reader is at first puzzled by their constant recurrence, but never weary of Goldoni's witty management of them.

They are the chief persons of the obsolete *commedia a braccio,* and have their nationality and peculiarities marked by immemorial attribution. Pantalon is a Venetian merchant, rich, and commonly the indulgent father of a wilful daughter or dissolute son, figuring also sometimes as the childless uncle of large fortune. The second old man is il Dottore, who is a Bolognese, and a doctor of the University. Brighella and Arlecchino are both of Bergamo. The one is a sharp and roguish servant, busy-body, and rascal; the other is dull and foolish, and always masked and dressd in motley,—a gibe at the poverty of the Bergamasks, among whom, moreover, the extremes of stupidity and cunning are most usually found, according to the popular notion in Italy.

The plays of the Marionette are written expressly for them, and are much shorter than the standard drama as it is known to us. They embrace, however, a wide range of subjects, from lofty melodrama to broad farce, as you may see by looking at the advertisements in the Venetian gazettes for any week past, where perhaps you shall find the plays performed to have been: The Ninety-nine Misfortunes of Facanapa; Arlecchino, the Sleeping King; Facanapa as Soldier in Catalonia; the Capture of Smyrna, with Facanapa and Arlecchino Slaves in Smyrna (this play being repeated several nights); and Arlecchino and Facanapa Hunting an Ass. If you can fancy people going night after night to this puppet-drama, and enjoying it with the keenest appetite, you will not only do something toward realizing to yourself the easily pleased Italian nature, but you will also suppose great excellence in the theatrical management. For my own part, I find few things in life equal to the Marionette. I am never tired of their bewitching absurdity, their inevitable defects, their irresistible touches of verisimilitude. At their theatre I have seen the relenting parent (Pantalon) twitchingly embrace his erring son, while Arlecchino, as the large-hearted cobbler who has paid the house-rent of the erring son when the prodigal was about to be cast into the street, looked on and rubbed his hands with amiable satisfaction and the conventional delight in benefaction which we all know. I have witnessed the base terrors of Facanapa at an apparition, and I have beheld the keen spiritual agonies of the Emperor Nicholas on hearing of the fall of Sebastopol. Not many passages of real life have affected me as deeply as the atrocious behavior of the brutal baronial brother-in-law, when he responds to the expostulations of his friend the Knight of Malta,—a puppet of shaky and vacillating presence, but a soul of steel and rock:—

"Why, O baron, detain this unhappy lady in thy dungeons? Remember, she is thy brother's wife. Remember thine own honor. Think on the sacred name of virtue." (Wrigglingly, and with a set countenance and gesticulations toward the pit.)

To which the ferocious baron makes answer, with a sneering laugh, "Honor?—I know it not? Virtue?—I detest it!" and attempting to pass the knight, in order to inflict fresh indignities upon his sister-in-law, he yields to the natural infirmities of rags and pasteboard, and topples against him.

Facanapa, also, in his great scene of the Haunted Poet, is tremendous. You discover him in bed, too much visited by the Muse to sleep, and reading his manuscripts aloud to himself, after the manner of poets when they cannot find other listeners. He is alarmed by various ghostly noises in the house, and is often obliged to get up and examine the dark corners of the room, and to look under the bed. When at last the spectral head appears at the foot-board, Facanapa vanishes with a miserable cry under the bed-clothes, and the scene closes. Intrinsically the scene is not much, but this great actor throws into it a life, a spirit, a drollery, wholly irresistible.

The ballet at the Marionette is a triumph of choreographic art, and is extremely funny. The *prima ballerina* has all the difficult grace and far-fetched arts of the *prima ballerina* of flesh and blood; and when the enthusiastic audience calls her back after the scene, she is humanly delighted, and acknowledges the compliment with lifelike *empressement*. I have no doubt the *corps de ballet* have their private jealousies and bickerings, when quietly laid away in boxes, and deprived of all positive power by the removal of the cords which agitate their arms and legs. The puppets are great in *pirouette* and *pas seul;* but I think the strictly dramatic part of such spectacular ballets, as The Fall of Carthage, is their strong point.

The people who witness their performances are of all ages and conditions,—I remember to have once seen a Russian princess and some German countesses in the pit,—but the greater number of spectators are young men of middle classes, pretty shop-girls, and artisans and their wives and children. The little theatre is a kind of trysting-place for lovers in humble life, and there is a great deal of amusing drama going on between the acts, in which the invariable Beppo and Nina of the Venetian populace take the place of the invariable Arlecchino and Facanapa of the stage. I one day discovered a letter at the bottom of the Canal of the Giudecca, to which watery resting-place some recreant, addressed as "Caro Antonio," had consigned it; and from this letter I came to know certainly of at least one love affair at the Marionette. "Caro Antonio" was humbly besought, "if his heart still felt the force of love," to meet the writer (who softly reproached him with neglect) at the Marionette the night of date, at six o'clock; and I would not like to believe he could resist so tender a prayer, though perhaps it fell out so. I fished up through the lucent water this despairing little epistle,—it was full of womanly sweetness and bad spelling,—and dried away its briny tears on the blade of my oar. If ever I though to keep it, with some vague purpose of offering it to any particularly anxious-looking Nina at the Marionette as to the probable writer, its unaccountable loss spared me the delicate office. Still, however, when I go to see the puppets, it is with an interest divided between the drolleries of Facanapa and the sad presence of expectation somewhere among the groups of dark-eyed girls there, who wear such immense hoops under such greasy dresses, who part their hair at one side, and call each other "Ciò!" Where are thou, O fickle and cruel, yet ever dear Antonio? All unconscious, I think,—gallantly posed against the wall, thy slouch hat brought forward to the point of thy long cigar, the arms of thy velvet jacket folded on thy breast, and thy ear-rings softly twinkling in the light.

CHAPTER VI

VENETIAN DINNERS AND DINERS

WHEN I first came to Venice, I accepted the fate appointed to young men on the Continent. I took lodgings, and I began dining drearily at the restaurants. Worse prandial fortunes may befall one, but it is hard to conceive of the continuance of so great unhappiness elsewhere; while the restaurant life is an established and permanent thing in Italy, for every bachelor and for many forlorn families. It is not because the restaurants are very dirty,—if you wipe your plate and glass carefully before using them, they need not stomach you; it is not because the rooms are

59

cold,—if you sit near the great vase of smouldering embers in the centre of each room, you may suffocate in comparative comfort; it is not because the prices are great,—they are really very reasonable; it is not for any very tangible fault that I object to life at the restaurants, and yet I cannot think of its hopeless home-lessness without rebellion against the whole system it implies, as something unnatural and insufferable.

But before we come to look closely at this aspect of Italian civilization, it is better to look first at a very noticeable trait of Italian character,—temperance in eating and drinking. As to the poorer classes, one observes without great surprise how slenderly they fare, and how, with a great habit of talking of meat and drink, the verb *mangiare* remains in fact for the most part inactive with them. But it is only just to say that this virtue of abstinence seems to be not wholly the result of necessity, for it prevails with other classes which could well afford the opposite vice. Meat and drink do not form the substance of conviviality with Venetians, as with the Germans and the English, and in degree with ourselves; and I have often noticed on the Mondays-at-the-Gardens, and other social festivals of the people, how the crowd amused itself with anything,—music, dancing, walking, talking,—anything but the great northern pastime of gluttony. Knowing the life of the place, I make quite sure that Venetian gayety is on few occasions connected with repletion; and I am ashamed to confess that I have not always been able to repress a feeling of stupid scorn for the empty stomachs everywhere, which do not even ask to be filled, or, at least, do not insist upon it. The truth is, the North has a gloomy pride in gastronomic excess, which unfits her children to appreciate the cheerful prudence of the south.

Venetians eat but one meal a day, which is dinner. They breakfast on a piece of bread with coffee and milk; supper is a little cup of black coffee, or an ice, taken at a *caffè*. The coffee, however, is repeated frequently throughout the day; and in the summer-time fruit is eaten, but eaten sparingly, like everything else. As to the nature of the dinner, it of course varies somewhat according to the nature of the diner; but in most families of the middle class a dinner at home consists of a piece of boiled beef, a *minestra* (a soup thickened with vegetables, tripe, and rice), a vegetable dish of some kind, and the wine of the country. The failings of the repast among all classes lean to the side of simplicity, and the abstemious character of the Venetian finds sufficient comment in his familiar invitation to dinner: "*Venga a mangiar quattro risi con me.*" (Come eat four grains of rice with me.)

But invitations to dinner have never formed a prime element of hospitality in Venice. Goldoni notices this fact in his memoirs, and, speaking of the city in the early half of the last century, he says that the number and excellence of the eating-houses in the city made invitations to dinner at private houses rare, and superfluous among the courtesies offered to strangers.

The Venetian does not, like the Spaniard, place his house at your disposition, and, having extended this splendid invitation, consider the duties of hospitality fulfilled; he does not appear to think you want to make use of his house for social purposes, preferring himself the *caffè*, and finding home and comfort there, rather than under his own roof. "What *caffè* do you frequent? Ah! so do I. We shall meet often there." This is frequently your new acquaintance's promise of friendship. And one may even learn to like the social footing on which people meet at the *caffè*, as well as that of the parlor or drawing-room. I could not help thinking one evening at Padua, while we sat talking with some pleasant Paduans in one of the magnificent saloons of the Caffè Pedrocchi, that I should like to go there for society, if I could always find it there, much better than to private houses. There is far greater ease and freedom, more elegance and luxury, and not the slightest weight of obligation laid upon you for the gratification your friend's company has given you. One has not to be a debtor in the sum of a friend's outlay for house, servants, refreshments, and the like. Nowhere in Europe is the senseless and wasteful American custom of *treating* known; and nothing could be more especially foreign to the frugal instincts and habits of the Italians. So, when a party of friends at a *caffè* eat or drink, each one pays for what he takes, and pecuniarily the enjoyment of the evening is uncostly or not, according as each prefers. Of course no one sits down in such a place without calling for something; but I have frequently seen people respond to this demand of custom by ordering a glass of water with anise, at the expense of two soldi. A cup of black coffee, for five soldi, secures a chair, a table, and as many journals as you like, for as long as you like.

I say, a stranger may learn to like the life of the *caffè*,—that of the restaurant never; though the habit of frequenting the restaurants, to which Goldoni somewhat vaingloriously refers, seems to have grown upon the Venetians with the lapse of time. The eating-houses are almost without number, and are of every degree, from the shop of the sausage-maker, who supplies gondoliers and *facchini* with bowls of *sguassetto,* to the Caffè Florian. They all have names which are not strange to European ears, but which are sufficiently amusing to people who come from a land where nearly every public thing is named from some inspiration of patriotism or local pride. In Venice the principal restaurants are called The Steamboat, The Savage, The Little Horse, The Black Hat, and The Pictures; and I do not know that any one of them is more uncomfortable, uncleanly, or noisy than another, or that any one of them suffers from the fact that all are bad.

You do not get breakfast at the restaurant for the reason, before stated, of the breakfast's unsubstantiality. The dining commences about three o'clock in the afternoon, and continues till nine o'clock, most people dining at five or six. As a rule the attendance is insufficient, and no guest is served until he has made a savage clapping on the tables, or clinking on his glass or plate. Then a hard-pushed waiter appears, and calls out, dramatically, "Behold me!" takes the order, shrieks it to the cook, and, returning with the dinner, cries out again, more dramatically than ever, "Behold it ready!" and arrays it with a great flourish on the table. I have dined in an hotel at Niagara, to the music of a brass band; but I did not find that so utterly bewildering, so destructive of the individual savor of the dishes, and so conducive to absent-minded gluttony as I at first found the constant rush and clamor of the waiters in the Venetian restaurants. The guests are, for the most part, patient and quiet enough, eating their *minestra* and boiled beef in such peace as the surrounding uproar permits them, and seldom making acquaintance with each other. It is a mistake, I think, to expect much talk from any people at dinner. The ingenious English tourists who visit the United States from time to time find us silent over our meat, and I have noticed the like trait among people of divers races in Europe.

As I have said, the greater part of the diners at the restaurants are single, and seem to have no knowledge of each other. Perhaps the gill of the fiendish wine of the country, which they drink at their meals, is rather calculated to chill than warm the heart. But, in any case, a drearier set of my fellow-beings I have never seen,—no, not at evening parties,—and I conceive that their life in lodgings, at the *caffè* and the restaurant, remote from the society of women and all the higher privileges of fellowship for which men herd together, is at once the most gross and insipid, the most selfish and comfortless, life in the world. Our boarding-house life in America, dull, stupid, and flat as it often is, seems to me infinitely better than the restaurant life of young Italy. It is creditable to Latin Europe that, with all this homelessness and domestic outlawry, its young men still preserve the gentleness of civilization.

The families that share the exile of the eating-houses sometimes make together a feeble buzz of conversation, but the unfriendly spirit of the place seems soon to silence them. Undoubtedly they frequent the restaurant for economy's sake. Fuel is costly, and the restaurant is cheap, and its cooking better than they could perhaps otherwise afford to have. Indeed, so cheap is the restaurant that actual experience proved the cost of a dinner there to be little more than the cost of the raw material in the market. From this inexpensiveness comes also the custom, which is common, of sending home to purchasers meals from the eating-houses.

As one descends in the scale of the restaurants, the difference is not so noticeable in the prices of the same dishes as in the substitution of cheaper varieties of food. At the best eating-houses, the Gallic traditions bear sway more or less, but in the poorer sort the cooking is done entirely by native artists, deriving their inspirations from the unsophisticated tastes of exclusively native diners. It is perhaps needless to say that they grow characteristic and picturesque as they grow dirty and cheap, until at last the cook-shop perfects the descent with a triumph of raciness and local coloring. The cook-shop in Venice opens upon you at almost every turn,—everywhere, in fact, but in the Piazza and the Merceria,—and looking in, you see its vast heaps of frying fish, and its huge caldrons of ever-boiling broth which smell to heaven with garlic and onions. In the seducing windows smoke golden mountains of *polenta* (a thicker kind of mush or hasty-pudding, made of Indian meal, and universally eaten in North Italy), platters of crisp minnows, bowls of rice, roast poultry, dishes of snails and liver; and around the fascinating walls hang huge plates of bronzed earthenware for a lavish and a hospitable show, and for the representation of those scenes of Venetian story which are modelled upon them in bas-relief. Here I like to take my unknown friend—my scoundrel *facchino* or rascal gondolier—as he comes to buy his dinner, and bargains eloquently with the cook, who stands with a huge ladle in his hand capable of skimming mysterious things from vasty depths. I am spellbound by the drama which ensues, and in which all the cords of the human heart are touched, from those that tremble at high tragedy to those that are shaken by broad farce. When the diner has bought his dinner, and issues forth with his *polenta* in one hand, and his fried minnows or stewed snails in the other, my fancy fondly follows him to his gondola-station, where he eats it, and quarrels volubly with other gondoliers across the Grand Canal.

A simpler and less ambitious sort of cook-shop abounds in the region of Rialto, where on market mornings I have seen it driving a prodigious business with peasants, gondoliers, and laborers. Its more limited resources consist chiefly of fried eels, fish, *polenta,* and *sguassetto.* The latter is a true *roba veneziana,* and is a loud-flavored broth, made of those desperate scraps of meat which are found impracticable even by the sausage-makers.

Another, but more delicate dish, peculiar to the place, is the clotted blood of poultry, fried in slices with onions. A great number of the families of the poor breakfast at these shops very abundantly, for three soldi each person.

In Venice every holiday has its appropriate viand. During carnival all the butter and cheese shop-windows are whitened with the snow of beaten cream,—*panamontata*. At San Martino the bakers parade troops of gingerbread warriors. Later, for Christmas, comes *mandorlato*, which is a candy made of honey and enriched with almonds. In its season only can any of these devotional delicacies be had; but there is a species of cruller, fried in oil, which has all seasons for its own. On the occasion of every *festa* and of every *sagra* (which is the holiday of one parish only), stalls are erected in the squares for the cooking and sale of these crullers, between which and the religious sentiment proper to the whole year there seems to be some occult relation.

In the winter, the whole city appears to abandon herself to cooking for the public, till she threatens to hopelessly disorder the law of demand and supply. There are, to begin with, the *caffè* and restaurants of every class. Then there are the cook-shops, and the poulterers', and the sausage-makers'. Then, also, every fruit-stall is misty and odorous with roast apples, boiled beans, cabbage, and potatoes. The chestnut-roasters infest every corner, and, women, and children cry roast pumpkin at every turn, till at last hunger seems an absurd and foolish vice, and the ubiquitous beggars, no less than the habitual abstemiousness of every class of the population, become the most perplexing and maddening of anomalies.

CHAPTER VII

HOUSEKEEPING IN VENICE

I HOPE that it is by a not unnatural progress I pass from speaking of dinners and diners to the kindred subject of thepresent chapter, and I trust the reader will not disdain the lowly-minded muse that sings this mild domestic lay. I was resolved in writing this book to tell what I had found most books of travel very slow to tell,—as much as possible of the every-day life of a people whose habits are so different from our own; endeavoring to develop a just notion of their character, not only from the show-traits which strangers are most likely to see, but also from experience of such things as strangers are most likely to miss.

The absolute want of society of my own nation in Venice would have thrown me upon study of the people for my amusement, even if I had cared to learn nothing of them; and the necessity of economical housekeeping would have caused me to live in the frugal Venetian fashion, even if I had been disposed to remain a foreigner in everything. Of bachelor lodgings I had sufficient experience during my first year; but as most prudent travellers who visit the city for a week take lodgings, I need not describe my own particularly. You can tell the houses in which there are rooms to let by the squares of white paper fastened to the window-shutters; and a casual glance as you pass through the streets gives you the idea that the chief income of the place is derived from letting lodgings. Carpetless, dreary barracks the rooms usually are, with an uncompromising squareness of prints upon the wall, an appalling breadth of husk-bed, a niggardness of wash-bowl, and an obduracy of sofa never, never to be dissociated in their victim's mind from the idea of the villainous hard bread of Venice on which the gloomy landlady sustains her life with its immutable purposes of plunder. Flabbiness without softness is the tone of these discouraging chambers, which are dear or not according to the season and the situation. On the sunlit Riva during winter, and on the Grand Canal in summer, they are costly enough, but they are to be found on nearly all the squares at reasonable rates. On the narrow streets, where most native bachelors have them, they are absurdly cheap.

As in nearly all places on the Continent, a house in Venice means a number of rooms, including a whole story in a building, or part of it only, but always completely separated from the other rooms on the same floor. Every house has its own entrance from the street, or by a common hall and stairway from the ground-floor, where are the cellars or store-rooms, while each kitchen is usually on a level with the other rooms of the house to which it belongs. The isolation of the different families is secured (as perfectly as where a building is solely appropriated to each) either by the exclusive possession of a street-door,[1] or by the unsocial domestic habits of Europe. You bow and give good-day to the people whom you meet in the common hall and on the common stairway, but you rarely know more of them than their names, and you certainly care nothing about them. The sociability of Europe, and more especially of Southern Europe, is shown abroad; under the domestic roof it dwindles and disappears. And indeed it is no wonder, considering how dispiriting and comfortless most of the houses are. The lower windows are heavily barred with iron; the wood-work is rude, even in many palaces in Venice; the rest is stone and stucco; the walls are not often papered, though they are sometimes painted: the most pleasing and inviting features of the interior is the frescoed ceiling of the better rooms. The windows shut imperfectly, the heavy wooden blinds imperviously (is it worth while to observe that there are no Venetian blinds in Venice?); the doors lift slantingly from the floor, in which their lower hinges are imbedded; the stoves are of plaster, and consume fuel without just return of heat; the balconies alone are always charming, whether they hang high over the streets or look out upon the canals, and, with the gayly painted ceilings, go far to make the houses habitable.

It happens in the case of houses, as with nearly everything else in Italy, that you pay about the same price for half the comfort that you get in America. In Venice, most of the desirable situations

---

[1] Where the street entrance is in common, every floor has its bell, which, being sounded, summons a servant to some upper window, with the demand, most formidable to strangers, *"Chi xe?"* (Who is it?) But you do not answer with your name. You reply, *"Amici!"* (Friends!) on which comforting reassurance the servant draws the latch of the door by a wire running upward to her hand, and permits you to enter and wander about at your leisure till you reach her secret height. This is, supposing the master or mistress of the house to be at home. If they are not in, she answers your *"Amici!"* with *"No ghe ne xe!"* (Nobody here!) and lets down a basket by a string outside the window, and fishes up your card.

are on the Grand Canal; but here the rents are something absurdly high when taken in consideration with the fact that the city is not made a place of residence by foreigners, like Florence, and that it has no commercial activity to enhance the cost of living. House-hunting, under these circumstances, becomes an office of constant surprise and disconcertment to the stranger. You look, for example, at a suite of rooms in a tumble-down old palace, where the walls, shamelessly smarted up with coarse paper, crumble at your touch; where the floor rises and falls like the sea, and the door-frames and window-cases have long lost all recollection of the plumb. Madama la Baronessa is at present occupying these pleasant apartments, and you only gain admission to them after an embassy to procure her permission. Madama la Baronessa receives you courteously, and you pass through her rooms, which are a little in disorder, the Baronessa being on the point of removal. Madama la Baronessa's hoop-skirts prevail upon the floors; and at the side of the couch which her form lately pressed in slumber you observe a French novel and a wasted candle in the society of a half-bottle of the wine of the country. A bedroomy smell pervades the whole suite, and through the open window comes a curious stench, explained as the odor of Madama la Baronessa's guinea-pigs, of which she is so fond that she has had their sty placed immediately under her window in the garden. It is this garden which has first taken your heart, with a glimpse caught through the great open door of the palace. It is disordered and wild, but so much the better; its firs are very thick and dark, and there are certain statues, fauns and nymphs, which weather-stains and mosses have made much decenter than the sculptor intended. You think that for this garden's sake you could put up with the house, which must be very cheap. What is the price of the rooms? you ask of the smiling landlord. He answers, without winking, "If taken for several years, a thousand florins a year." At which you suppress the whistle of disdainful surprise, and say you think it will not suit. He calls your attention to the sun, which comes in at every side, which will roast you in summer, and will not (as he would have you think) warm you in winter. "But there is another apartment," through which you drag languidly. It is empty now, being last inhabited by an English Ledi,—and her stove-pipes went out of the windows and blackened the shabby stucco front of the villainous old palace.

In a back court, upon a filthy canal, you chance on a house, the curiously frescoed front of which tempts you within. A building which has a lady and gentleman painted in fresco, and making love from balcony to balcony, on the façade, as well as Arlecchino depicted in the act of leaping from the second to the third story, promises something. Promises something, but does not fulfil the promise. The interior is fresh, clean, and new, and cold and dark as a cellar. This house—that is to say, a floor of the house—you may have for four hundred florins a year; and then farewell the world and the light of the sun! for neither will ever find you in that back court, and you will never see anybody but the neighboring laundresses and their children, who cannot enough admire the front of your house.

E via in seguito! This is of house-keeping, not house-hunting. There are pleasant and habitable houses in Venice, but they are not cheap, as many of the uninhabitable houses also are not. Here, discomfort and ruin have their price, and the tumble-down is patched up and sold at rates astonishing to innocent strangers who come from countries in good repair, where the tumble-down is worth nothing. If I were not ashamed of the idle and foolish old superstitions in which I once believed concerning life in Italy, I would tell how I came gradually to expect very little for a great deal; and how a knowledge of many houses to let made me more and more contented with the house we had taken.

It was in one corner of an old palace on the Grand Canal, and the window of the little parlor looked down upon the water, which had made friends with its painted ceiling, and bestowed tremulous, golden smiles upon it when the sun shone. The dining-room was not so much favored by the water, but it gave upon some green and ever-rustling tree-tops, that rose to it from a tiny garden-ground, no bigger than a pocket handkerchief. Through this window, also, we could see the quaint, picturesque life of the canal; and from another room we could reach a little terrace above the water. We were not in the *appartamento signorile*,[2]—that was above,—but we were more snugly quartered on the first story from the ground-floor, commonly used as a winter apartment in the old times. But it had been cut up, and suites of rooms had been broken according to the caprice of successive landlords, till it was not at all palatial any more. The upper stories still retained something of former grandeur, and had acquired with time more than former discomfort. We were not envious of them, for they were humbly let at a price less than we paid; though we could not quite repress a covetous yearning for their arched and carven windows, which we saw sometimes from the canal, above the tops of the garden trees.

The gondoliers used always to point out our palace (which was called Casa Falier) as the house in which Marino Faliero was born; and for a long time we clung to the hope that it might be so. But however pleasant it was, we were forced, on reading up the subject a little, to relinquish our illusion, and accredit an old palace at Santi Apostoli with the distinction we would fain have claimed for ours. I am rather at a loss to explain how it made our lives in Casa Falier any pleasanter to think that a beheaded traitor had been born in it, but we relished the superstition amazingly as long as we could possibly believe in it. What went far to confirm us at first in our credulity was the residence, in another part of the palace, of the Canonico Falier, a lineal descendant of the unhappy Doge. He was a very mild-faced old priest, with a white head, which he carried downcast, and crimson legs, on which he moved but feebly. He owned the rooms in which he lived, and the apartment in the front of the palace just above our own. The rest of the house belonged to another; for in Venice many of the palaces are divided up and sold among different purchasers, floor by floor, and sometimes even room by room.

But the tenantry of Casa Falier was far more various than its proprietorship. Over our heads dwelt a Dalmatian family; below

---

[2] The noble floor, as the second or third story of the palace is called.

our feet a Frenchwoman; at our right, upon the same floor, an English gentleman; under him a French family; and over him the family of a marquis in exile from Modena. Except with Mr.——, the Englishman, who was at once our friend and landlord (impossible as this may appear to those who know anything of landlords in Italy), we had no acquaintance, beyond that of salutation, with the many nations represented in our house. We could not help holding the French people in some sort responsible for the invasion of Mexico; and, though opportunity offered for cultivating the acquaintance of the Modenese, we did not improve it.

As for our Dalmatian friends, we met them and bowed to them a great deal, and we heard them overhead in frequent athletic games, involving noise as of the manœuvring of cavalry; and as they stood a good deal on their balcony, and looked down upon us on ours, we sometimes enjoyed seeing them admirably fore-shortened, like figures in a frescoed ceiling. The father of this family was a little man of a solemn and impressive demeanor, who had no other occupation but to walk up and down the city and view its monuments, for which purpose, he one day informed us, he had left his native place in Dalmatia, after forty years' study of Venetian history. He further told us that this was by no means worth the time given it; that whereas the streets of Venice were sepulchres in point of narrowness and obscurity, he had a house in Zara, from the windows of which you might see for miles uninterruptedly! This little gentleman wore a black hat, in the last vivid polish of respectability, and I think fortune was not his friend. The hat was too large for him, as the hats of Italians always are; it came down to his eyes, and he carried a cane. Every evening he marched solemnly at the head of a procession of his handsome young children, who went to hear the military music in St. Mark's Square.

The entrance to the house of the Dalmatians—we never knew their names—gave access also to a house in the story above them, which belonged to some mysterious person described on his door-plate as "Co. Prata." I think we never saw Co. Prata himself, and only by chance some members of his family when they came back from their summer in the country to spend the winter in the city. Prata's "Co.," we gradually learnt, meant "Conte," and the little counts and countesses, his children, immediately on their arrival took an active part in the exercises of the Dalmatian cavalry. Later in the fall, certain of the count's vassals came to the *riva*[3] in one of the great boats of the Po, with a load of brush and corncobs for fuel,—and this is all we ever knew of our neighbors on the fourth floor. As long as he remained "Co." we yearned to know who and what he was; being interpreted as Conte Prata, he ceased to interest us.

Such, then, was the house, and such the neighborhood, in which two little people, just married, came to live in Venice.

They were by nature of the order of shorn lambs, and Providence, tempering the inclemency of the domestic situation, gave them Giovanna.

The house was furnished throughout, and Giovanna had been furnished with it. She was at hand to greet the new-comers, and "This is my wife, the new mistress," said the young *Paron*,[4] with the bashful pride proper to the time and place.

Giovanna glowed welcome, and said, with adventurous politeness, she was very glad of it.

"*Serva sua!*"

The *Parona,* not knowing Italian, laughed in English.

So Giovanna took possession of us, and, acting upon the great truth that handsome is that handsome does, began at once to make herself a thing of beauty.

As a measure of convenience and of deference to her feelings, we immediately resolved to call her G., merely, when speaking of her in English, instead of Giovanna, which would have troubled her with conjecture concerning what was said of her. And as G. thus became the centre around which our domestic life revolved,

---

[3] The gondola landing-stairs which descend to the water before palace-doors and at the ends of streets.

[4] *Padrone* in Italian. A salutation with Venetian friends, and the title by which Venetian servants always designate their employers.

she must be somewhat particularly treated of in this account of our housekeeping. I suppose that, given certain temperaments and certain circumstances, this would have been much like keeping play-house anywhere; in Venice it had, but for the unmistakable florins it cost, a curious property of unreality and impermanency. It is sufficiently bad to live in a rented house; in a house which you have hired ready-furnished, it is long till your life takes root, and Home blossoms up in the alien place. For a great while we regarded our house merely as very pleasant lodgings, and we were slow to form any relations which could take from our residence its temporary character. Had we but thought to get in debt to the butcher, the baker, and the grocer, we might have gone far to establish ourselves at once; but we imprudently paid our way, and consequently had no ties to bind us to our fellow-creatures. In Venice provisions are bought by housekeepers on a scale surprisingly small to one accustomed to wholesale American ways, and G., having the purse, made our little purchases in cash, never buying more than enough for one meal at a time. Every morning, the fruits and vegetables are distributed from the great market at the Rialto among a hundred greengrocers' stalls in all parts of the city; bread (which is never made at home) is found fresh at the baker's; there is a butcher's stall in each campo with fresh meat. These shops are therefore resorted to for family supplies day by day; and the poor lay in provisions there in portions graduated to a soldo of their ready means. A great Bostonian, whom I remember to have heard speculate on the superiority of a state of civilization in which you could buy two cents' worth of beef to that in which so small a quantity was unpurchasable, would find the system perfected here, where you can buy half a cent's worth. It is a system friendly to poverty, and the small retail prices approximate very closely the real value of the stuff sold, as we sometimes proved by offering to purchase in quantity. Usually no reduction would be made from the retail rate, and it was sufficiently amusing to have the dealer figure up the cost of the quantity we proposed to buy, and then exhibit an exact multiplication of his retail rate by our twenty or fifty. Say an orange is worth a soldo: you get no more than a hundred for a florin, though the dealer will cheerfully go under that number if he can cheat you in the count. So in most things we found it better to let G. do the marketing in her own small Venetian fashion, and "guard our strangeness."

But there were some things which must be brought to the house by the dealers, such as water for drinking and cooking, which is drawn from public cisterns in the squares, and carried by stout young girls to all the houses. These *bigolanti* all come from the mountains of Friuli; they all have rosy cheeks, white teeth, bright eyes, and no waists whatever (in the fashionable sense), but abundance of back. The cisterns are opened about eight o'clock in the morning, and then their day's work begins with chatter, and splashing, and drawing up buckets from the wells; and each sturdy little maiden in turn trots off under a burden of two buckets,—one appended from either end of a bow resting upon the right shoulder. The water is very good, for it is the rain which falls on the shelving surface of the campo, and soaks through a bed of sea-sand around the cisterns into the cool depths below. The *bigolante* comes every morning and empties her brazen buckets into the great picturesque jars of porous earthenware which ornament Venetian kitchens; and the daily supply of water costs a moderate family about a florin a month.

Fuel is likewise brought to your house, but this arrives in boats. It is cut upon the eastern shore of the Adriatic, and comes to Venice in small coasting vessels, each of which has a plump captain in command, whose red face is so cunningly blended with his cap of scarlet flannel that it is hard on a breezy day to tell where the one begins and the other ends. These vessels anchor off the Custom House in the Giudecca Canal in the fall, and lie there all winter (or until their cargo of fuel is sold), a great part of the time under the charge solely of a small yellow dog of the irascible breed common to the boats of the Po. Thither the smaller dealers in firewood resort, and carry thence supplies of fuel to all parts of the city, melodiously crying their wares up and down the canals, and penetrating the land on foot with specimen bundles of fagots in their arms. They are not, as a class, imaginative, I think,—their fancy seldom rising beyond the invention that their fagots are beautiful and sound and dry. But our particular woodman was, in his way, a gifted man.

Long before I had dealings with him, I knew him by the superb song, or rather incantation, with which he announced his coming on the Grand Canal. The purport of this was merely that his bark was called the Beautiful Caroline, and that his fagots were fine; but he so dwelt upon the hidden beauties of this idea, and so prolonged their effect upon the mind by artful repetition and the full, round, and resonant roar with which he closed his triumphal hymn, that the spirit was taken with the charm, and held in breathless admiration. By all odds, this woodman's cry was the most impressive of all the street cries of Venice. There may have been an exquisite sadness and sweetness in the wail of the chimney-sweep; a winning pathos in the voice of the vender of roast pumpkin; an oriental fancy and splendor in the fruiterers who cried "Melons with hearts of fire!" and "Juicy pears that bathe your beard!"—there may have been something peculiarly effective in the song of the chestnut-man who shouted "Fat chestnuts," and added, after a lapse in which you got almost beyond hearing, "and well cooked!"—I do not deny that there was a seductive sincerity in the proclamation of one whose peaches could *not* be called beautiful to look upon, and were consequently advertised as "Ugly, but good!"—I say nothing to detract from the merits of harmonious chair-menders;—to my ears the shout of the melodious fisherman was delectable music, and all the birds of summer sang in the voices of the countrymen who sold finches and larks in cages, and roses and pinks in pots;—but I say, after all, none of these people combined the vocal power, the sonorous movement, the delicate grace, and the vast compass of our woodman. Yet this man, as far as virtue went, was *vox et præterea nihil*. He was a vagabond of the most abandoned; he was habitually in drink, and I think his sins had gone near to make him mad,—at any rate, he was of a most lunatical deportment. In other lands, the man of whom you are a regular purchaser serves you well; in Italy, he conceives that his long service gives him the right to plunder you if possible. I felt in every fibre that this woodman invariably cheated me in measurement, and, indeed, he scarcely denied it on accusation. But my single experience of the more magnificent scoundrels of whom *he* bought the wood originally contented me with the swindle with which I had become familiarized. On this occasion I took a boat and went to the Custom House, to get my fuel at first hand. The captain of the ship which I boarded wished me to pay more than I gave for fuel delivered at my door, and thereupon ensued the tragic scene of bargaining, as these things are conducted in Italy. We stood up and bargained, we sat down and bargained; the captain turned his back upon me in indignation; I parted from him and took to my boat in scorn; he called me back and displayed the wood,—good, sound, dryer than bones; he pointed to the threatening heavens, and declared that it would snow that night, and on the morrow I could not get wood for twice the present price; but I laughed incredulously. Then my captain took another tack, and tried to make the contract in obsolete currencies, in Austrian pounds, in Venetian pounds; but as I inexorably reduced these into familiar money, he paused desperately, and made me an offer which I accepted with mistaken exultation. For my captain was shrewder than I, and held arts of measurement in reserve against me. He agreed that the measurement and transportation should not cost me the value of his tooth-pick—quite an old and worthless one—which he showed me. Yet I was surprised into the payment of a youth whom this man called to assist at the measurement, and I had to give the boatman drink-money at the end. He promised that the measure should be just: yet if I lifted my eye from the work he placed the logs slantingly on the measure, and threw in knotty chunks that crowded wholesome fuel out, and let the daylight through and through the pile. I protested, and he admitted the wrong when I pointed it our: "*Ga razon, lu!*" (He's right!) he said to his fellows in infamy, and throwing aside the objectionable pieces, proceeded to evade justice by new artifices.

When I had this memorable load of wood housed at home, I found that it had cost me just what I paid my woodman, and that I had additionally lost my self-respect in being plundered before my face, and I resolved thereafter to be cheated in quiet dignity behind my back. The woodman exulted in his restored sovereignty, and I lost nothing in penalty for my revolt.

Among other provisioners who come to your house in Venice are those ancient peasant-women who bring fresh milk in bottles, carefully packed in baskets filled with straw. They set off the whiteness of their wares by the brownness of their sunburnt hands and faces, and bear in their general stoutness and burliness of presence a curious resemblance to their own comfortable bottles. They wear broad straw hats, and dangling ear-rings of yellow gold, and are the pleasantest sight of the morning streets of Venice, to the stoniness of which they bring a sense of the country's clovery pasturage in the milk just drawn from the great cream-colored cows.

Fishermen also come down the little *calli*—with shallow baskets of fish upon their heads and under either arm, and cry their soles and mackerel to the neighborhood, stopping now and then at some door to bargain away the eels which they chop into sections as the thrilling drama proceeds, and hand over as a denouement at the purchaser's own price. "Beautiful and all alive!" is the engaging cry with which they hawk their fish.

Besides these daily purveyors, there are men of divers arts who come to exercise their crafts at your house: not chimney-sweeps merely, but glaziers, and that sort of workmen, and, best of all, chair-menders,—who bear a mended chair upon their shoulders for a sign, with pieces of white wood for further mending, a drawing-knife, a hammer, and a sheaf of rushes, and who sit down at your door, and plait the rush bottoms of your kitchen-chairs anew, and make heaps of fragrant whittlings with their knives, and gossip with your serving-woman.

But in the mean time our own serving-woman Giovanna, the great central principle of our housekeeping, is waiting to be personally presented to the company. In Italy there are old crones so haggard that it is hard not to believe them created just as crooked and foul and full of fluff and years as you behold them, and you cannot understand how so much frowziness and so little hair, so great show of fangs and so few teeth, are growths from any ordinary human birth. G. is no longer young, but she is not after the likeness of these old women. It is of a middle age, unbeginning, interminable, of which she gives you the impression. She has brown apple-cheeks, just touched with frost; her nose is of a strawberry formation, abounding in small dints, and having the slightly shrunken effect observable in tardy perfections of the fruit mentioned. A tough, pleasant, indestructible woman—for use, we thought, not ornament—the mother of a family, a good Catholic, and the flower of serving-women.

I do not think that Venetian servants are, as a class, given to pilfering; but knowing ourselves subject by nature to pillage, we cannot repress a feeling of gratitude to G. that she does not prey upon us. She strictly accounts for all money given her at the close of each week, and to this end keeps a kind of account-book, which I cannot help regarding as in some sort an inspired volume, being privy to the fact, confirmed by her own confession, that G. is not good for reading and writing. On settling with her I have been permitted to look into this book, which is all in capital letters,— each the evident result of serious labor,—with figures representing combinations of the pot-hook according to bold and original conceptions. The spelling is also a remarkable effort of creative genius. The only difficulty under which the author labors in regard to the book is the confusion naturally resulting from the effort to get literature right side up when it has got upside down. The writing is a kind of pugilism—the strokes being made straight out from the shoulder. The account-book is always carried about with her in a fathomless pocket overflowing with the aggregations of a housekeeper who can throw nothing away, to wit: match-boxes, now appointed to hold buttons and hooks-and-eyes; beeswax in the lump; the door-key (which in Venice takes a formidable size, and impresses you at first sight as ordnance); a patch-bag; a porte-monnaie; many lead-pencils in the stump;

scissors, pincushions, and the Beata Vergine in a frame. Indeed, this incapability of throwing things away is made to bear rather severely upon us in some things, such as the continual reappearance of familiar dishes at table, particularly veteran *bifsteca*. But we fancy that the same frugal instinct is exercised to our advantage and comfort in other things, for G. makes a great show and merit of denying our charity to those bold and adventurous children of sorrow who do not scruple to ring your doorbell and demand alms. It is true that with G., as with every Italian, almsgiving enters into the theory and practice of Christian life, but she will not suffer misery to abuse its privileges. She has no hesitation, however, in bringing certain objects of compassion to our notice, and she procures small services to be done for us by many lame and halt of her acquaintance. Having bought my boat (I come, in time, to be willing to sell it again for half its cost to me), I require a menial to clean it now and then, and Giovanna first calls me a youthful Gobbo for the work,—a festive hunchback, a bright-hearted whistler of comic opera. Whether this blithe humor is not considered decent, I do not know, but though the Gobbo serves me faithfully, I find him one day replaced by a venerable old man, whom—from his personal resemblance to Time—I should think much better occupied with an hour-glass, or engaged with a scythe in mowing me and other mortals down, than in cleaning my boat. But all day long he sits on my *riva* in the sun, when it shines, gazing fixedly at my boat; and when the day is dark, he lurks about the street, accessible to my slightest boating impulse. He salutes my going out and coming in with grave reverence, and I think he has no work to do but that which G.'s wise compassion has given him from me. Suddenly, like the Gobbo, the Veccio also disappears, and I hear vaguely—for in Venice you never know anything with precision—that he has found a regular employment in Padua, and again that he is dead. While he lasts, G. has a pleasant, even a sportive manner with this poor old man, calculated to cheer his declining years; but, as I say, cases of insolent and aggressive misery fail to touch her. The kind of wretchedness that comes breathing woe and *sciampagnin*[5] under our window, and there spends a leisure hour in the rehearsal of distress, establishes no claim either upon her pity or her weakness. She is deaf to the voice of that sorrow, and the monotonous whine of that dolor cannot move her to the purchase of a guilty tranquillity. I imagine, however, that she is afraid to deny charity to the fat Capuchin friar in spectacles and bare feet, who comes twice a month to levy contributions of bread and fuel for his convent, for we hear her declare from the window that the master is not at home, whenever the good brother rings; and at last, as this excuse gives out, she ceases to respond to his ring at all.

Sometimes, during the summer weather, comes down our street a certain tremulous old troubadour with an aged cithern, on which he strums feebly with bones which remain to him from former fingers, and in a thin, quivering voice pipes wornout ditties of youth and love. Sadder music I have never heard, but though it has at times drawn from me the sigh of sensibility without referring sympathy to my pocket, I always hear the compassionate soldo of Giovanna clink reproof to me upon the pavement. Perhaps that slender note touches something finer than habitual charity in her middle-aged bosom, for these were songs, she says, that they used to sing when she was a girl, and Venice was gay and glad, and different from now—*veramente, tutt' altro, signor!*

It is through Giovanna's charitable disposition that we make the acquaintance of two weird sisters, who live not far from us in Calle Falier, and whom we know to this day merely as the Creatures—*creatura* being in the vocabulary of Venetian pity the term for a fellow-being somewhat more pitiable than a *poveretta*. Our Creatures are both well stricken in years, and one of them has some incurable disorder which frequently confines her to the wretched cellar in which they live with the invalid's husband,—a mild, pleasant-faced man, a tailor by trade, and of batlike habits,

---

[5] Little champagne,—the name which the Venetian populace gave to a fierce and deadly kind of brandy drunk during the scarcity of wine. After the introduction of coal-oil this liquor came to be jocosely know as *petrolio*.

who hovers about their dusky doorway in the summer twilight. These people have but one room, and a little nook of kitchen at the side; and not only does the sun never find his way into their habitation, but even the daylight cannot penetrate it. They pay about four florins a month for the place, and I hope their landlord is as happy as his tenants. For though one is sick, and all are wretchedly poor, they are far from being discontented. They are opulent in the possession of a small dog, which they have raised from the cradle, as it were, and adopted into the family. They are never tired of playing with their dog,—the poor old children,— and every slight display of intelligence on his part delights them. They think it fine in him to follow us as we go by, but pretend to beat him; and then they excuse him, and call him ill names, and catch him up, and hug him and kiss him. He feeds upon their slender means and the pickings that G. carefully carries him from our kitchen, and gives to him on our doorstep in spite of us, while she gossips with his mistresses, who chorus our appearance at such times with "*I miei rispetti, signori!*" We often see them in the street, and at a distance from home, carrying mysterious bundles of clothes; and at last we learn their vocation, which is one not known out of Italian cities, I think. There the state is Uncle to the hard-pressed, and instead of many pawnbrokers' shops there is one large municipal spout, which is called the Monte di Pietà, where the needy pawn their goods. The system is centuries old in Italy, but there are people who to this day cannot summon courage to repair in person to the Mount of Pity, and, to meet their wants, there has grown up a class of frowzy old women who transact the business for them, and receive a small percentage for their trouble. Our poor old Creatures were of this class, and as there were many persons in impoverished, decaying Venice who had need of the succor they procured, they made out to earn a living when both were well, and to eke out existence by charity when one was ill. They were harmless neighbors, and I believe they regretted our removal, when this took place, for they used to sit down under an arcade opposite our new house, and spend the duller intervals of trade in the contemplation of our windows.

The alarming spirit of nepotism which Giovanna developed at a later day was, I fear, a growth from the encouragement we gave her charitable disposition. But for several months it was merely from the fact of a boy who came and whistled at the door until Giovanna opened it and reproved him in the name of all the saints and powers of darkness, that we knew her to be a mother; and we merely had her word for the existence of a husband, who dealt in poultry. Without seeing Giovanna's husband, I nevertheless knew him to be a man of downy exterior, wearing a canvas apron, thickly crusted with the gore of fowls, who sat at the door of his shop and plucked chickens forever, as with the tireless hand of Fate. I divined that he lived in an atmosphere of scalded pullet; that three earthen cups of clotted chickens' blood, placed upon his window-shelf, formed his idea of an attractive display, and that he shadowed forth his conceptions of the beautiful in symmetrical rows of plucked chickens, presenting to the public eye rear views embellished with a single feather erect in the tail of each bird; that he must be, through the ethics of competition, the sworn foe of those illogical peasants who bring dead poultry to town in cages, like singing birds, and equally the friend of those restaurateurs who furnish you a meal of victuals and a feather-bed in the same *mezzo-pollo arrosto*. He turned out on actual appearance to be all I had prefigured him, with the additional merit of having a large red nose, a sidelong, fugitive gait, and a hangdog countenance. He furnished us poultry at rates slightly advanced, I think.

As for the boy, he turned up after a while as a constant guest, and took possession of the kitchen. He came near banishment at one time for catching a large number of sea-crabs in the canal, and confining them in a basket in the kitchen, which they left at the dead hour of night, to wander all over our house,—making a mysterious and alarming sound of snapping, like an army of death-watches, and eluding the cunningest efforts at capture. On another occasion, he fell into the canal before our house, and terrified us by going under twice before the arrival of the old gondolier, who called out to him "*Petta! petta!*" (Wait! wait!) as he placidly pushed his boat to the spot. Developing other disagreeable traits, Beppi was finally driven into exile, from which he nevertheless furtively returned on holidays.

The family of Giovanna thus gradually encroaching upon us, we came also to know her mother,—a dread and loathly old lady, whom we would willingly have seen burned at the stake for a witch. She was commonly encountered at nightfall in our street, where she lay in wait, as it were, to prey upon the fragrance of dinner drifting from the kitchen windows of our neighbor, the Duchess of Parma. Here was heard the voice of cooks and of scullions, and the ecstasies of helpless voracity in which we sometimes beheld this old lady were fearful to witness. Nor did we find her more comfortable in our own kitchen, where we often saw her. The place itself is weird and terrible,—low ceiled, with the stone hearth built far out into the room, and the melodramatic implements of Venetian cookery dangling tragically from the wall. Here is no every-day cheerfulness of cooking-range, but grotesque andirons wading into the bristling embers, and a long crane with villainous pots gibbeted upon it. When Giovanna's mother, then (of the Italian hags, haggard), rises to do us reverence from the darkest corner of this kitchen, and croaks her good wishes for our long life, continued health, and endless happiness, it has the effect upon our spirits of the darkest malediction.

Not more pleasing, though altogether lighter and cheerfuller, was Giovanna's sister-in-law, whom we knew only as the Cognata. Making her appearance first upon the occasion of Giovanna's sickness, she slowly but surely established herself as an habitual presence, and threatened at one time, as we fancied, to become our paid servant. But a happy calamity, which one night carried off a carpet and the window curtains of an unoccupied room, cast an evil suspicion upon the Cognata, and she never appeared after the discovery of the theft. We suspected her of having invented some dishes of which we were very fond, and we hated her for oppressing us with a sense of many surreptitious favors. Objectively, she was a slim, hoopless little woman, with a tendency to be always at the street-door when we opened it. She had a narrow, narrow face, with eyes of terrible slyness, an applausive smile, and a demeanor of slavish patronage. Our kitchen, after her addition to the household, became the banqueting-hall of Giovanna's family, who dined there every day upon dishes of fish and garlic, that gave the house the general savor of a low cook-shop.

As for Giovanna herself, she had the natural tendency of excellent people to place others in subjection. Our servitude at first was not hard, and consisted chiefly in the stimulation of appetite to extraordinary efforts when G. had attempted to please us with some novelty in cooking. She held us to a strict account in this respect; but indeed our applause was for the most part willing enough. Her culinary execution, first revealing itself in a noble rendering of our ideas of roast potatoes,—a delicacy foreign to the Venetian kitchen,—culminated at last in the same style of *polpetti*[6] which furnished forth the table of our neighbor, the Duchess, and was a perpetual triumph with us.

But G.'s spirit was not wholly that of the serving-woman. We noted in her the liveliness of wit seldom absent from the Italian poor. She was a great babbler, and talked willingly to herself and to inanimate things, when there was no other chance for talk. She was profuse in maledictions of bad weather, which she held up to scorn as that dog of a weather. The crookedness of the fuel transported her, and she upbraided the fagots as springing from races of ugly old curs. (The vocabulary of Venetian abuse is inexhaustible, and the Venetians invent and combine terms of opprobrium with endless facility, but all abuse begins and ends with the attribution of doggishness.) The conscription was held in the campo near us, and G. declared the place to have become unendurable,—"*proprio un campo di sospiri!*" (Really a field of sighs.) "*Staga comodo!*" she said to a guest of ours who would have moved his chair to let her pass between him and the wall. "Don't move; the way to Paradise is not wider than this."

We sometimes lamented that Giovanna, who did not sleep in

---

[6] I confess a tenderness for this dish, which is a delicater kind of hash, skilfully flavored and baked in rolls of a mellow complexion and fascinating appearance.

the house, should come to us so late in the morning; but we could
not deal harshly with her on that account, met, as we always were
with plentiful and admirable excuses. Who were we, indeed, to
place our wishes in the balance against the welfare of the sick
neighbor with whom Giovanna passed so many nights of vigil?
Should we reproach her with tardiness when she had not closed
the eye all night for a headache properly of the devil? If she came
late in the morning, she stayed late at night; and it sometimes
happened that when the Paron and Parona, supposing her gone,
made a stealthy expedition to the kitchen for cold chicken, they
found her there at midnight, in the fell company of the Cognata,
bibbing the wine of the country, and holding a mild Italian revel
with that vinegar and the stony bread of Venice.

I have said G. was the flower of serving-women; and so at first
she seemed, and it was long till we doubted her perfection. We knew
ourselves to be very young and weak and unworthy. The Parona
had the rare gift of learning to speak less and less Italian every day,
and fell inevitably into subjection. The Paron in a domestic point
of view was naturally nothing. It had been strange indeed if Giovanna, beholding the great contrast we presented to herself in many
respects, had forborne to abuse her advantage over us. But we
trusted her implicitly, and I hardly know how or when it was that
we began to waiver in our confidence. It is certain that with the lapse
of time we came gradually to have breakfast at twelve o'clock,
instead of nine, as we had originally appointed it, and that G. grew
to consume the greater part of the day in making our small purchases, and to give us our belated dinners at seven o'clock. We
protested, and temporary reforms ensued, only to be succeeded by
more hopeless lapses; but it was not till all entreaties and threats
failed that we began to think seriously it would be well to have done
with Giovanna, as an unprofitable servant. I give the result, not all
the nice causes from which it came. But the question was, How to
get rid of a poor woman and a civil, and the mother of a family
dependent in great part upon her labor? We solemnly resolve a
hundred times to dismiss G., and we shrink a hundred times from
inflicting the blow. At last, somewhat in the spirit of Charles Lamb's

Chinaman who invented roast pig, and discovered that the sole method of roasting it was to burn down a house in order to consume the adjacent pig-sty, and thus cook the roaster in the flames, we hit upon an artifice by which we could dispense with Giovanna, and keep an easy conscience. We had long ceased to dine at home, in despair; and now we resolved to take another house, in which there were other servants. But even then, it was a sore struggle to part with the flower of serving-women, who was set over the vacated house to put it in order after our flitting, and with whom the imprudent Paron settled the last account in the familiar little dining-room, surrounded by the depressing influences of the empty chambers. The place was peopled after all, though we had left it, and I think the tenants who come after us will be haunted by our spectres, crowding them on the pleasant little balcony, and sitting down with them at table. G. stood there, the genius of the place, and wept six regretful tears, each one of which drew a florin from the purse of the Paron. She had hoped to remain with us always while we lived in Venice; but now that she could no longer look to us for support, the Lord must take care of her. The gush of grief was transient: it relieved her, and she came out sunnily a moment after. The Paron went his way more sorrowfully, taking leave at last with the fine burst of Christian philosophy: "We are none of us masters of ourselves in this world, and cannot do what we wish. *Ma! Come si fa? Ci vuol pazienza!*" Yet he was undeniably lightened in heart. He had cut adrift from old moorings, and had crossed the Grand Canal. G. did not follow him, nor any of the long line of pensioners who used to come on certain feast-days to levy tribute of eggs at the old house. (The postman was among these, on Christmas and New Year's, and as he received eggs at every house, it was a problem with us, unsolved to this hour, how he carried them all, and what he did with them.) Not the least among the Paron's causes for self-gratulation was the non-appearance at his new abode of two local newspapers, for which in an evil hour he subscribed, which were delivered with unsparing regularity, and which, being never read, formed the keenest reproach of his imprudent outlay and his idle neglect of their contents.

CHAPTER VIII

THE BALCONY ON THE GRAND CANAL

THE history of Venice reads like a romance; the place seems a fantastic vision at the best, from which the world must at last awake some morning, and find that after all it has only been dreaming, and that there never was any such city. There our race seems to be in earnest in nothing. People sometimes work, but as if without any aim; they suffer, and you fancy them playing at wretchedness. The Church of St. Mark, standing so solidly, with a thousand years under the feet of its innumerable pillars, is not in the least gray with time,—no grayer than a Greek lyric.

"All has suffered a sea-change
Into something rich and strange,"

in this fantastic city. The prose of earth has risen poetry from its baptism in the sea.

And if, living constantly in Venice, you sometimes for a little while forget how marvellous she is, at any moment you may be startled into vivid remembrance. The cunning city beguiles you street by street, and step by step, into some old court, where a flight of marble stairs leads high up to the pillared gallery of an empty palace, with a climbing vine, green and purple on its old decay, and one or two gaunt trees stretching their heads to look into the lofty windows,—blind long ago to their leafy tenderness,—while at their feet is some sumptuously carven well, with the beauty of the sculptor's soul wrought forever into the stone. Or Venice lures you in a gondola into one of her remote canals, where you glide through an avenue as secret and as still as if sea-deep under our work-day world; where the grim heads carven over the water-gates of the palaces stare at you in austere surprise; where the innumerable balconies are full of the Absences of gay cavaliers and gentle dames, gossiping and making love to one another, from their airy perches. Or if the city's mood is one of bolder charm, she fascinates you in the very places where you think her power is the weakest, and as if impatient of your forgetfulness dares a wilder beauty, and enthralls with a yet more unearthly and incredible enchantment. It is in the Piazza, and the Austrian band is playing, and the promenaders pace solemnly up and down to the music, and the gentle Italian loafers at Florian's brood vacantly over their little cups of coffee, and nothing can be more stupid; when suddenly everything is changed, and a memorable tournament flashes up in many-glittering action upon the scene, and there upon the gallery of the church, before the horses of bronze, sit the Senators, bright-robed, and in the midst the bonneted Doge with his guest Petrarch at his side. Or the old Carnival, which had six months of every year to riot in, comes back and throngs the place with motley company,—dominoes, harlequins, pantaloni, illustrissimi and illustrissime, and perhaps even the Doge himself, who has the right of incognito when he wears a little mask of wax at his button-hole. Or may be the grander day revisits Venice when Doria has sent word from his fleet of Genoese at Chioggia that he will listen to the Senate when he has bridled the horses of Saint Mark,—and the whole Republic of rich and poor crowds the square, demanding the release of Pisani, who comes forth from his prison to create victory from the dust of the crumbling commonwealth.

But whatever surprise of memorable or beautiful Venice may prepare for your forgetfulness, be sure it will be complete and resistless. Nay, what potenter magic needs my Venice to revivify her past whenever she will than the serpent cunning of her Grand Canal? Launched upon this great S have I not seen hardened travellers grow sentimental, and has not this prodigious sibilant, in my hearing, inspired white-haired Puritan ministers of the gospel to attempt to quote out of the guide-book "that line from Byron"? Upon my word, I have sat beside wandering editors in their gondolas, and witnessed the expulsion of the newspaper from their nature, while, lulled by the fascination of the place, they were powerless to take their own journals from their pockets, and instead of politics talked some bewildered nonsense about coming back with their families next summer. For myself, I must count as half lost the year spent in Venice before I took a house upon the Grand Canal. There alone can existence have the perfect local flavor. But by what witchery touched one's being suffers the common sea-change, till life at last seems to ebb and flow with the tide in that wonder-avenue of palaces, it would be idle to attempt to tell. I can only take you to our dear little balcony at Casa Falier, and comment not very coherently on the scene upon the water under us.

And I am sure (since it is either in the spring or the fall) you will not be surprised to see, the first thing, a boat-load of those English, who go by from the station to their hotels, every day, in well-freighted gondolas. These parties of travelling Englishry are all singularly alike, from the "Pa'ty" travelling alone with his opera-glass and satchel to the party which fills a gondola with well-cushioned English middle age, ruddy English youth, and substantial English baggage. We have learnt to know them all very well: the father and the mother sit upon the back seat, and their comely girls at the sides and front. These girls all have the honest cabbage-roses of English health upon their cheeks; they all wear little rowdy English hats, and invariable waterfalls of hair tumble upon their broad English backs. They are coming from Switzerland and Germany, and they are going south to Rome and to Naples, and they always pause at Venice a few days. To-morrow we shall see them in the Piazza, and at Florian's, and St. Mark's and the Ducal Palace; and the young ladies will cross the Bridge of Sighs, and will sentimentally feed the vagabond pigeons of St. Mark which loaf about the Piazza and defile the sculptures. But now our travellers are themselves very hungry, and are more anxious than Americans can understand about the *table d'hôte* of their hotel. It is perfectly certain that if they fall into talk there with any of our nation, the respectable English father will remark that this war in America is a very sad war, and will ask to know when it will all end. The truth is Americans do not like these people, and I believe there is no love lost on the other side. But in many things they are travellers to be honored, if not liked: they voyage through all countries, and without awaking fervent affection in any land through which they pass; but their sterling honesty and truth have made the English tongue a draft upon the unlimited confidence of the Continental peoples, and French, Germans, and Italians trust and respect private English faith as cordially as they hate public English perfidy.

They come to Venice chiefly in the autumn, and October is the month of the Sunsets and the English. The former are best seen from the Public Gardens, whence one looks westward, and beholds them glorious behind the domes and towers of San Giorgio Maggiore and the church of the Redentore. Sometimes, when the sky is clear, your sunset on the lagoon is a fine thing; for then the sun goes down into the water with a broad trail of bloody red behind him, as if, wounded far out at sea, he had dragged himself landward across the crimsoning expanses, and fallen and died as he reached the land. But we (upon whom the idleness of Venice grows daily, and from whom the Gardens, therefore, grow farther and farther) are commonly content to take our bit of sunset as we get it from our balcony, through the avenue opened by the narrow canal opposite. We like the earlier afternoon to have been a little rainy, when we have our sunset splendid as the fury of a passionate beauty,—all tears and fire. There is a pretty but impertinent little palace on the corner which is formed by this canal as it enters the Canalazzo, and from the palace, high over the smaller channel, hands an airy balcony. When the sunset sky, under and over the balcony, is of that pathetic and angry red which I have tried to figure, we think ourselves rich in the neighborhood of that part of the "Palace of Art," whereon

> "The light aerial gallery, golden railed,
> Burnt like a fringe of fire."

And so, after all, we do not think we have lost any greater thing in not seeing the sunset from the Gardens, where half a dozen artists are always painting it, or from the quay of the Zattere, where it is splendid over and under the island church of San Giorgio in Alga.

It is only the English and the other tourist strangers who go by upon the Grand Canal during the day. But in the hours just before the summer twilight the gondolas of the citizens appear, and then you may seen whatever is left of Venetian gayety, and looking down upon the groups in the open gondolas may witness something of the home-life of the Italians, who live out-of-doors.

The groups do not vary a great deal one from another: inevitably the pale-faced papa, the fat mamma, the overdressed, handsome young girls. We learned to look for certain gondolas, and grew to feel a fond interest in a very mild young man who took the air in company and contest with a ferocious bull-dog,—boule-dogue he called him, I suppose. He was always smoking languidly, that mild young man, and I fancied I could read in his countenance a gentle, gentle antagonism to life,—the proportionate Byronic misanthropy, which might arise from sugar and water taken instead of gin. But we really knew nothing about him, and our conjecture was conjecture. Officers went by in their brilliant uniforms, and gave the scene an alien splendor. Among these we enjoyed best the spectacle of an old major, or perhaps general, in whom the arrogance of youth had stiffened into a chill hauteur, and who frowned above his gray overwhelming mustache upon the passers, like a citadel grim with battle and age. We used to fancy, with a certain luxurious sense of our own safety, that one broadside from those fortressed eyes could blow from the water the slight pleasure-boats in which the young Venetian idlers were innocently disporting. But again this was merely conjecture. The general's glance may have had no such power. Indeed, the furniture of our apartment sustained no damage from it, even when concentrated through an opera-glass, by which means the brave officer at times perused our humble lodging from the balcony of his own over against us. He may have been no more dangerous in his way than two aged sisters (whom we saw every evening) were in theirs. They represented Beauty in its most implacable and persevering form, and perhaps they had one day been belles and could not forget it. They were very old indeed, but their dresses were new and their paint fresh, and as they glided by in the good-natured twilight one had no heart to smile at them. We gave our smiles, and now and then our soldi, to the swarthy beggar, who, being short of legs, rowed up and down the canal in a boat, and overhauled Charity in the gondolas. He was a singular compromise, in his vocation and his equipment, between the mendicant and corsair: I fear he would not have hesitated to assume the pirate altogether in lonelier waters; and had I been a heavily laden oyster-boat returning by night through some remote and dark canal, I would have steered clear of that truculent-looking craft, of which the crew must have fought with a desperation proportioned to the lack of legs and the difficulty of running away, in case of defeat.

About nightfall came the market boats on their way to the Rialto market, bringing heaped fruits and vegetables from the mainland; and far into the night the soft dip of the oar and the gurgling progress of the boats were company and gentlest lullaby. By which time, if we looked out again, we found the moon risen, and the ghost of dead Venice shadowily happy in haunting the lonesome palaces, and the sea, which had so loved Venice, kissing and caressing the tide-worn marble steps where her feet seemed to rest.

At night sometimes we saw from our balcony one of those *freschi,* which once formed the chief splendor of festive occasions in Venice, and are peculiar to the city, where alone their fine effects are possible. The fresco is a procession of boats with music and lights. Two immense barges, illumined with hundreds of paper lanterns, carry the military bands; the boats of the civil and military dignitaries follow, and then the gondolas of such citizens as choose to take part in the display,—though since 1859 no Italian, unless a government official, has been seen in the procession. No gondola has less than two lanterns, and many have eight or ten, shedding mellow lights of blue and red and purple, over uniforms and silken robes. The soldiers of the bands breathe from their instruments music the most perfect and exquisite of its kind in the world: and as the procession takes the width of the Grand Canal in its magnificent course, soft crimson flushes play upon the old, weather-darkened palaces, and die tenderly away, giving to light and then to shadow the opulent sculptures of pillar and arch and spandrel, and weirdly illuminating the grim and bearded visages of stone that peer down from doorway and window. It is a sight more gracious and fairy than ever poet dreamed; and I feel that the lights and the music have only got into my description by name, and that you would not know them when you saw and heard them, from anything I say. In other days, people tell you, the fresco was much more impressive than now. At intervals, rockets used to be sent up, and the Bengal lights, burned during the progress of the boats, threw the gondoliers' spectral shadows, giant-huge, on the palace walls. But, for my part, I do not care to have the fresco other than I know it: indeed, for my own selfish pleasure, I should be sorry to have Venice in any way less fallen and forlorn than she is.

Without doubt the most picturesque craft ever seen on the
Grand Canal are the great boats of the river Po, which, crossing
the lagoons from Chioggia, come up to the city with the swelling
sea. They are built with a pointed stern and bow rising with the
sweep of a short curve from the water high above the cabin roof,
which is always covered with a straw matting. Black is not the
color of the gondolas alone, but of all boats in Venetia; and these
of the Po are like immense funeral barges, and any one of them
might be sent to take King Arthur and bear him to Avilon, whither
I think most of them are bound. A path runs along either gunwale,
on which the men pace as they pole the boat up the canal,—her
great sail folded and lying with the prostrate mast upon the deck.
The rudder is a prodigious affair, and the man at the helm is
commonly kind enough to wear a red cap with a blue tassel, and
to smoke. The other persons on board are not less obliging and
picturesque, from the dark-eyed young mother who sits with her
child in her arms at the cabin-door, to the bronze boy who figures
in play at her feet with a small yellow dog of the race already
noticed in charge of the fuel-boats from Dalmatia. The father of
the family, whom we take to be the commander of the vessel,
occupies himself gracefully in sitting down and gazing at the babe
and its mother. It is an old habit of mine, formed in childhood
from looking at rafts upon the Ohio, to attribute, with a kind of
heart-ache, supreme earthly happiness to the navigators of lazy
river craft; and as we glance down upon these people from our
balcony, I choose to think them immensely contented, and try, in
a feeble, tacit way, to make friends with so much bliss. But I am
always repelled in these advances by the small yellow dog, who is
rendered extremely irascible by my contemplation of the boat
under his care, and who, ruffling his hair as a hen ruffles her
feathers, never fails to bark furious resentment of my longing.

Far different from the picture presented by this boat's
progress—the peacefulness of which even the bad temper of the
small yellow dog could not mar—was another scene which we
witnessed upon the Grand Canal, when one morning we were
roused from our breakfast by a wild and lamentable outcry. Two

large boats, attempting to enter the small canal opposite at the same time, had struck together with a violence that shook the boatmen to their inmost souls. One barge was laden with lime, and belonged to a plasterer of the city; the other was full of fuel, and commanded by a virulent rustic. These rival captains advanced toward the bows of their boats, with murderous looks,

> "Con la test' alta e con rabbiosa fame,
> Sì che parea che l'aer ne temesse,"

and there stamped furiously, and beat the wind with hands of deathful challenge, while I looked on with that noble interest which the enlightened mind always feels in people about to punch each other's heads.

But the storm burst in words.

"Figure of a pig!" shrieked the Venetian, "you have ruined my boat forever!"

"Thou liest, son of an ugly old dog!" returned the countryman, "and it was my right to enter the canal first."

They then, after this exchange of insult, abandoned the main subject of dispute, and took up the quarrel laterally and in detail. Reciprocally questioning the reputation of all their female relatives to the third and fourth cousins, they defied each other as the offspring of assassins and prostitutes. As the peace-making tide gradually drifted their boats asunder, their anger rose, and they danced back and forth and hurled opprobrium with a foamy volubility that quite left my powers of comprehension behind. At last the townsman, executing a *pas seul* of uncommon violence, stooped and picked up a bit of lime, while the countryman, taking shelter at the stern of his boat, there attended the shot. To my infinite disappointment it was not fired. The Venetian seemed to have touched the climax of his passion in the mere demonstration of hostility, and gently gathering up his oar gave the countryman the right of way. The courage of the latter rose as the danger passed, and as far as he could be heard he continued to exult in the wildest excesses of insult: "Ah-heigh! brutal executioner! Ah, hideous headsman!" *Da capo.* I now know that these people never intended to do more than quarrel, and no doubt they parted as well pleased as if they had actually carried broken heads from the encounter. But at the time I felt affronted and trifled with by the result, for my disappointments arising out of the dramatic manner of the Italians had not yet been frequent enough to teach me to expect nothing from it.

There was some compensation for me—coming, like all compensation, a long while after the loss—in the spectacle of a funeral procession on the Grand Canal, which had a singular and imposing solemnity only possible to the place. It was the funeral of an Austrian general, whose coffin, mounted on a sable catafalco, was borne upon the middle boat of three that moved abreast. The barges on either sides bristled with the bayonets of soldiery, but the dead man was alone in his boat, except for one strange figure that stood at the head of the coffin, and rested its glittering hand upon the black fall of the drapery. This was a man clad *cap-a-pie* in a perfect suit of gleaming mail, with his visor down, and his shoulders swept by the heavy raven plumes of his helm. As at times he moved from side to side, and glanced upward at the old palaces, sad in the yellow morning light, he put out of sight, for me, everything else upon the canal, and seemed the ghost of some crusader come back to Venice, in wonder if this city, lying dead under the hoofs of the Croat, were indeed that same haughty Lady of the Sea who had once sent her blind old Doge to beat down the pride of an empire and disdain its crown.

CHAPTER IX

A DAYBREAK RAMBLE

ONE summer morning the mosquitoes played for me with
sleep, and won. It was half past four, and as it had often
been my humor to see Venice at that hour I got up and sallied
forth for a stroll through the city.

This morning walk did not lay the foundation of a habit of early
rising in me, but I nevertheless advise people always to get up at
half past four, if they wish to receive the most vivid impressions,
and to take the most absorbing interest in everything in the world.
It was with a feeling absolutely novel that I looked about me that

morning, and there was a breezy freshness and clearness in my perceptions altogether delightful, and I fraternized so cordially with Nature that I do not think, if I had sat down immediately after to write out the experience, I should have at all patronized her, as I am afraid scribbling people have sometimes the custom to do. I know that my feeling of brotherhood in the case of two sparrows, which obliged me by hopping down from a garden wall at the end of Calle Falier and promenading on the pavement, was quite humble and sincere; and that I resented the ill-nature of a cat,

"Whom love kept wakeful and the muse,"

and who at that hour was spitefully reviling the morn from a window grating. As I went by the gate of the Canonico's little garden, the flowers saluted me with a breath of perfume,—I think the white honeysuckle was first to offer me this politeness,—and the dumpy little statues looked far more engaging than usual.

After passing the bridge, the first thing to do was to drink a cup of coffee at the Caffè Ponte di Ferro, where the eyebrows of the waiter expressed a mild surprise at my early presence. There was no one else in the place but an old gentleman talking thoughtfully to himself on the subject of two florins, while he poured his coffee into a glass of water, before drinking it. As I lingered a moment over my cup, I was reinforced by the appearance of a company of soldiers, marching to parade in the Campo di Marte. Their officers went at their head, laughing and chatting, and one of the lieutenants, smoking a long pipe, gave me a feeling of satisfaction only comparable to that which I experienced shortly afterward in beholding a stoutly built small dog on the Ponte di San Moisè. The creature was only a few inches high, and it must have been through some mist of dreams yet hanging about me that he impressed me as having something elephantine in his manner. When I stooped down and patted him on the head, I felt colossal.

On my way to the Piazza, I stopped in the church of Saint Mary of the Lily, where, in the company with one other sinner, I found a relish in the early sacristan's deliberate manner of lighting the candles on the altar. Saint Mary of the Lily has a façade in the taste of the declining Renaissance. The interior is in perfect keeping, and all is hideous, abominable, and abandoned. My fellow-sinner was kneeling, and repeating his prayers. He now and then tapped himself absent-mindedly on the breast and forehead, and gave a good deal of his attention to me as I stood at the door, hat in hand. The hour and the place invested him with so much interest that I parted from him with emotion. My feelings were next involved by an abrupt separation from a young English East-Indian, whom I overheard asking the keeper of a *caffè* his way to the Campo di Marte. He was a claret-colored young fellow, tall, and wearing folds of white muslin around his hat. In another world I trust to know how he liked the parade that morning.

I discovered that Piazza San Marco is every morning swept by troops of ragged *facchini*, who gossip noisily and quarrelsomely together over their work. Bootblacks, also, were in attendance, and several followed my progress through the square, in the vague hope that I would relent and have my boots blacked. One peerless waiter stood alone amid the desert elegance of Caffè Florian, which is never shut, day or night, from year to year. At the Caffè of the Greeks, two individuals of the Greek nation were drinking coffee.

I went upon the Molo, passing between the pillars of the Lion and the Saint, and walked freely back and forth, taking in the glory of that prospect of water and of vague islands breaking the silver of the lagoons, like those scenes cunningly wrought in apparent relief on old Venetian mirrors. I walked there freely, for though there were already many gondoliers at the station, not one took me for a foreigner or offered me a boat. At that hour, I was in myself so improbable that, if they saw me at all, I must have appeared to them as a dream. My sense of security was sweet, but it was false, for, on going into the church of St. Mark, the keener eye of the sacristan detected me. He instantly offered to show me the Zeno Chapel; but I declined, preferring the church, where I found the space before the high altar filled with market-people come to hear the early mass. As I passed out of the church, I witnessed the partial awaking of a Venetian gentleman who had spent the night in a sitting posture, between the columns of the main entrance. He looked puffy, scornful, and uncomfortable, and at the moment of falling back to slumber tried to smoke an unlighted cigarette, which he held between his lips. I found none of the shops open as I passed through the Merceria, and but for myself, and here and there a laborer going to work, the busy thoroughfare seemed deserted. In the mere wantonness of power and the security of solitude, I indulged myself in snapping several door-latches, which gave me a pleasure as keen as that enjoyed in boyhood from passing a stick along the pickets of a fence. I was in no wise abashed to be discovered in this amusement by an old peasant-woman, bearing at either end of a yoke the usual basket with bottles of milk packed in straw.

Entering Campo San Bartolomeo, I found trade already astir in that noisy place; the voice of cheap bargains, which by noonday swells into an intolerable uproar, was beginning to be heard. Having lived in Campo San Bartolomeo, I recognized several familiar faces there, and particularly noted among them that of a certain fruit-vender, who frequently swindled me in my small dealings with him. He now sat before his stand, and for a man of a fat and greasy presence looked very fresh and brisk, and as if he had passed a pleasant night.

On the other side of the Rialto Bridge, the market was preparing for the purchasers. Butchers were arranging their shops; fruit-stands, and stands for the sale of crockery, and—as I must say for want of a better word, if there is any—notions, were in a state of tasteful readiness. The person on the steps of the bridge, who had exposed his stock of cheap clothing and coarse felt hats on the parapet, had so far completed his preparations as to have leisure to be talking himself hot and hoarse with the neighboring barber. He was in a perfectly good humor, and was merely giving a dramatic flavor to some question of six soldi.

At the landings of the market-place, squadrons of boats loaded with vegetables were arriving and unloading. Peasants were building cabbages into pyramids; collective squashes and cucumbers were taking a picturesque shape; wreaths of garlic and garlands of onions graced the scene. All the people were clamoring at the tops of their voices; and in the midst of the tumult and confusion, resting on heaps of cabbage-leaves and garbage, men lay on their bellies sweetly sleeping. Numbers of eating-houses were sending forth a savory smell, and everywhere were breakfasters with bowls of *sguassetto*. In one of the shops, somewhat prouder than the rest, a heated brunette was turning sections of eel on a gridiron, and hurriedly coquetting with the purchasers. Singularly calm amid all this bustle was the countenance of the statue called the Gobbo, as I looked at it in the centre of the market-place. The Gobbo (who is not a hunchback, either) was patiently supporting his burden, and looking with a quiet, thoughtful frown upon the ground, as if pondering some dream of change that had come to him since the statutes of the haughty Republic were read aloud to the people from the stone tribune on his shoulders.

Indeed, it was a morning for thoughtful meditation; and as I sat at the feet of the four granite kings shortly after, waiting for the gate of the Ducal Palace to be opened, that I might see the girls drawing the water, I studies the group of the Judgment of Solomon, on the corner of the palace, and arrived at an entirely new interpretation of that Bible story, which I have now wholly forgotten.

The gate remained closed too long for my patience, and I turned away from a scene momently losing its interest. The brilliant little shops opened like hollyhocks as I went home; the swelling tide of life filled the streets, and brought Venice back to my day-time remembrance, robbing her of that keen, delightful charm with which she greeted my early morning sense.

CHAPTER X

THE MOUSE

WISHING to tell the story of our Mouse, because I think it illustrates some amusing traits of character in a certain class of Italians, I explain at once that he was not a mouse, but a man so called from his wretched, trembling little manner, his fugitive expression and peaked visage.

He first appeared to us on the driver's seat of that carriage in which we posted so splendidly one spring-time from Padua to Ponte Lagoscuro. But though he mounted to his place just outside the city gate, we did not regard him much, nor, indeed, observe what a mouse he was, until the driver stopped to water his horses near Battaglia, and the Mouse got down to stretch his forlorn little legs. Then I got down, too, and bade him good-day, and told him it was a very hot day,—for he was a mouse apparently so plunged in wretchedness that I doubted if he knew what kind of day it was.

When I had spoken, he began to praise (in the wary manner of the Venetians when they find themselves in the company of a foreigner who does not look like an Englishman) the Castle of the Obizzi near by, which is now the country-seat of the ex-Duke of Modena; and he presently said something to imply that he thought me a German.

"But I am not a German," said I.

"As many excuses," said the Mouse sadly, but with evident relief; and then began to talk more freely, and of the evil times.

"Are you going all the way with us to Florence?" I asked.

"No, signor, to Bologna; from there to Ancona."

"Have you ever been in Venice? We are just coming from there."

"Oh, yes."

"It is a beautiful place. Do you like it?"

"Sufficiently. But one does not enjoy himself very well there."

"But I thought Venice interesting."

"Sufficiently, signor. *Ma!*" said the Mouse, shrugging his shoulders, and putting on the air of being luxuriously fastidious in his choice of cities, "the water is so bad in Venice."

The Mouse is dressed in a heavy winter overcoat, and has no garment to form a compromise with his shirt-sleeves, if he should wish to render the weather more endurable by throwing off the surtout. In spite of his momentary assumption of consequence, I suspect that his coat is in the Monte di Pietà. It comes out directly that he is a ship-carpenter who has worked in the Arsenal of Venice and at the ship-yards in Trieste.

But there is no work any more. He went to Trieste lately to get a job on the three frigates which the Sultan had ordered to be built there. *Ma!* After all, the frigates are to be built in Marseilles instead. There is nothing. And everything is so dear. In Venetia you spend much and gain little. Perhaps there is work at Ancona.

By this time the horses are watered; the Mouse regains his seat, and we almost forget him, till he jumps from his place, just before we reach the hotel in Rovigo, and disappears—down the first hole in the side of a house, perhaps. He might have done much worse, and spent the night at the hotel, as we did.

The next morning at four o'clock, when we start, he is on the box again, nibbling bread and cheese, and glancing furtively back at us to say good-morning. He has little twinkling black eyes, just like a mouse, and a sharp mustache, and sharp tuft on his chin,—as like Victor Emanuel's as a mouse's tuft can be.

The cold morning air seems to shrivel him, and he crouches into a little gelid ball on the seat beside the driver, while we wind along the Po on the smooth gray road; while the twilight lifts slowly from the distances of field and vineyard; while the black boats of the Po, with their gaunt white sails, show spectrally through the mists; while the trees and the bushes break into innumerable voice, and the birds are glad of another day in Italy; while the peasant drives his mellow-eyed, dun oxen afield; while his wife comes in her scarlet bodice to the door, and the children's faces peer out from behind her skirts; while the air freshens, the east flushes, and the great miracle is wrought anew.

Once again, before we reach the ferry of the Po, the Mouse leaps down and disappears as mysteriously as at Rovigo. We see him no more till we meet in the station on the other side of the river, where we hear him bargaining long and earnestly with the ticket-seller for a third-class passage to Bologna. He fails to get it, I think, at less than the usual rate, for he retires from the contest more shrunken and forlorn than ever, and walks up and down the station, startled at a word, shocked at any sudden noise.

For curiosity, I ask how much he paid for crossing the river, mentioning the fabulous sum it had cost us.

It appears that he paid sixteen soldi only. "What could they do when a man was in misery? I had nothing else."

Even while thus betraying his poverty the Mouse did not beg, and we began to respect his poverty. In a little while we pitied it, witnessing the manner in which he sat down on the edge of a chair, with a smile of meek desperation.

It is a more serious case when an artisan is our of work in the Old World than one can understand in the New. There the struggle for bread is so fierce and the competition so great; and, then, a man bred to one trade cannot turn his hand to another, as in America.

Even the rudest and least skilled labor has more to do it than are wanted. The Italians are very good to the poor, but the tradesman out of work must become a beggar before charity can help him.

We, who are poor enough to be wise, consult foolishly together concerning the Mouse. It blesses him that gives and him that takes,—this business of charity. And then, there is something irresistibly relishing and splendid in the consciousness of being the instrument of a special providence! Have I all my life admired those beneficent characters in novels and comedies who rescue innocence, succor distress, and go about pressing gold into the palm of poverty, and telling it to take it and be happy, and now shall I reject an occasion, made to my hand, for emulating them in real life?

"I think I will give the Mouse five francs," I say.

"Yes, certainly."

"But I will be prudent," I continue. "I will not *give* him this money. I will tell him it is a loan which he may pay me back again whenever he can. In this way I shall relieve him now and furnish him an incentive to economy."

I call to the Mouse, and he runs tremulously toward me.

"Have you friends in Ancona?"

"No, signor."

"How much money have you left?"

He shows me three soldi. "Enough for a coffee."

"And then?"

"God knows."

So I give him the five francs, and explain my little scheme of making it a loan, and not a gift; and then I give him my address.

He does not appear to understand the scheme of the loan; but he takes the money, and is quite stunned by his good fortune. He thanks me absently, and goes and shows the piece to the guards, with a smile that illumines and transfigures his whole person. At Bologna, he has come to his senses; he loads me with blessings, he is ready to weep; he reverences me, he wishes me a good voyage, endless prosperity, and innumerable days; and takes the train for Ancona.

"Ah, ah!" I congratulate myself,—"is it not a fine thing to be the instrument of a special providence?"

It is pleasant to think of the Mouse during all that journey, and if we are never so tired it rests us to say, "I wonder where the Mouse is by this time?" When we get home, and coldly count up our expenses, we rejoice in the five francs lent to the Mouse. "And I know he will pay it back if ever he can," I say. "That was a Mouse of integrity."

Two weeks later comes a comely young woman, with a young child,—a child strong on its legs, a child which tries to open everything in the room, which wants to pull the cloth off the table, to throw itself out of the open window,—a child of which I have never seen the peer for restlessness and curiosity. This young woman has been directed to call on me as a person likely to pay her way to Ferrara.

"But who sent you? But, in fine, why should I pay your way to Ferrara? I have never seen you before."

"My husband, whom you benefited on his way to Ancona, sent me. Here is his letter and the card you gave him."

I call out to my fellow-victim, "My dear, here is news of the Mouse!"

"Don't *tell* me he's sent you that money already!"

"Not at all. He has sent me his wife and child, that I may forward them to him at Ferrara, out of my goodness and the boundless prosperity which has followed his good wishes,—I, who am a great signor in his eyes, and an insatiable giver of five-franc pieces,—the instrument of a perpetual special providence. The Mouse has found work at Ferrara, and his wife comes here from Trieste. As for the rest, I am to send her to him, as I said."

"You are deceived," I say solemnly to the Mouse's wife. "I am not a rich man. I lent your husband five francs because he had nothing. I am sorry; but I cannot spare twenty florins to send you to Ferrara. If *one* will help you?"

"Thanks the same," said the young woman, who was well dressed enough; and blessed me, and gathered up her child, and went her way.

But her blessing did not lighten my heart, depressed and troubled by so strange an end to my little scheme of a beneficent loan. After all, perhaps the Mouse may have been as keenly disappointed as myself. With the ineradicable idea of the Italians, that persons who speak English are wealthy by nature, and *tutti originali,* it was not such an absurd conception of the case to suppose that if I had lent him five francs once I should like to do it continually. Perhaps he may yet pay back the loan with usury. But I doubt it. In the mean time, I am far from blaming the Mouse. I merely feel that there is a misunderstanding, which I can pardon if he can.

CHAPTER XI

CHURCHES AND PICTURES

ONE day, in the gallery of the Venetian Academy, a family party of the English, whom we had often seen from our balcony in their gondolas, were kind enough to pause before Titian's John the Baptist. It was attention that the picture could scarcely demand in strict justice, for it hangs at the end of a suite of smaller rooms, through which visitors usually return from the great halls spent with looking at much larger paintings. As these people stood gazing at the sublime figure of the Baptist,—one of the most impressive, if not the most religious, that the master has painted,—and the wild and singular beauty of the landscape made itself felt through the infinite depths of their respectability, the father of the family and the head of the group uttered approval of the painter's conception: "quite my idea of the party's character," he said; and then silently and awfully led his domestic train away.

I am so far from deriding the criticism of this honest gentleman that I would wish to have equal sincerity and boldness in saying what I thought—if I really thought anything at all—concerning the art which I spent so great a share of my time at Venice in looking at. But I fear I should fall short of the terseness as well as the candor I applaud, and should presently find myself tediously rehearsing criticisms which I neither respect for their honesty nor regard for their justice. It is the sad fortune of him who desires to arrive at full perception of the true and beautiful in art to find that critics have no agreement except upon a few loose general principles; and that among the artists, to whom he turns in his despair, no two think alike concerning the same master, while his own little learning has made him distrust his natural likings and mislikings. Ruskin is undoubtedly the best guide you can have in your study of the Venetian painters; and after reading him, and suffering confusion and ignominy from his theories and egotisms, the exercises by which you are chastised into admission that he has taught you anything cannot fail to end in a humility very favorable to your future as a Christian. But even in this subdued state you must distrust the methods by which he pretends to relate the æsthetic truths you perceive to certain civil and religious conditions: you scarcely understand how Tintoretto, who gen-teelly disdains (on one page) to paint well any person baser than a saint or senator, and with whom "exactly in proportion to the dignity of the character is the beauty of the painting," comes (on the next page) to paint a very "weak, mean, and painful" figure of Christ; and knowing a little the loose lives of the great Venetian painters, you must reject, with several other humorous postulates, the idea that good colorists are better men than bad colorists. Without any guide, I think, these painters may be studied and understood, up to a certain point, by one who lives in the atmosphere of their art at Venice, and who, insensibly breathing in its influence, acquires a feeling for it which all the critics in the world could not impart where the works themselves are not to be seen. I am sure that no one strange to the profession of artist ever received a just notion of any picture by reading the most accurate and faithful description of it: stated dimensions fail to convey ideas of size; adjectives are not adequate to the ideas of movement; and the names of the colors, however artfully and vividly introduced and repeated, cannot tell the reader of a painter's coloring. I should be glad to hear what Titian's Assumption is like from some one who knew it by descriptions. Can any one who has seen it tell its likeness, or forget it? Can any cunning critic describe intelligibly the difference between the styles of Titian, of Tintoretto, and of Paolo Veronese,—that difference which no one with the slightest feeling for art can fail to discern after looking thrice at their works? It results from all this that I must believe special criticisms on art to have their small use only in the presence of the works they discuss. This is my sincere belief, and I could not, in any honesty, lumber my pages with descriptions or speculations which would be idle to most readers, even if I were a far wiser judge of art than I affect to be. As it is, doubting if I be gifted in that way at all, I think I may better devote myself to discussion of such things in Venice as can be understood by comparison with things elsewhere, and so rest happy in the thought that I have thrown no additional darkness on any of the pictures half obscured now by the religious dimness of the Venetian churches.

Doubt, analogous to that expressed, has already made me hesitate to spend the reader's patience upon many well-known wonders of Venice; and, looking back over the preceding chapters, I find that some of the principal edifices of the city have scarcely got into my book even by name. It is possible that the reader, after all, loses nothing by this; but I should regret it, if it seemed ingratitude to that expression of the beautiful which beguiled many dull hours for me, and kept me company in many lonesome ones. For kindnesses of this sort, indeed, I am under obligations to edifices in every part of the city; and there is hardly a bit of sculptured stone in the Ducal Palace to which I do not owe some pleasant thought or harmless fancy. Yet I am shy of endeavoring, in my gratitude, to transmute the substance of the Ducal Palace into some substance that shall be sensible to the eyes that look on this print; and I forgive myself the reluctance the more readily when I remember how, just after reading Mr. Ruskin's description of St. Mark's Church, I, who had seen it every day for three years, began to have dreadful doubts of its existence.

To be sure, this was only for a moment, and I do not think all the descriptive talent in the world could make me again doubt St. Mark's, which I remember with no less love than veneration. This church indeed has a beauty which touches and wins all hearts, while it appeals profoundly to the religious sentiment. It is as if there were a sheltering friendliness in its low-hovering domes and arches, which lures and caresses while it awes; as if here, where the meekest soul feels welcome and protection, the spirit oppressed with the heaviest load of sin might creep nearest to forgiveness, hiding the anguish of its repentance in the temple's dim cavernous recesses, faintly starred with mosaic, and twilighted by twinkling altar-lamps.

Though the temple is enriched with incalculable value of stone and sculpture, I cannot remember at any time to have been struck by its mere opulence. Preciousness of material has been sanctified to the highest uses, and there is such unity and justness in the solemn splendor that wonder is scarcely appealed to. Even the priceless and rarely seen treasures of the church—such as the famous golden altar-piece, whose costly blaze of gems and gold was lighted in Constantinople six hundred years ago—failed to impress me with their pecuniary worth, though I

"Value the giddy pleasure of the eyes,"

and like to marvel at precious things. The jewels of other churches are conspicuous and silly heaps of treasure; but St. Mark's, where every line of space shows delicate labor in rich material, subdues the jewels to their place of subordinate adornment. So, too, the magnificence of the Romish service seems less vainly ostentatious there. In other churches the ceremonies may sometimes impress you with a sense of their grandeur, and even spirituality, but they all need the effect of twilight upon them. You want a foreground of kneeling figures, and faces half visible through heavy bars of shadow; little lamps must tremble before the shrines; and in the background must rise the high altar, all ablaze with candles from vault to pavement, while a hidden choir pours music from behind, and the organ shakes the heart with its heavy tones. But with the daylight on its splendors even the grand function of the Te Deum fails to awe, and wearies by its length, except in St. Mark's alone, which is given grace to spiritualize what elsewhere would be mere theatric pomp.[1] The basilica, however, is not in everything the edifice best adapted to the Romish worship; for the incense, which is a main element of the function, is gathered and held there in choking clouds under the low wagon-roofs of the cross-naves.— Yet I do not know if I would banish incense from the formula of worship even in St. Mark's. There is certainly a poetic if not a religious grace in the swinging censer and its curling fumes; and I think the perfume, as it steals mitigated to your nostrils, out of the open church door, is the reverendest smell in the world.

The music in Venetian churches is not commonly very good: the best is to be heard at St. Mark's, though the director of the choir always contrives to make so odious a slapping with his *bâton* as nearly to spoil your enjoyment. The great musical event of the year is the performance (immediately after the Festa del Redentore) of the Soldini Masses. These are offered for the repose of one Giuseppe Soldini of Verona, who, dying possessed of about a

---

[1] The cardinal-patriarch officiates in the Basilica San Marco with some ceremonies which I believe are peculiar to the patriarchate of Venice, and which consist of an unusual number of robings and disrobings, and putting on and off of shoes. All this is performed with great gravity, and has, I suppose, some peculiar spiritual significance. The shoes are brought by a priest to the foot of the patriarchal throne, when a canon removes the profane, out-of-door *chaussure,* and places the sacred shoes on the patriarch's feet. A like ceremony replaces the patriarch's every-day gaiters, and the pious rite ends.

million francs, bequeathed a part (some six thousand francs) annually to the church of St. Mark, on conditions named in his will. The terms are that during three successive days, every year, there shall be said for the peace of his soul a certain number of masses,—all to be done in the richest and costliest manner. In case of delinquency, the bequest passes to the Philharmonic Society of Milan; but the priesthood of the basilica so strictly regard the wishes of the deceased that they never say less than four masses over and above the prescribed number.[2]

As there is so little in St. Mark's of the paltry or revolting character of modern Romanism, one would form too exalted an idea of the dignity of Catholic worship if he judged it there. The truth is, the sincerity and nobility of a spirit well-nigh unknown to the Romish faith of these times are the ruling influences in that temple: the past lays its spell upon the present, transfiguring it, and the sublimity of the early faith honors the superstition which

---

[2] After hearing these masses, curiosity led me to visit the Casa di Ricovero, in order to look at Soldini's will, and there I had the pleasure of recognizing the constantly recurring fact that beneficent humanity is of all countries and religions. The Casa di Ricovero is an immense edifice dedicated to the shelter and support of the decrepit and helpless of either sex, who are collected there to the number of five hundred. The more modern quarter was erected from a bequest by Soldini; and eternal provision is also made by his will for ninety of the inmates. The Secretary of the Casa went through all the wards and infirmaries with me, and everywhere I saw cleanliness and comfort (and such content as is possible to sickness and old age), without surprise; for I had before seen the Civil Hospital of Venice, and knew something of the perfection of Venetian charities.

At last we came to the wardrobe, where the clothes of the pensioners are made and kept. Here we were attended by a little, slender, pallid young nun, who exhibited the dresses with a simple pride altogether pathetic. She was a woman still, poor thing, though a nun, and she could not help loving new clothes. They called her Madre, who would never be it except in name and motherly tenderness. When we had seen all, she stood a moment before us, and as one of the coarse woollen lappets of her cape had hidden it she drew out a heavy crucifix of gold, and placed it in sight, with a heavenly little ostentation, over her heart. Sweet and beautiful vanity! An angel could have done it without harm, but she blushed repentance, and glided away with downcast eyes. Poor little mother!

has succeeded it. To see this superstition in all its proper grossness and deformity you must go into some of the Renaissance churches,—fit tabernacles for that droning and mumming spirit which has deprived all young and generous men in Italy of religion; which has made the priests a bitter jest and by-word; which has rendered the population ignorant, vicious, and hopeless; which gives its friendship to tyranny and its hatred to freedom; which destroys the life of the Church that it may sustain the power of the Pope. The idols of this superstition are the foolish and hideous dolls which people bow to in most of the Venetian temples, and of which the most abominable is in the church of the Carmelites. It represents the Madonna with the Child, elevated breast-high to the worshippers. She is crowned with tinsel and garlanded with paper flowers; she has a blue ribbon about her tightly corseted waist; and she wears an immense spreading hoop. On her painted, silly face of wood, with its staring eyes shadowed by a wig, is figured a pert smile, and people come constantly and kiss the cross that hangs by a chain from her girdle, and utter their prayers to her; while the column near which she sits is hung over with pictures celebrating the miracles she has performed.

These votive pictures, indeed, are to be seen on most altars of the Virgin, and are no less interesting as works of art than as expressions of hopeless superstition. That Virgin, who, in all her portraits, is dressed in a churn-shaped gown, and who holds a Child similarly habited, is the Madonna most efficacious in cases of dreadful accident and hopeless sickness, if we may trust the pictures which represent her interference. You behold a carriage overturned and dragged along the ground by frantic horses, and the fashionably dressed lady and gentleman in the carriage about to be dashed into millions of pieces, when the havoc is instantly arrested by this Madonna, who breaks the clouds, leaving them with jagged and shattered edges, like broken panes of glass, and visibly holds back the fashionable lady and gentleman from destruction. It is the fashionable lady and gentleman who have thus recorded their obligation; and it is the mother, doubtless, of the little boy miraculously preserved from death in his fall from

the second floor balcony, who has gratefully caused the miracle to
be painted and hung at the Madonna's shrine. Now and then you
also find offerings of corn and fruits before her altar, in acknowledgment of good crops which the Madonna has made to grow;
and again you find rows of silver hearts, typical of the sinful hearts
which her intercession has caused to be purged. The greatest
number of these, at any one shrine, is to be seen in the church of
San Nicolò dei Tolentini, where I should think there were three
hundred.

Whatever may be the popularity of the Madonna della Salute in
pestilent times, I do not take it to be very great when the health of
the city is good, if I may judge from the spareness of the
worshippers in the church of her name: it is true that on the
annual holiday commemorative of her interposition to save
Venice from the plague there is an immense concourse of people
there; but at other times I found the masses and vespers slenderly
attended, and I did not observe a great number of votive offerings
in the temple,—though the great silver lamp placed there by the
city, in memory of the Madonna's goodness during the visitation
of the cholera in 1849, may be counted, perhaps, as representative
of much collective gratitude. It is a cold, superb church, lording it
over the noblest breadth of the Grand Canal; and I do not know
what it is saves it from being as hateful to the eye as other temples
of the Renaissance architecture. But it has certainly a fine effect,
with its twin bell-towers and single massive dome, its majestic
breadth of steps rising from the water's edge, and the man-statued
sculpture of its façade. Strangers go there to see the splendor of its
high altar (where the melodramatic Madonna, as the centre of a
marble group, responds to the prayer of the operatic Venezia, and
drives away the haggard, theatrical Pest), and the excellent Titians
and the grand Tintoretto in the sacristy.

The Salute is one of the great show-churches, like that of San
Giovanni e Paolo, which the common poverty of imagination has
decided to call the Venetian Westminster Abbey, because it
contains many famous tombs and monuments. But there is only
one Westminster Abbey; and I am so far a believer in the

perfectibility of our species as to suppose that vergers are nowhere possible but in England. There would be nothing to say, after Mr. Ruskin, in praise or blame of the great monuments in San Giovanni e Paolo, even if I cared to discuss them; I only wonder that, in speaking of the bad art which produced the tomb of the Venieri, he failed to mention the successful approach to its depraved feeling, made by the single figure sitting on the base of a slender shaft, at the side of the first altar on the right of the main entrance. I suppose this figure typifies Grief, but it really represents a drunken woman, whose drapery has fallen, as if in some vile debauch, to her waist, and who broods, with a horrible, heavy stupor and chopfallen vacancy, on something which she supports with her left hand upon her knee. It is a round of marble, and if you have the daring to peer under the arm of the debauchee, and look at it as she does, you find that it contains the bas-relief of a skull in bronze. Nothing more ghastly and abominable than the whole thing can be conceived, and it seemed to me the fit type of the abandoned Venice which produced it; for one even less Ruskinian than I might have fancied that in the sculptured countenance could be seen the dismay of the pleasure-wasted harlot of the sea when, from time to time, death confronted her amid her revels.

People go into the Chapel of the Rosary here to see the painting of Titian representing the Death of Peter Martyr. Behind it stands a painting of equal size by John Bellini,—the Madonna, Child, and Saints, of course,—and it is curious to study in the two pictures those points in which Titian excelled and fell short of his master. The treatment of the sky in the landscape is singularly alike in both, but where the greater painter has gained in breadth and freedom he has lost in that indefinable charm which belonged chiefly to Bellini, and only to that brief age of transition of which his genius was the fairest flower and ripest fruit. I have looked again and again at nearly every painting of note in Venice, having a foolish shame to miss a single one, and having also a better wish to learn something of the beautiful from them; but at last I must say that, while I wondered at the greatness of some, and tried to wonder at the greatness of others, the only paintings which gave me genuine and hearty pleasure were those of Bellini, Carpaccio, and a few others of that school and time.

Every day we used to pass through the court of the old Augustinian convent adjoining the church of San Stefano. It is a long time since the monks were driven out of their snug hold; and the convent is now the headquarters of the Austrian engineer corps, and the colonnade surrounding the court is become a public thoroughfare. On one wall of this court are remains—very shadowy remains indeed—of frescos painted by Pordenone at the period of his fiercest rivalry with Titian; and it is said that Pordenone, while he wrought upon the scenes of scriptural story here represented, wore his sword and buckler, in readiness to repel an attack which he feared from his competitor. The story is very vague, and I hunted it down in divers authorities only to find it grow more and more intangible and uncertain. But it gave a singular relish to our daily walk through the old cloister, and I added, for my own pleasure (and chiefly out of my own fancy, I am afraid, for I can nowhere localize the fable on which I built), that the rivalry between the painters was partly a love-jealousy, and that the disputed object of their passion was that fair Violante, daughter of the elder Palma, who is to be seen in so many pictures painted by her father and by her lover, Titian. No doubt there are readers who will care less for this idleness of mine than for the fact that the hard-headed German monk, Martin Luther, once said mass in the adjoining church of San Stefano, and lodged in the convent, on his way to Rome. The unhappy Francesco Carrara, last Lord of Padua, is buried in this church; but Venetians are chiefly interested there now by the homilies of those fervent preacher-monks, who deliver powerful sermons during Lent. The monks are gifted men, with a most earnest and graceful eloquence, and they attract immense audiences, like popular and eccentric ministers among ourselves. It is a fashion to hear them, and although the atmosphere of the churches in the season of Lent is raw, damp, and most uncomfortable, the Venetians then throng the churches where they preach. After Lent the sermons and church-going cease, and the sanctuaries are once more abandoned to the possession of the priests, droning from the altars to the scattered kneelers on the floor,—the foul old women and the young girls of the poor, the old-fashioned old gentlemen and devout ladies of the better class, and that singular race of poverty-stricken old men proper to Italian churches, who, having dabbled themselves with holy water, wander forlornly and aimlessly about, and seem to consort with the foreigners looking at the objects of interest. Lounging young fellows of low degree appear with their caps in their hands long enough to tap themselves upon the breast and nod recognition to the high altar; and lounging young fellows of high degree step in to glance at the faces of the pretty girls, and then vanish. The droning ends, presently, and the devotees disappear, the last to go being that thin old woman, kneeling before a shrine, with a grease-gray shawl falling from her head to the ground. The sacristan, in his perennial enthusiasm about the great picture of the church, almost treads upon her as he brings the strangers to see it, and she gets meekly up and begs of them in a whispering whimper. The sacristan gradually expels her with the visitors, and at one o'clock locks the door and goes home.

By chance I have got a fine effect in churches at the five o'clock mass in the morning, when the worshippers are nearly all peasants who have come to market, and who are pretty sure, each one, to have a bundle or basket. At this hour the sacristan is heavy with sleep; he dodges uncertainly at the tapers as he lights and extinguishes them; and his manner to the congregation, as he passes through it to the altar, is altogether rasped and nervous. I think it is best to be one's self a little sleepy,—when the barefooted friar at the altar (if it is in the church of the Scalzi, say) has a habit of getting several centuries back from you, and of saying mass to the patrician ghosts from the tombs under your feet; and there is nothing at all impossible in the Renaissance angels and cherubs in marble, floating and fatly tumbling about on the broken arches of the altars.

I have sometimes been puzzled in Venice to know why churches should keep cats, church-mice being proverbially so poor, and so little capable of sustaining a cat in good condition; yet I have repeatedly found sleek and portly cats in the churches, where they seem to be on terms of perfect understanding with the priests, and to have no quarrel even with the little boys who assist at mass. There is, for instance, a cat in the sacristy of the Frari which I have often seen in familiar association with the ecclesiastics there, when they came into his room to robe or disrobe or warm their hands, numb with supplication, at the great brazier in the middle of the floor. I do not think this cat has the slightest interest in the lovely Madonna of Bellini which hangs in the sacristy; but I suspect him of dreadful knowledge concerning the tombs of the church. I have no doubt he has passed through the open door of Canova's monument, and that he sees some coherence and meaning in Titian's; he has been all over the great mausoleum of the Doge Pesaro, and he knows whether the griffins descend from their perches at the midnight hour to bite the naked knees of the ragged black caryatides. This profound and awful animal I take to be a blood relation of the cat in the church of San Giovanni e Paolo, who sleeps like a Christian during divine service, and loves a certain glorious bed on the top of a bench, where the sun strikes upon him through the great painted window, and dapples his tawny coat with lovely purples and crimsons.

The church cats are apparently the friends of the sacristans, with whom their amity is maintained probably by entire cession of the spoils of visitors. In these, therefore, they seldom take any interest, merely opening a lazy eye now and then to wink at the sacristans as they drag the deluded strangers from altar to altar, with intense enjoyment of the absurdity and a wicked satisfaction in the incredible stories rehearsed. I fancy, being Italian cats, they feel something like a national antipathy toward those troops of German tourists, who always seek the Sehenswürdigkeiten in companies of ten or twenty,—the men wearing their beards, and the women their hoops and hats, to look as much like English people as possible; while their valet marshals them forward with a stream of guttural information, unbroken by a single punctuation point. These wise cats know the real English by their Murrays; and I think they make a shrewd guess at the nationality of us Americans by the speed with which we pass from one thing to another, and by our national ignorance of all languages but English. They must also hear us vaunt the superiority of our own land in unpleasant comparisons, and I do not think they believe us, or like us, for our boastings. I am sure they would say to us, if they could, "*Quando finirà mai quella guerra? Che sangue! che orrore!*"[3] The French tourist they distinguish by his evident skepticism concerning his own wisdom in quitting Paris for the present purpose; and the travelling Italian by his attention to his badly dressed, handsome wife, with whom he is now making his wedding trip.

I have found churches undergoing repairs (as most of them always are in Venice) rather interesting. Under these circumstances, the sacristan is obliged to take you into all sorts of secret places and odd corners, to show you the objects of interest; and you may often get glimpses of pictures which, if not removed from their proper places, it would be impossible to see. The carpenters and masons work most deliberately, as if in a place so set against progress that speedy workmanship would be a kind of impiety. Besides the mechanics, there are always idle priests standing about, and vagabond boys clambering over the scaffolding. In San Giovanni e Paolo I remember we one day saw a small boy appear through an opening in the roof, and descend by means of some hundred feet of dangling rope. The spectacle, which made us ache with fear, delighted his companions so much that their applause was scarcely subdued by the sacred character of the place. As soon as he reached the ground in safety, a gentle, good-natured-looking priest took him by the arm and cuffed his ears. It was a scene for a painter.

---

[3] "When will this war ever be ended? What blood! what horror!" I have often heard the question and the comment from many Italians who were not cats.

CHAPTER XII

SOME ISLANDS OF THE LAGOONS

NOTHING can be fairer to the eye than these "summer isles of Eden" lying all about Venice, far and near. The water forever trembles and changes, with every change of light, from one rainbow glory to another, as with the restless hues of an opal; and even when the splended tides recede and go down with the sea, they leave a heritage of beauty to the empurpled mud of the shallows, all strewn with green, dishevelled seaweed. The lagoons have almost as wide a bound as your vision. On the east and west you can see their borders of sea-shore and main-land; but looking north and south, there seems no end to the charm of their vast, smooth, all but melancholy expanses. Beyond their southern limit rise the blue Euganean Hills, where Petrarch died; on the north, loom the Alps, white with snow. Dotting the stretches of lagoon in every direction lie the islands,—now piles of airy architecture that the water seems to float under and bear upon its breast, now

"Sunny spots of greenery,"

with the bell-towers of demolished cloisters shadowily showing
above their trees; for in the days of the Republic nearly every one
of the islands had its monastery and its church. At present the
greater number have been fortified by the Austrians, whose
sentinel paces the once peaceful shores, and challenges all passers
with his sharp "*Halt! Wer da!*" and warns them not to approach
too closely. Other islands have been devoted to different utilitarian
purposes, and few are able to keep their distant promises of
loveliness. One of the more faithful is the island of San Clemente,
on which the old convent church is yet standing, empty and
forlorn within, but without all draped in glossy ivy. After I had
learned to row in the gondolier fashion, I voyaged much in the
lagoon with my boat, and often stopped at this church. It has a
curious feature in the chapel of the Madonna di Loreto, which is
built in the middle of the nave, faced with marble, roofed, and
isolated from the walls of the main edifice on all sides. On the
back of this there is a bas-relief in bronze, representing the
Nativity,—a work much in the spirit of the bas-reliefs in San
Giovanni e Paolo; and one of the chapels has an exquisite little
altar, with gleaming columns of porphyry. There has been no
service in the church for many yers; and this altar had a strangely
pathetic effect, won from the black four-cornered cap of a priest
that lay before it, like an offering. I wondered who the priest was
that wore it, and why he had left it there, as if he had fled away
in haste. I might have thought it looked like the signal of the
abdication of a system; the gondolier who was with me took it up
and reviled it as representative of *birbanti matricolati,* who fed
upon the poor, and in whose expulsion from that island he
rejoiced. But he had little reason to do so, since the last use of the
place was for the imprisonment of refractory ecclesiastics. Some of
the tombs of the Morosini are in San Clemente,—villainous
monuments, with bronze Deaths popping out of apertures, and
holding marble scrolls inscribed with undying deeds. Indeed,
nearly all the decorations of the poor old church are horrible, and
there is one statue in it, meant for an angel, with absolutely the
most lascivious face I ever saw in marble.

The islands near Venice are all small, except the Giudecca (which is properly a part of the city), the Lido, and Murano. The Giudecca, from being anciently the bounds in which certain factious nobles were confined, was later laid out in pleasure-gardens and built up with summer palaces. The gardens still remain to some extent; but they are now chiefly turned to practical account in raising vegetables and fruits for the Venetian market, and the palaces have been converted into warehouses and factories. This island produces a variety of beggar, the most truculent and tenacious in all Venice, and it has a convent of lazy Capuchin friars, who are likewise beggars. To them belongs the church of the Redentore, which only the Madonnas of Bellini in the sacristy make worthy to be seen,—though the island is hardly less famed for this church than for the difficult etymology of its name.

At the eastern extremity of the Giudecca lies the island of San Giorgio Maggiore, with Palladio's church of that name. There are some great Tintorettos in the church, and I like the beautiful wood-carvings in the choir. The island has a sad interest from the political prison into which part of the old convent has been perverted; and the next island eastward is the scarcely sadder abode of the mad. Then comes the fair and happy seat of Armenian learning and piety, San Lazzaro, and then the Lido.

The Lido is the sea-shore, and thither in more cheerful days the Venetians used to resort in great numbers on certain holidays, called the Mondays of the Lido, to enjoy the sea-breeze and the country scenery, and to lunch upon the flat tombs of the Hebrews, buried there in exile from the consecrated Christian ground. On a summer's day there the sun glares down upon the sand and flat gravestones, and it seems the most desolate place where one's bones might be laid. The Protestants were once also interred on the Lido, but now they rest (apart from the Catholics, however) in the cemetery of San Michele.

The island is long and narrow: it stretches between the lagoons and the sea, with a village at either end, and with bath-houses on the beach, which is everywhere faced with forts. There are some poor little trees there, and grass,—things which we were thrice a week grateful for, when we went thither to bathe. I do not know whether it will give the place further interest to say that it was among the tombs of the Hebrews Cooper's ingenious Bravo had the incredible good luck to hide himself from the *sbirri* of the Republic; or to relate that it was the habit of Lord Byron to gallop up and down the Lido in search of that conspicuous solitude of which the sincere bard was fond.

One day of the first summer I spent in Venice (three years of Venetian life afterward removed it back into times of the remotest antiquity), a friend and I had the now incredible enterprise to walk from one end of the Lido to the other,—from the port of San Nicolò (through which the Bucintoro passed when the Doges went to espouse the Adriatic) to the port of Malamocco, at the southern extremity.

We began with that delicious bath which you may have in the Adriatic, where the light surf breaks with a pensive cadence on the soft sand, all strewn with brilliant shells. The Adriatic is the bluest water I have ever seen; and it is an ineffable, lazy delight to lie and watch the fishing sails of purple and yellow dotting its surface, and the greater ships dipping down its utmost rim. It was particularly good to do this after coming out of the water; but our American blood could not brook much repose, and we got up presently, and started on our walk to the little village of Malamocco, some three miles away. The double-headed eagle keeps watch and ward from a continuous line of forts along the shore, and the white-coated sentinels never cease to pace the bastions, night or day. Their vision of the sea must not be interrupted by even so much as the form of a stray passer; and as we went by the forts, we had to descend from the sea-wall, and walk under it, until we got beyond the sentry's beat. The crimson poppies grow everywhere on this sandy little isle, and they fringe the edges of the bastions with their bloom, as if the "blood-red blossoms of war" had there sprung from the seeds of battle sown in old forgotten fights. But otherwise the forts were not very engaging in appearance. A sentry-box of yellow and black, a sentry, a row of seaward frowning cannon,—

there was not much in all this to interest us; and so we walked idly along, and looked either to the city rising from the lagoons on one hand, or the ships going down the sea on the other. In the fields, along the road, were vines and Indian corn; but instead of those effigies of humanity, doubly fearful from their wide unlikeness to anything human, which we contrive to scare away the birds, the devout peasant-folks had here displayed on poles the instruments of the Passion of the Lord,—the hammer, the cords, the nails,— which at once protected and blessed the fields. But I doubt if even these would save them from the New World pigs, and cetainly the fences here would not turn pork, for they are made of a matting of reeds, woven together, and feebly secured to tremulous posts. The fields were well cultivated, and the vines and garden vegetables looked flourishing; but the corn was spindling, and had, I thought, a homesick look, as if it dreamed vainly of wide ancestral bottom-lands, on the mighty streams that run through the heart of the Great West. The Italians call our corn *gran turco;* but I knew that it was for the West that it yearned, and not for the East.

No doubt there were once finer dwellings than the peasants' houses which are now the only habitations on the Lido; and I suspect that a genteel villa must formerly have stood near the farm-gate, which we found surmounted by broken statues of Venus and Diana. The poor goddesses were both headless, and some cruel fortune had struck off their hands, and they looked strangely forlorn in the swaggering attitudes of the absurd period of art to which they belonged: they extended their mutilated arms toward the sea for pity, but it regarded them not; and we passed before them scoffing at their bad taste, for we were hungry, and it was yet some distance to Malamocco.

This dirty little village was the capital of the Venetian islands before King Pepin and his Franks burned it, and the shifting sands of empire gathered solidly about the Rialto in Venice. It is a thousand years since that time, and Malamocco has long been given over to fishermen's families and the soldiers of the forts. We found the latter lounging about the unwholesome streets; and the former seated at their thresholds, engaged in those pursuits of the chase which the use of a fine-tooth comb would undignify to mere slaughter.

There is a church at Malamocco, but it was closed, and we could not find the sacristan; so we went to the little restaurant, as the next best place, and demanded something to eat. What had the padrone? He answered pretty much to the same effect as the innkeeper in Don Quixote, who told his guests that they could have anything that walked on the earth, or swam in the sea, or flew in the air. We would take, then, some fish, or a bit of veal, or some mutton chops. The padrone sweetly shrugged the shoulders of apology. There was nothing of all this, but what would we say to some liver or gizzards of chickens, fried upon the instant and ready the next breath? No, we did not want them; so we compromised on some ham fried in a batter of eggs, and reeking with its own fatness. The truth is, it was a very bad little lunch we made, and nothing redeemed it but the amiability of the smiling padrone and the bustling padrona, who served us as kings and princes. It was a clean hostelry, though, and that was a merit in Malamocco, of which the chief modern virtue is that it cannot hold you long. No doubt it was more interesting in other times. In the days when the Venetians chose it for their capital, it was a walled town, and fortified with towers. It has been more than once inundated by the sea, and it might again be washed out with advantage.

In the spring, two years after my visit to Malamocco, we people in Casa Falier made a long-intended expedition to the island of Torcello, which is perhaps the most interesting of the islands of the lagoons. We had talked of it all winter, and had acquired enough property there to put up some light Spanish castles on the desolate site of the ancient city that so many years ago sickened of the swamp air and died. A Count from Torcello is the title which Venetian *persiflage* gives to improbable noblemen; and thus even the pride of the dead Republic of Torcello has passed into matter of scornful jest, as that of the dead Republic of Venice may likewise in its day.

When we leave the *riva* of Casa Falier, we pass down the Grand

Canal, cross the Basin of St. Mark, and enter one of the narrow canals that intersect the Riva degli Schiavoni, whence we wind and deviate south-westward till we emerge near the church of San Giovanni e Paolo, on the Fondamenta Nuove. On our way we notice that a tree hanging over the water from a little garden, is in full leaf, and at Murano we see the tender bloom of peaches and the drifted blossom of cherry-trees.

As we go by the Cemetery of San Michele, Piero, the gondolier, and Giovanna improve us with a little solemn pleasantry.

"It is a small place," says Piero, "but there is room enough for all Venice in it."

"It is true," assents Giovanna, "and here we poor folks become landholders at last."

At Murano we stop a moment to look at the old Duomo, and to enjoy its quaint mosaics within, and the fine and graceful spirit of the *apsis* without. It is very old, this architecture; but the eternal youth of the beautiful belongs to it, and there is scarce a stone fallen from it that I would replace.

The manufacture of glass at Murano, of which the origin is so remote, may be said to form the only branch of industry which still flourishes in the lagoons. Muranese beads are exported to all quarters in vast quantities, and the process of making them is one of the things tht strangers feel they must see when visiting Venice. The famous mirrors are no longer made, and the glass has deteriorated in quality, as well as in the beauty of the thousand curious forms it took. The test of the old glass, which is now imitated a great deal, is its extreme lightness. I suppose the charming notion that glass was once wrought at Murano of such fineness that it burst into fragments if poison were poured into it must be fabulous. And yet it would have been an excellent thing in the good old toxicological days of Italy: and people of noble family would have found a sensitive goblet of this sort as sovereign against the arts of venomers as an exclusive diet of boiled eggs.

The city of Murano has dwindled from thirty to five thousand in population. It is intersected by a system of canals like Venice and has a Grand Canal of its own, of as stately breadth as that of the capital. The finer houses are built on this canal; but the beautiful palaces, once occupied in *villeggiatura* by the noble Venetians, are now inhabited by herds of poor, or converted into glass-works. The famous Cardinal Bembo and other *literati* made the island their retreat, and beautified it with gardens and fountains. Casa Priuli in that day was, according to Venetian ideas, "a terrestrial Paradise," and a proper haunt of "nymphs and demi-gods." But the wealth, the learning, and the elegance of former times, which planted "groves of Academe" at Murano, have passed away, and the fair pleasure-gardens are now weed-grown wastes, or turned into honest cabbage and potato patches. It is a poor, dreary little town, with an inexplicable charm in its decay. The city arms are still displayed upon the public buildings (for Murano was ruled, independently of Venice, by its own council); and the heraldic cock, with a snake in its beak, has yet a lusty and haughty air amid the ruin of the place.

The way in which the spring made itself felt upon the lagoon was full of curious delight. It was not so early in the season that we should know the spring by the first raw warmth in the air, and there was as yet no assurance of her presence in the growth—later so luxuriant—of the coarse grasses of the shallows. But somehow the spring was there, giving us new life with every breath. There were fewer gulls than usual, and those we saw sailed far overhead, debating departure. There was deeper languor in the laziness of the soldiers of finance, as they lounged and slept upon their floating custom-houses in every channel of the lagoons; and the hollow voices of the boatmen, yelling to each other, as their wont is, had an uncommon tendency to diffuse themselves in echo. Over all, the heavens had put on their summer blue, in promise of that delicious weather which in the laggons lasts half the year, and which makes every other climate seem niggard of sunshine and azure skies. I know we have beautiful days at home,—days of which the sumptuous splendor used to take my memory with unspeakable longing and regret even in Italy,—but we do not have, week after week, month after month, that

"Blue, unclouded weather,"

which, at Venice, contents all your senses, and makes you exult to be alive with the inarticulate gladness of children, or of the swallows that there all day wheel and dart through the air, and shriek out a delight too intense and precipitate for song.

The island of Torcello is some five miles away from Venice, in the northern lagoon. The city was founded far back in the troubled morning of Christian civilization, by refugees from barbarian invasion, and built with stones quarried from the ruins of old Altinum, over which Attila had passed desolating. During the first ages of its existance Torcello enjoyed the doubtful advantage of protection from the Greek emperors, but fell afterward under the domination of Venice. In the thirteenth century the *débris* of the river that emptied into the lagoon there began to choke up the wholesome salt canals, and to poison the air with swampy malaria; and in the seventeenth century the city had so dwindled that the Venetian *podestà* removed his residence from the depopulated island to Burano,—though the bishopric established immediately after the settlement of the refugees at Torcello continued there till 1814, to the satisfaction, no doubt, of the frogs and mosquitoes that had long inherited the former citizens.

I confess that I know little more of the history of Torcello than I found in my guidebook. There I read that the city had once stately civic and religious edifices, and that in the tenth century the Emperor Porphorygenitus called it *"magnum emporium Torcellanorum."* The much-restored cathedral of the seventh century, a little church, a building supposed to have been the public palace, and other edifices so ruinous and so old that their exact use in other days is not now known, are all that remain of the *magnum emporium,* except some lines of mouldering wall that wander along the canals and through pastures and vineyards, in the last imbecile stages of dilapidation and decay. There is a lofty bell-tower, also, from which, no doubt, the Torcellani used to descry afar off the devouring hordes of the barbarians on the main-land, and prepare for defence. As their city was never actually invaded, I am at a loss to account for the so-called Throne of Attila, which stands in the grass-grown piazza before the cathedral; and I fear that it may really have been after all only the seat which the ancient Tribunes of Torcello occupied on public occasions. It is a stone arm-chair, of a rude stateliness, and though I questioned its authenticity I went and sat down in it a little while, to give myself the benefit of a doubt in case Attila had really pressed the same seat.

As soon as our gondola touched the grassy shores at Torcello, Giovanna's children, Beppi and Nina, whom we had brought with us to give a first experience of trees and flowers and mother earth, leaped from the boat and took possession of land and water. By a curious fatality the little girl, who was bred safely amid the hundred canals of Venice, signalized her absence from their perils by presently falling into the only canal in Torcello, whence she was taken dripping, to be confined at a farm-house during the rest of our stay. The children were wild with pleasure, being absolutely new to the country, and ran over the island, plucking bouquets of weeds and flowers by armsful. A rake, borne afield upon the shoulder of a peasant, afterwhile fascinated the Venetian Beppi, and drew him away to study its strange and wonderful uses.

The simple inhabitants of Torcello came forth with gifts, or rather bargains, of flowers, to meet their discoverers, and in a little while exhausted our soldi. They also attended us in full force when we sat down to lunch,—the old, the young men and maidens, and the little children, all alike sallow, tattered, and dirty. Under these circumstances, a sense of the idyllic and the patriarchal gave zest to our collation, and moved us to bestow, in a splendid manner, fragments of the feast among the poor Torcellani. Knowing the abstemiousness of Italians everywhere, and seeing the hungry fashion in which the islanders clutched our gifts and devoured them, it was our doubt whether any one of them had ever experienced perfect repletion. I inclined to think that a chronic famine gnawed their entrails, and that they never filled their bellies but with draughts of the east wind disdained of Job. The smaller among them even scrambled with the dog for the bones until a little girl was bitten, when a terrific tumult arose, and the dog was driven home by the whole multitude. The children presently returned. They all had that gift of beauty which Nature seldom denies to the children of their race; but being, as I said, so dirty, their beauty shone forth chiefly from their large, soft eyes. They had a very graceful, bashful archness of manner, and they insinuated beggary so winningly tht it would have been impossible for hungry people to deny them. As for us, having lunched, we gave them everything that remained, and went off to feast our enthusiasm for art and antiquity in the cathedral.

Of course, I have not the least intention of describing it. I remember best among its wonders the bearing of certain impenitents in one of the mosaics on the walls, whom the earnest early artist had meant to represent as suffering in the flames of torment. I think, however, I have never seen complacence equal to that of these sinners, unless it was in the countenances of the seven fat kine, which, as represented in the vestibule of St. Mark's, wear an air of the sleepiest and laziest enjoyment, while the seven lean kine, having just come up from the river, devour steaks from their bleeding haunches. There are other mosaics in the Torcello cathedral, especially those in the *apsis* and in one of the side chapels, which are in a beautiful spirit of art, and form the widest possible contrast to the eighteenth-century high altar, with its insane and ribald angels flying off at the sides, and poising themselves in the rope-dancing attitudes favored by statues of heavenly persons in the decline of the Renaissance. The choir is peculiarly built, in the form of a half-circle, with seats rising one above another, as in an amphitheatre, and a flight of steps ascending to the bishop's seat above all,—after the manner of the earliest Christian churches. The partition parapet before the high altar is of almost transparent marble, delicately and quaintly sculptured with peacocks and lions, as the Byzantines loved to carve them; and the capitals of the columns dividing the naves are of infinite richness. Part of the marble pulpit has a curious bas-relief, said to be representative of the worship of Mercury; and indeed the Torcellani owe much of the beauty of their Duomo

to unrequited antiquity. (They came to be robbed in their turn: for
the opulence of their churches was so great that in the fifteenth
and sixteenth centuries the severest penalties had to be enacted
against those who stole from them. No one will be surprised to
learn that the clergy themselves participated in these spoliations;
but I believe no ecclesiastic was ever lashed in the piazza, or
deprived of an eye or a hand, for his offence.) The Duomo has the
peculiar Catholic interest and the horrible fascination of a dead
saint's mortal part in a glass case.

An arcade runs along the façade of the cathedral, and around
the side and front of the adjoining church of Santa Fosca, which
is likewise very old. But we found nothing in it but a dusty,
cadaverous stench, and so we came away and ascended the
campanile. From the top of this you have a view of the lagoon in
all its iridescent hues, and of the heaven-blue sea. Here, looking
toward the main-land, I would have been glad to experience the
feelings of the Torcellani of old, as they descried the smoking
advance of Huns or Vandals. But the finer emotions are like gifted
children, and are seldom equal to occasions. I am ashamed to say
that mine got no further than Castle Bluebeard, with Lady
Bluebeard's sister looking out for her brothers, and tearfully
responding to Lady B.'s repeated and agonized entreaty, "O sister,
do you see them yet?"

The old woman who had opened the door of the campanile was
surprised into hospitality by the sum of money we gave her, and
took us through her house (which was certainly very neat and
clean) into her garden, where she explained the nature of many
familiar trees and shrubs to us poor Venetians.

We went back home over the twilight lagoon, and Giovanna
expressed the general feeling when she said: "*Torsello xe beo—no
si pol negar—la campagna xe bea; ma benedetta la mia Venezia!*"
(The country is beautiful—it can't be denied—Torcello is beautiful; but blessed be my Venice!)

The panorama of the southern lagoon is best seen in a voyage
to Chioggia, or Ciozza, the quaint and historic little city that lies
twenty miles away from Venice, at one of the ports of the harbor.

The Giant Sea-wall, built there by the Republic in her decline, is a work of Roman grandeur which impresses you more deeply than any other monument of the past with a sense of her former industrial and commercial greatness. Strips of village border the narrow Littorale all the way to Chioggia, and on the right lie the islands of the lagoon. Chioggia itself is hardly more than a village,—a Venice in miniature, like Murano, with canals and boats and bridges. But here the character of life is more amphibious than in brine-bound Venice; and though there is no horse to be seen in the central streets of Chioggia, peasants' teams penetrate her borders by means of a long bridge from the main-land.

Of course Chioggia has passed through the customary vicissitudes of Italian towns, and has been depopulated at divers times by pestilence, famine, and war. It suffered cruelly in the war with the Genoese in 1380, when it was taken by those enemies of St. Mark; and its people were so wasted by the struggle that the Venetians, on regaining it, were obliged to invite immigration to repopulate its emptiness. I do not know how great comfort the Chiozzotti of that unhappy day took in the fact that some of the earliest experiments with cannon were made in the contest that destroyed them, but I can hardly offer them less tribute than to mention it here. At present the place is peopled almost entirely by sailors and fishermen, whose wives are more famous for their beauty than their amiability. Goldoni's Baruffe Chiozzotte is an amusing and vivid picture of the daily battles which the high-spirited ladies of the city fought in the dramatist's[1] time, and which are said to be of frequent occurrence at this day. The Chiozzotte are the only women of this part of Italy who still preserve a semblance of national costume; and this remnant of more picturesque times consists merely of a skirt of white, which, being open in front, is drawn from the waist over the head and gathered in the hand under the chin, giving to the flashing black

---

[1] Goldoni's family went from Venice to Chioggia when the dramatist was very young. The descriptions of his life there form some of the most interesting chapters of his Memoirs.

eyes and swarthy features of the youthful wearer a look of very
dangerous slyness and cunning. The dialect of the Chiozzotti is
said to be that of the early Venetians, with an admixture of Greek,
and it is infinitely more sweet and musical than the dialect now
spoken in Venice. "Whether derived," says the author of the Fiore
di Venezia, alluding to the speech of these peculiar people, "from
those who first settled these shores, or resulting from other
physical and moral causes, it is certain that the tone of the voice
is here more varied and powerful: the mouth is thrown wide open
in speaking; a passion, a lament, mingles with laughter itself, and
there is a continual *ritornello* of words previously spoken. But this
speech is full of energy; whoever would study brief and strong
modes of expression should come here."

Chioggia was once the residence of noble and distinguished
persons, among whom was the painter Rosalba Carrera, famed
throughout Europe for her crayon miniatures; and the place produced, in the sixteenth century, the great maestro Giuseppe
Zarlino, "who passes," says Cantù, "for the restorer of modern
music," and "whose Orfeo heralded the invention of the musical
drama." This composer claimed for his birthplace the doubtful
honor of the institution of the order of the Capuchins, which he
declared to have been founded by Fra Paolo (Giovanni Sambi) of
Chiogga. There is not much now to see in poor little Chioggia
except its common people, who, after a few minutes' contemplation, can hardly interest any one but the artist. There are no
dwellings in the town which approach palatial grandeur, and nothing in the Renaissance churches to claim attention, unles it be an
attributive Bellini in one of them. Yet if you have the courage to
climb the bell-tower of the cathedral, you get from its summit the
loveliest imaginable view of many-purpled lagoon and silver-
flashing sea; and if you are sufficiently acquainted with Italy and
Italians to observe a curious fact, and care to study the subject, you
may note the great difference between the inhabitants of Chioggia
and those of Palestrina,—an island divided from Chioggia by a half
mile of lagoon, and by quite different costume, type of face, and
accent.

Just between Chioggia and the sea lies the lazy town of Sottomarina, and I should say that the population of Sottomarina chiefly spent its time in lounging up and down the Sea-wall; while that of Chioggia, when not professionally engaged with the net, gave its leisure to playing *mora*[2] in the shade, or pitilessly pursuing strangers, and offering them boats. For my own part, I refused the subtlest advances of this kind which were made me in Chiozzotto, but fell a helpless prey to a boatman who addressed me in some words of wonderful English, and then rowed me to the Sea-wall at about thrice the usual fare.

These primitive people are bent, in their out-of-the-world, remote way, upon fleecing the passing stranger quite as earnestly as other Italians, and they naively improve every occasion for plunder. As we passed up the shady side of their wide street, we came upon a plump little blonde boy, lying asleep on the stones, with his head upon his arm; and as no one was near, the artist of our party stopped to sketch the sleeper. Atmospheric knowledge of the fact spread rapidly, and in a few minutes we were the centre of a general assembly of the people of Chioggia, who discussed us and the artist's treatment of her subject in open congress. They handed round the airy chaff, as usual, but were very orderly and respectful, nevertheless,—one father of the place quelling every tendency to tumult by kicking his next neighbor, who passed on the penalty, till, by this simple and ingenious process, the guilty cause of the trouble was infallibly reached and kicked at last. I placed a number of soldi in the boy's hand, to the visible sensation of the crowd, and then we moved away and left him, heading, as we went, a procession of Chiozzotti, who could not make up their minds to relinquish us till we took refuge in a church. When we came out the procession had disappeared, but all round the church

---

[2] *Mora* is the game which the Italians play with their fingers, one throwing out two, three, or four fingers, as the case may be, and calling the number at the same instant. If (so I understood the game) the player mistakes the number of the fingers he throws out, he loses; if he hits the number with both voice and fingers, he wins. It is played with tempestuous interest, and is altogether fiendish in appearance.

door, and picturesquely scattered upon the pavement in every direction, lay boys asleep, with their heads upon their arms. As we passed, laughing, through the midst of these slumberers, they rose and followed us with cries of "*Mi tiri zu! Mi tiri zu!*" (Take me down! Take me down!) They ran ahead, and fell asleep again in our path, and round every corner we came upon a sleeping boy; and, indeed, we never got out of that atmosphere of slumber till we returned to the steamer for Venice, when Chioggia shook off her drowsy stupor, and began to tempt us to throw soldi into the water, to be dived for by her awakened children.

CHAPTER XIII

THE ARMENIANS

AMONG the pleasantest friends we made in Venice were the monks of the Armenian Convent, whose cloistral buildings rise from the glassy lagoon, upon the south of the city, near a mile away. This bulk

"Of mellow brick-work on an isle of bowers"

is walled in with solid masonry from the sea, and encloses a garden-court, filled with all beautiful flowers and with the memorable trees of the East; while another garden encompasses the

141

monastery itself, and yields those honest fruits and vegetables which supply the wants of the well-cared-for mortal part of the good brothers. The island is called San Lazzaro, and the convent was established in 1717 by a learned and devoted Armenian priest named Mechithar, from whom the present order of monks is called Mechitharist. He was the first who formed the idea of educating a class of priests to act as missionaries among the Armenian nation in the East, and infuse into its civil and religious decay the life of European piety and learning. He founded at Sebaste, therefore, a religious order, of which the seat was presently removed to Constantinople, where the friars met with so much persecution from Armenian heterodoxy that it was again transferred, and fixed at Modone in Morea. That territory falling into the hands of the Turks, the Mechitharists fled with their leader to Venice, where the Republic bestowed upon them a vast and desolate island, which had formerly been used as a place of refuge for lepers; and the monks made it the loveliest spot in all the lagoons.

The little island has such a celebrity in travel and romance that I feel my pen catching in the tatters of a threadbare theme. And yet I love the place and its people so well that I could scarcely pass it without mention. Every tourist who spends a week in Venice goes to see the convent, and every one is charmed with it and the courteous welcome of the fathers. Its best interest is the intrinsic interest attaching to it as a seat of Armenian culture; but persons who relish the cheap sentimentalism of Byron's life find the convent all the more entertaining from the fact that he did the Armenian language the favor to study it there, a little. The monks show his autograph, together with those of other distinguished persons, and the Armenian Bible which he used to read. I understood from one of the friars, Padre Giacomo Issaverdanz, that the brothers knew little or nothing of Byron's celebrity as a poet while he studied with them, and that his proficiency as an Armenian scholar was not such as to win high regard from them.

I think most readers who have visited the convent will recall the pleasant face and manners of the young father mentioned, who shows the place to English-speaking travellers, and will care to know that Padre Giacomo was born at Smyrna, and dwelt there, in the family of an English lady, till he came to Venice and entered on his monastic life at San Lazzaro.

He came one morning to breakfast with us, bringing with him Padre Alessio, a teacher in the Armenian College in the city. As for the latter, it was not without a certain shock that I heard Mesopotamia mentioned as his birthplace, having somehow in childhood learned to regard that formidable name as little better than a kind of profane swearing. But I soon came to know Padre Alessio apart from his birthplace, and to find him very interesting as a scholar and an artist. He threw a little grace of poetry around our simple feast by repeating some Armenian verses,—grace all the more ethereal from our entire ignorance of what the verses meant. Our breakfast-table talk wrought to friendship the acquaintance made some time before, and the next morning we received the photograph of Padre Giacomo, and the compliments of the Orient, in a heaped basket of ripe and luscious figs from the garden of the Convent San Lazzaro. When, in turn, we went to visit him at the convent, we had experience of a more curious oriental hospitality. Refreshments were offered to us as to friends, and we lunched fairly upon little dishes of rose leaves, delicately preserved, with all their fragrance, in a "lucent sirup." It seemed that this was a common conserve in the East; but we could hardly divest ourselves of the notion of sacrilege, as we thus fed upon the very most luxurious sweetness and perfume of the soul of summer. Pleasant talk accompanied the dainty repast,—Padre Giacomo recounting for us some of his adventures with the people whom he had to show about the convent, and of whom many were disappointed at not finding a gallery or museum, and went away in extreme disgust; and relating with a sly, sarcastic relish, that blent curiously with his sweetness and gentleness of spirit, how some English people once came with the notion that Lord Byron was an Armenian; how an unhappy French gentleman, who had been robbed in Southern Italy, would not be parted a moment from a huge bludgeon which he carried in his hand, and (probably disordered by his troubles) could hardly be persuaded from attacking the mummy which is in one of the halls; how a sharp, bustling, go-ahead Yankee rushed in one morning, rubbing his hands, and demanding, "Show me all you can in five minutes."

As a seat of learning, San Lazzaro is famed throughout the Armenian world, and gathers under its roof the best scholars and poets of that nation. In the printing-office of the convent books are printed in some thirty languages; and a number of the fathers employ themselves constantly in works of translation. The most distinguished of the Armenian literati now living at San Lazzaro is the Reverend Father Gomidas Pakraduni, who has published an Armenian version of Paradise Lost, and whose great labor, the translation of Homer, has been recently issued from the convent press. He was born at Constantinople of an ancient and illustrious family, and took religious orders at San Lazzaro, where he was educated, and where for twenty-five years after his consecration he held the professorship of his native tongue. He devoted himself especially to the culture of the ancient Armenian, and developed it for the expression of modern ideas; he made exhaustive study of the vast collection of old manuscripts at San Lazzaro, and then went to Paris in pursuance of his purpose, and acquainted himself with all the treasures of Armenian learning in the Bibliothèque Royale. He became the first scholar of the age in his national language, and acquired at the same time a profound knowledge of Latin and Greek.

Returning to Constantinople, Father Pakraduni, whose fame had preceded him, took up his residence in the family of a noble Armenian, high in the service of the Turkish government; and, while assuming the care of educating his friend's children, began those labors of translation which have since so largely employed him. He made an Armenian version of Pindar, and wrote a work on Rhetoric, both of which were destroyed by fire while yet in the manuscript. He labored, meanwhile, on his translation of the Iliad,—a youthful purpose which he did not see fulfilled till the year 1860, when he had already touched the Psalmist's limit of life. In this translation he revived with admirable success an ancient species of Armenian verse, which bears, in flexibility and strength, comparison with the original Greek. Another of his great labors was the production of an Armenian Grammar, in which he reduced to rule and order the numerous forms of his native tongue, never before presented by one work in all its Eastern variety.

Padre Giacomo, to whose great kindness I am indebted for a biographic and critical notice in writing of Father Pakraduni, considers the epic poem by that scholar a far greater work than any of his philological treatises, profound and thorough as they are. When nearly completed, this poem perished in the same conflagration which consumed the Pindar and the Rhetoric; but the poet patiently began his work anew, and after eight years gave his epic of twenty books and twenty-two thousand verses to the press. The hero of the poem is Häik, the first Armenian patriarch after the flood, and the founder of a kingly dynasty. Nimrod, the great hunter, drunk with his victories, declares himself a god, and ordains his own worship throughout the Orient. Häik refuses to obey the commands of the tyrant, takes up arms against him, and finally kills him in battle. "In the style of this poem," writes Padre Giacomo, "it is hard to tell whether to admire most its richness, its energy, its sweetness, its melancholy, its freedom, its dignity, or its harmony, for it has all these virtues in turn. The descriptive parts are depicted with the faithfullest pencil; the battle scenes can only be matched in the Iliad."

Father Pakraduni returned, after twenty-five years' sojourn at Constantinople, to publish his epic at San Lazzaro, where he still lives, a tranquil, gentle old man, with a patriarchal beauty and goodness of face. In 1861 he printed his translation of Milton, with a dedication to Queen Victoria. His other works bear witness to the genuineness of his inspiration and piety and the diligence of his study: they are poems, poetic translations from the Italian, religious essays, and grammatical treatises.

Indeed, the existence of all the friars at San Lazzaro is one of close and earnest study; and life grows so fond of these quiet of monks that it will hardly part with them at last. One of them is ninety-five years old, and, until 1863, there was a lay-brother among them whose years numbered a hundred and eight, and who

died of old age, on the 17th of September, after passing fifty-eight
years at San Lazzaro. From biographic memoranda furnished me
by Padre Giacomo, I learn that the name of this patriarch was
George Karabagiak, and that he was a native of Kutaieh in Asia
Minor. He was for a long time the disciple of Dèdè Vartabied, a
renowned preacher of the Armenian faith, and he afterward
taught the doctrines of his master in the Armenian schools. Failing
in his desire to enter upon the sacerdotal life at Constantinople, he
procured his admission as lay-brother at San Lazzaro, where all
his remaining days were spent. He was but little learned; but he
had a great passion for poetry, and he was the author of some
thirty small works on different subjects. During the course of his
long and diligent life, which was chiefly spent in learning and
teaching, he may be said to have hardly known a day's sickness.
And at last he died of no perceptible disorder. The years tired him
to death. He had a trifling illness in August, and as he convalesced
he grew impatient of the tenacious life which held him to earth.
Slowly pacing up and down the corridors of the convent, he used
to crave the prayers of the brothers whom he met, beseeching
them to intercede with Heaven that he might be suffered to die.
One day he said to the archbishop, "I fear that God has
abandoned me, and I shall live." Only a little while before his
death he wrote some verses, as Padre Giacomo's memorandum
witnesses, "with a firm and steady hand," and the manner of his
death was this,—as recorded in the grave and simple words of my
friend's note: "Finally, on the 17th of September, very early in the
morning, a brother, entering his chamber, asked him how he was.
'Well,' he replied, turning his face to the wall, and spoke no more.
He had passed to a better life."

It seems to me there is a pathos in the close of this old man's
life,—which I hope has not been lost by my way of describing
it,—and there is certainly a moral. I have read of an unlucky sage
who discovered the Elixir of Life, and who, after thrice renewing
his existence, at last voluntarily resigned himself to death, because
he had exhausted all that life had to offer of pleasure or of pain,
and knew all its vicissitudes but the very last. Brother Karabagiak

seems to have had no humor to take even a second lease of life. It is perhaps as well that most men die before reaching the over-ripeness of a hundred and eight years; and, doubtless, with all our human wilfulness and ignorance, we would readily consent, if we could fix the time, to go sooner,—say, at a hundred and seven years, friends?

Besides the Convent of San Lazzaro, where Armenian boys from all parts of the East are educated for the priesthood, the nation has a college in the city in which boys intended for secular careers receive their schooling. The Palazzo Zenobia is devoted to the use of this college, where, besides room for study, the boys have abundant space and apparatus for gymnastics and ample grounds for gardening. We once passed a pleasant summer evening there, strolling through the fragrant alleys of the garden, in talk with the father-professors, and looking on at the gymnastic feats of the boys; and when the annual exhibition of the school took place in the fall, we were invited to be present.

The room appointed for the exhibition was the great hall of the palace, which in other days had evidently been a ball-room. The ceiling was frescoed in the manner of the last century, with Cupids and Venuses, Vices and Virtues, fruits and fiddles, dwarfs and blackamoors; and the painted faces looked down on a scene of as curious interest as ever the extravagant loves and graces of Tiepolo might hope to see, when the boys of the college, after assisting at Te Deum in the chapel, entered the room, and took their places.

At the head of the hall sat the archbishop in his dark robes, with his heavy gold chain about his neck,—a figure and a countenance in all things spiritual, gracious, and reverend. There is small difference, I believe, between the creeds of the Armenians and the Roman Catholics, but a very great disparity in the looks of the two priesthoods, which is all in favor of the former. The Armenian wears his beard, and the Latin shaves,—which may have a great deal to do with the holiness of appearance. Perhaps, also, the gentle and mild nature of the oriental yields more sweetly and entirely to the self-denials of the ecclesiastical vocation, and thus wins a fairer grace from them. At any rate, I have not seen anything but content and calm in the visages of the Armenian fathers, among whom the priest-face, as a type, does not exist, though it would mark the Romish ecclesiastic in whatever dress he wore. There is, moreover, a look of such entire confidence and unworldly sincerity in their eyes that I could not help thinking, as I turned from the portly young fathers to the dark-faced, grave, old-fashioned school-boys, that an exchange of beard only was needed to effect an exchange of character between those youthful elders and their pupils. The gray-haired archbishop is a tall and slender man; but nearly all the fathers take kindly to curves and circles, and glancing down a row of these amiable priests I could scarcely repress a smile at the constant recurrence of the line of beauty in their well-rounded persons.

On the right and left of the archbishop were the few invited guests, and at the other end of the saloon sat one of the fathers, the plump key-stone of an arch of comfortable young students expanding toward us. Most of the boys are from Turkey (the Armenians of Venice, though acknowledging the Pope as their spiritual head, are the subjects of the Sultan), others are of Asiatic birth, and two are Egyptians.

As to the last, I think the Sphinx and the Pyramid could hardly have impressed me more than their dark faces, that seemed to look vaguely on our modern world from the remote twilights of old, and in their very infancy to be reverend through the antiquity of their race. The mother of these boys—a black-eyed, olive-cheeked lady, very handsome and stylish—was present with their younger brother. I hardly know whether to be ashamed of having been awed by hearing of the little Egyptian that his native tongue was Arabic, and that he spoke nothing more occidental than Turkish. But, indeed, was it wholly absurd to offer a tacit homage to this favored boy, who must know the Arabian Nights in the original?

The exercises began with a theme in Armenian,—a language which, but for its English abundance of sibilants and a certain German rhythm, was wholly outlandish to our ears. Themes in Italian, German, and French succeeded, and then came one in

English. We afterward had speech with the author of this essay, who expressed the liveliest passion for English, in the philosophy and poetry of which, it seemed, he particularly delighted. He told us that he was a Constantinopolitan, and that in six months more he would complete his collegiate course, when he would return to his native city, and take employment in the service of the Turkish Government. Many others of the Armenian students here also find this career open to them in the East.

The literary exercises closed with another essay in Armenian; and then the archbishop delivered, very gracefully and impressively, an address to the boys. After this, the distribution of the premiums—medals of silver and bronze and books—took place at the desk of the archbishop. Each boy, as he advanced to receive his premium, knelt and touched the hand of the priest with his lips and forehead,—a quaint and pleasing ceremony which had preceded and followed the reading of all the themes.

The social greetings and congratulations that now took place ended an entertainment throughout which everybody was pleased, and the good-natured fathers seemed to be moved with a delight no less hearty than that of the boys themselves. Indeed, the ground of affection and confidence on which the lads and their teachers seemed to meet was something very novel and attractive. We shook hands with our smiling friends among the padri, took leave of the archbishop, and then visited the studio of Padre Alessio, who had just finished a faithful and spirited portrait of monsignore. Adieux to the artist and to Padre Giacomo brought our visit to an end; and so, from that scene of oriental learning, simplicity, and kindliness, we walked into our western life once more, and resumed our citizenship and burden in the Venetian world,—out of the waters of which, like a hydra or other water beast, a bathing boy instantly issued and begged of us.

A few days later our good Armenians went to pass a month on the main-land near Padua, where they have comfortable possessions. Peace followed them, and they came back as plump as they went.

CHAPTER XIV

THE GHETTO AND THE JEWS OF VENICE

AS I think it extremely questionable whether I could get through a chapter on this subject without some feeble pleasantry about Shylock, and whether, if I did, the reader would be at all satisfied that I had treated the matter fully and fairly, I say at the beginning that Shylock is dead; that, if he lived, Antonio would hardly spit upon his gorgeous pantaloons or his Parisian coat, as he met him on the Rialto; that he would far rather call out

to him, *"Ciò Shylock! Bon dì! Go piaser vederla;"*[1] that, if
Shylock by any chance entrapped Antonio into a foolish promise
to pay him a pound of his flesh on certain conditions, the honest
commissary of police before whom they brought their affair
would dismiss them both to the madhouse at San Servolo. In a
word, the present social relations of Jew and Christian in this city
render the Merchant of Venice quite impossible; and the reader,
though he will find the Ghetto sufficiently noisome and dirty, will
not find an oppressed people there, nor be edified by any of those
insults or beatings which it was once a large share of Christian
duty to inflict upon the enemies of our faith. The Catholic
Venetian certainly understands that his Jewish fellow-citizen is
destined to some very unpleasant experiences in the next world,
but *Corpo di Bacco!* that is no reason why he should not be
friends with him in this. He meets him daily on exchange and at
the Cassino, and he partakes of the hospitality of his *conversazioni.* If he still despises him,—and I think he does a little,—he keeps
his contempt to himself; for the Jew is gathering into his own
hands great part of the trade of the city, and has the power that
belongs to wealth. He is educated, liberal, and enlightened, and
the last great name in Venetian literature is that of the Jewish
historian of the Republic, Romanin. The Jew's political sympathies are invariably patriotic, and he calls himself not Ebreo, but
Veneziano. He lives, when rich, in a palace or a fine house on the
Grand Canal, and he furnishes and lets many others (I must say at
rates which savor of the loan secured by the pound of flesh) in
which he does not live. The famous and beautiful Ca'Doro now
belongs to a Jewish family; and an Israelite, the most distinguished
physician in Venice, occupies the *appartamento signorile* in the
palace of the famous Cardinal Bembo. The Jew is a physician, a
banker, a manufacturer, a merchant; and he makes himself
respected for his intelligence and his probity,—which perhaps
does not infringe more than that of Italian Catholics. He dresses
well,—with that indefinable difference, however, which distin-

---

[1] "Shylock, old fellow, good-day. Glad to see you."

guishes him in everything from a Christian,—and his wife and daughter are fashionable and stylish. They are sometimes, also, very pretty; and I have seen one Jewish lady who might have stepped out of the sacred page, down from the patriarchal age, and been known for Rebecca, with her oriental grace and delicate, sensitive, high-bred look and bearing,—no more western and modern than a lily of Palestine.

But it is to the Ghetto I want to take you now (by the way we went one sunny day late last fall), that I may show you something of the Jewish past, which has survived to the nineteenth century in much of the discomfort and rank savor of the dark ages.

In the fifteenth century all the riches of the Orient had been poured into the lap of Venice, and a spirit of reckless profusion took possession of her citizens. The money, hastily and easily amassed, went as rapidly as it came. It went chiefly for dress, in which the Venetian still indulges very often to the stint of his stomach; and the ladies of that bright-colored, showy day bore fortunes on their delicate persons in the shape of costly vestments of scarlet, black, green, white, maroon, or violet, covered with gems, glittering with silver buttons, and ringing with silver bells. The fine gentlemen of the period were not behind them in extravagance; and the priests were peculiarly luxurious in dress, wearing gay silken robes, with cowls of fur and girdles of gold and silver. Sumptuary laws were vainly passed to repress the general license, and fortunes were wasted and wealthy families reduced to beggary.[2] At this time, when so many worthy gentlemen and ladies had need of the Uncle to whom hard-pressed nephews fly to pledge the wrecks of prosperity, there was yet no Monte di Pietà, and the demand for pawnbrokers becoming imperative, the Republic was obliged to recall the Hebrews from the exile into which they had been driven some time before, that they might set up pawnshops and succor necessity. They came back, however, only for a limited time, and were obliged to wear a badge of yellow color upon the breast, to distinguish them from the

---

[2] Galliciolli, *Memorie Venete.*

Christians, and later a yellow cap, then a red hat, and then a hat of oil-cloth. They could not acquire houses or lands in Venice, nor practise any trades, nor exercise any noble art but medicine. They were assigned a dwelling place in the vilest and unhealthiest part of the city, and their quarter was called Ghetto, from the Hebrew *nghedah,* a congregation.[3] They were obliged to pay their landlords a third more rent than Christians paid; the ghetto was walled in, and its gates were kept by Christian guards, who every day opened them at dawn and closed them at dark, and who were paid by the Jews. They were not allowed to issue at all from the Ghetto on holidays, and two barges, with armed men, watched over them night and day, while a special magistracy had charge of their affairs. Their synagogues were built at Mestre, on the mainland, and their dead were buried in the sand upon the sea-shore, whither, on the Mondays of September, the baser sort of Venetians went to make merry, and drunken men and women danced above their desecrated tombs. These unhappy people were forced also to pay tribute to the state, at first every third year, then every fifth year, and then every tenth year, the privilege of residence being ingeniously renewed to them at these periods for a round sum; but, in spite of all, they flourished upon the waste and wickedness of their oppressors, waxed rich as these waxed poor, and were not again expelled from the city.[4]

There never was any attempt to disturb the Hebrews by violence, except on one occasion, about the close of the fifteenth century, when a tumult was raised against them for child-murder. This, however, was promptly quelled by the Republic before any harm was done them; and they dwelt peacefully in their Ghetto till the lofty gates of their prison caught the sunlight of modern civilization, and crumbled beneath it. Then many of the Jews came forth and fixed their habitations in different parts of the city, but many others clung to the spot where their temples still remain, and which was hallowed by long suffering, and soaked with the blood

---

[3] Mutinelli.
[4] *Del Commercio dei Veneziani.* Mutinelli.

of innumerable generations of geese. So, although you find Jews everywhere in Venice, you never find a Christian in the Ghetto, which is held to this day by a large Hebrew population.

We had not started purposely to see the Ghetto, and for this reason it had that purely incidental relish, which is the keenest possible savor of the object of interest. We were on an expedition to find Sior Antonio Rioba, who has been from time immemorial the means of ponderous practical jokes in Venice. Sior Antonio is a rough-hewn statue set in the corner of an ordinary grocery, near the Ghetto. He has a pack on his back and a staff in his hand; his face is painted, and is habitually dishonored with dirt thrown upon it by boys. On the wall near him is painted a bell-pull, with the legend *Sior Antonio Rioba*. Rustics, raw apprentices, and honest Germans new to the city are furnished with packages to be carried to Sior Antonio Rioba, who is very hard to find, and not able to receive the messages when found, though there is always a crowd of loafers near to receive the unlucky simpleton who brings them. "*E poi, che commedia vederli arrabiarsi! Che ridere!*" That is the Venetian notion of fun, and no doubt the scene is amusing. I was curious to see Sior Antonio, because a comic journal bearing his name had been published during the time of the Republic of 1848, and from the fact that he was then a sort of Venetian Pasquino. But I question now if he was worth seeing, except as something that brought me into the neighborhood of the Ghetto, and suggested to me the idea of visiting that quarter.

As we left him and passed up the canal in our gondola, we came unawares upon the church of Santa Maria dell' Orto, one of the most graceful Gothic churches in the city. The façade is exquisite, and has two Gothic windows of that religious and heavenly beauty which pains the heart with its inexhaustible richness. One longed to fall down on the space of green turf before the church, now bathed in the soft golden October sunshine, and recant these happy, commonplace centuries of heresy, and have back again the good old believing days of bigotry, and superstition, and roasting, and racking, if only to have once more the men who dreamed those windows out of their faith and piety (if they did, which I doubt), and made them with their patient, reverent hands (if their hands *were* reverent, which I doubt). The church is called Santa Maria dell' Orto from the miraculous image of Our Lady which was found in an orchard where the temple now stands. We saw this miraculous sculpture, and thought it reflected little credit upon the supernatural artist. The church is properly that of Saint Christopher, but the saint has been titularly vanquished by the Madonna, though he comes out gigantically triumphant in a fresco above the high altar, and leads to confused and puzzling reminiscences of Bluebeard and Morgante Maggiore, to both of which characters he bears a bewildering personal resemblance.

There were once many fine paintings by Tintoretto and Bellini in this church; but as the interior is now in course of restoration, the paintings have been removed to the Academy, and we only saw one, which was by the former master, and had all his striking imagination in the conception, all his strength in the drawing, and all his lamp-black in the faded coloring. In the centre of the church, the sacristan scraped the carpenter's rubbish away from a flat tablet in the floor, and said that it was Tintoretto's tomb. It is a sad thing to doubt even a sacristan, but I pointed out that the tomb bore any name in the world rather than Robusti. "Ah!" said the sacristan, "it is just that which makes it so curious,—that Tintoretto should wish to be buried under another name!"[5]

It was a warm, sunny day in the fall, as I said; yet as we drew near the Ghetto we noticed in the air many white, floating particles, like lazy, straggling flakes of snow. These we afterward found to be the down of multitudes of geese, which are forever plucked by the whole apparent force of the populace,—the fat of the devoted birds being substituted for lard in the kitchens of the ghetto, and their flesh for pork. As we approached the obscene little *riva* at which we landed, a blonde young Israelite, lavishly adorned with feathers, came running to know if we wished to see

---

[5] Members of the family of Tintoretto are actually buried in this church; and no sacristan of right feeling could do less than point out some tomb as that of the great painter himself.

the church,—by which name he put the synagogue to the Gentile comprehension. The street through which we passed had shops on either hand, and at the doors groups of jocular Hebrew youth sat plucking geese; while within, long files of all that was mortal of geese hung from the rafters and the walls. The ground was webbed with the feet of geese, and certain loutish boys, who paused to look at us, had each a goose dragging at his heels, in the forlorn and elongated manner peculiar to dead poultry. The ground was stained with the blood of geese, and the smell of roasting geese came out of the windows of the grim and lofty houses.

Our guide was picturesque, but the most helpless and inconclusive cicerone I ever knew; and while his long, hooked Hebrew nose caught my fancy, and his soft blue eyes excused a great deal of inefficiency, the aimless fashion in which he mounted dirty staircases for the keys of the synagogue, and came down without them, and the manner in which he shouted to the heads of unctuous Jessicas thrust out of windows, and never gained the slightest information by his efforts, were imbecilities that we presently found insupportable, and we gladly cast him off for a dark-faced Hebrew boy who brought us at once to the door of the Spanish synagogue.

Of seven synagogues in the Ghetto, the principal was built in 1655, by the Spanish Jews who had fled to Venice from the terrors of the Holy Office. Its exterior has nothing to distinguish it as a place of worship, and we reached the interior of the temple by means of some dark and narrow stairs. In the floor and on the walls of the passage-way were set tablets to the memory of rich and pious Israelites who had bequeathed their substance for the behoof of the sanctuary; and the sacristan informed us that the synagogue was also endowed with a fund by rich descendants of Spanish Jews in Amsterdam. These moneys are kept to furnish indigent Israelitish couples with the means of marrying, and any who claim the benefit of the fund are entitled to it. The sacristan— a little wiry man, with bead-black eyes, and of a shoemakerish presence—told us with evident pride that he was himself a

descendent of the Spanish Jews. Howbeit, he was now many
centuries from speaking the Castilian, which, I had read, was still
used in the families of the Jewish fugitives from Spain to the
Levant. He spoke, instead, the abominable Venetian of Cannaregio, with that Jewish thickness which distinguishes the race's
utterance, no matter what language its children are born to. It is
a curious philological fact, which I have heard repeatedly alleged
by Venetians, and which is perhaps worth noting here, that Jews
speaking their dialect have not only this thickness of accent, but
also a peculiarity of construction which marks them at once.

We found the contracted interior of the synagogue hardly worth
looking at. Instead of having anything oriental or peculiar in its
architecture, it was in a bad spirit of Renaissance art. A gallery
encircled the inside, and here the women, during worship, sat
apart from the men, who had seats below, running back from
either side of the altar. I had no right, coming from a Protestant
land of pews, to indulge in that sentimentality; but I could not
help being offended to see that each of these seats might be lifted
up and locked into the upright back and thus placed beyond
question at the disposal of the owner: I like the freedom and
equality in the Catholic churches much better. The sacristan
brought a ponderous silver key, and, unlocking the door behind
the pulpit, showed us the Hebrew Scriptures used during the
service by the Rabbi. They formed an immense parchment
volume, and were rolled in silk upon a wooden staff. This was the
sole object of interest in the synagogue, and its inspection
concluded our visit.

We descended the narrow stairs, and emerged upon the piazza
which we had left. It was only partly paved with brick, and was
very dirty. The houses which surrounded it were on the outside
old and shabby, and, even in this Venice of lofty edifices,
remarkably high. A wooden bridge crossed a vile canal to another
open space, where once congregated the merchants who sell
antique furniture, old pictures, and objects of vertu. They are
now, however, found everywhere in the city, and most of them are
on the Grand Canal, where they heap together marvellous collec-

tions, and establish authenticities beyond cavil. "Is it an original?" asked a young lady who was visiting one of their shops, as she paused before an attributive Veronese, or—what know I?— perhaps a Titian. "*Sì, signora, originalissimo!*"

I do not understand why any class of Jews should still remain in the Ghetto, but it is certain, as I said, that they do remain there in great numbers. It may be that the impurity of the place and the atmosphere is conducive to purity of race; but I question if the Jews buried on the sandy slope of the Lido, and blown over by the sweet sea wind,—it must needs blow many centuries to cleanse them of the Ghetto,—are not rather to be envied by the inhabitants of those high dirty houses and low dirty lanes. There was not a touch of anything wholesome, or pleasant, or attractive, to relieve the noisomeness of the Ghetto to its visitors; and they applauded, with a common voice, the neatness which had prompted Andrea the gondolier to roll up the carpet from the floor of his gondola, and not to spread it again within the limits of that quarter.

In the good old times when pestilence avenged the poor and oppressed upon their oppressors, what grim and dismal plagues may not have stalked by night and noonday out of those hideous streets, and passed the marble bounds of patrician palaces, and brought to the bedsides of the rich and proud the filthy misery of the Ghetto turned to poison! Thank God that the good old times are gone and going! One learns in these aged lands to hate and execrate the past.

CHAPTER XV

SOME MEMORABLE PLACES

WE came away from the Ghetto, as we had arrived, in a gentle fall of goose-down, and, winding crookedly through a dirty canal, glided into purer air and cleaner waters. I cannot well say how it was we came upon the old Servite Convent, which I had often looked for in vain, and which, associated with the great name of Paolo Sarpi, is to me one of the most memorable places in Venice. We reached it, after passing by that old, old palace, which was appointed in the early ages of Venetian commerce for the reception of oriental traffic and traffickers, and where it is said the Moorish merchants resided till the later time of the Fondaco dei Turchi on the Grand Canal. The façade of the palace is richly sculptured; and near one corner is the bas-relief of a camel and his turbaned driver,—in token, perhaps, that man and beast (as orientals would understand them) were here entertained.

We had lived long enough in Venice to know that it was by no means worth while to explore the interior of this old palace because the outside was attractive, and so we left it; and, turning a corner, found ourselves in a shallow canal, with houses on one side, and a grassy bank on the other. The bank sloped gently from the water up to the walls of some edifice, on which ruin seemed to have fastened soon after the architect had begun his work. The vast walls, embracing several acres in their close, rose only some thirty or forty feet from the ground,—only high enough, indeed, to join over the top of the great Gothic gates, which pierced them on two façades. There must have been barracks near; for on the sward, under the walls, muskets were stacked, and Austrian soldiers were practising the bayonet-exercise with long poles padded at the point. "*Ein, zwei, drei,—vorwärts! Ein, zwei, drei,—rückwärts!*" snarled the drill-sergeant, and the dark-faced Hungarian soldiers—who may have soon afterward prodded their Danish fellow-beings all the more effectively for that day's training—stooped, writhed, and leaped obedient. I, who had already caught sight of a little tablet in the wall bearing the name of Paolo Sarpi, could not feel the propriety of the military performance on that scene; yet I was very glad, dismounting from the gondola, to get by the soldiers without being forced back at the padded point of a pole, and offered no audible objection to their presence.

So passing to the other side, I found entrance through a disused chapel to the interior of the convent. The gates on the outside were richly sculptured, and were reverend and clean; tufts of harsh grass grew from their arches, and hung down like the "overwhelming brows" of age. Within, at first sight, I saw nothing but heaps of rubbish, piles of stone, and here and there a mutilated statue. I remember two pathetic caryatides, that seemed to have broken and sunk under too heavy a weight for their gentle beauty, and everywhere the unnamable filth with which ruin is always dishonored in Italy, and which makes the most picturesque and historic places inaccessible to the foot, and intolerable to the senses and the soul. I was thinking with a savage indignation on this incurable *porcheria* of the Italian poor (who are guilty of such desecrations), when my eye fell upon an enclosed space in one corner, where some odd-looking boulders were heaped together. It was a space about six feet in depth and twenty feet square; and the boulders, on closer inspection, turned out to be human skulls, nestling on piles of human bones. In any other land than Italy I think I should have turned from the grisly sight with a cowardly sickness and shuddering; but here!—Why, heaven and earth seem to take the loss of men so good-naturedly,—so many men have died and passed away with their difficult, ambitious, and trouble-some little schemes,—and the great mass of mankind is taken so small account of in the course of destiny, that the idea of death does not appear so alien and repulsive as elsewhere, and the presence of such evidences of our poor mortality can scarcely offend sensibility. These were doubtless the bones of the good Servite friars who had been buried in their convent, and had been digged up to make way for certain improvements now taking place within its walls. I have no doubt that their deaths were a rest to their bodies, to say nothing of their souls. If they were at all in their lives like those who have come after them, the sun baked their bald brows in summer, and their naked feet—poor feet! clapping round in wooden-soled sandals over the frozen stones of Venice—were swollen and gnawed with chilblains in winter; and no doubt some fat friar of their number, looking all the droller in his bare feet for the spectacles on his nose, came down Calle Falier then, as now, to collect the charity of bread and fuel, far oftener than the dwellers in that aristocratic precinct wished to see him.

The friars' skulls looked contented enough, and smiled after the hearty manner of skulls; and some of the leg-bones were thrust through the enclosing fence, and hung rakishly over the top. As to their spirits, I suppose they must have found out by this time that these confused and shattered tabernacles which they left behind them are not nearly so corrupt and dead as the monastic system which still cumbers the earth. People are building on the site of the old convent a hospital for indigent and decrepit women, where a religious sisterhood will have care of the inmates. It is a good end enough, but I think it would be the true compensation if all the rubbish of the old cloister were cleared from the area of those walls, and a great garden planted in the space, where lovers might whisper their wise nonsense, and children might romp and frolic, till the crumbling masonry forgot its old office of imprisonment and the memory of its prisoners. For here one could only think of the moping and mumming herd of monks, who were certainly not worth remembering, while the fame of Paolo Sarpi, and the good which he did, refused to be localized. That good is an inheritance which has enriched the world; but the share of Venice has been comparatively small in it, and that of this old convent ground still less. I rather wondered, indeed, that I should have taken the trouble to look up the place; but it is a harmless, if even a very foolish, pastime to go seeking for the sublime secret of the glory of the palm in the earth where it struck root and flourished. So far as the life-long presence and the death of a man of clear brain and true heart could hallow any scene, this ground was holy; for here Sarpi lived, and here in his cell he died, a simple Servite friar,—he who had caught the bolts of excommunication launched against the Republic from Rome, and broken them in his hand,—who had breathed upon the mighty arm of the temporal power, and withered it to the juiceless stock it now remains. And yet I could not feel that the ground *was* holy, and it did not make me think of Sarpi; and I believe that only those travellers who invent in cold blood their impressions of memorable places ever have remarkable impressions to record.

Once, before the time of Sarpi, an excommunication was pronounced against the Republic with a result as terrible as that of the later interdict was absurd. Venice took possession, early in the fourteenth century, of Ferrara, by virtue of a bargain which the

high contracting parties—the Republic and an exiled claimant to
the ducal crown of Ferrara—had no right to make. The father of
the banished prince had displeased him by marrying late in life,
when the thoughts of a good man should be turned on other
things, and the son compassed the sire's death. For this the
Ferrarese drove him away, and as they would not take him back
to reign over them at the suggestion of Venice, he resigned his
rights in favor of the Republic, and the Republic at once annexed
the city to its territories. The Ferrarese appealed to the Pope for his
protection, and Clement V., supporting an ancient but long
quiescent claim to Ferrara on the part of the Church, called upon
the Venetians to surrender the city, and, on their refusal, excommunicated them. All Christian peoples were commanded "to arm
against the Venetians, to spoil them of their goods, as separated
from the union of Christians, and as enemies of the Roman
Church." They were driven out of Ferrara, but their troubles did
not end with their loss of the city. Giustina Renier-Michiel says
the nations, under the shelter of the Pope's permission and
command, "exercised against them every species of cruelty: there
was no wrong or violence of which they were not victims. All the
rich merchandise which they had in France, in Flanders, and in
other places was confiscated; their merchants were arrested,
maltreated, and some of them killed. Woe to us, if the Saracens
had been baptized Christians! Our nation would have been utterly
destroyed. Such was the ruin brought upon us by this excommunication that to this day it is a popular saying, concerning a man
of gloomy aspect, *'He looks as if he were bringing the excommunication of Ferrara.'* "

No proverb sprung from the popular terror commemorates the
interdict of the Republic which took place in 1606, and which, I
believe, does not survive in popular recollection at Venice. It was
at first a collision of the Venetian and Papal authorities at Ferrara,
and then an interference of the Pope to prevent the execution of
secular justice upon certain ecclesiastical offenders in Venetia,
which resulted in the excommunication of the Republic, and
finally in the defeat of St. Peter and the triumph of St. Mark. Chief

among the ecclesiastical offenders mentioned were the worthy
Abbate Brandolino of Narvesa, who was accused, among other
things, of poisoning his own father; and the good Canonico
Saraceni of Vicenza, who was repulsed in overtures made to his
beautiful cousin, and who revenged himself by defaming her
character, and "filthily defacing" the doors of her palace. The
abbate was arrested, and the canon, on this lady's complaint to
the Ten at Venice, was thrown into prison, and the weak and
furious Pope Paul V., being refused their release by the Ten,
excommunicated the whole Republic.

In the same year, that is to say 1552, the bane and antidote,
Paul the Pope and Paul Sarpi the friar, were sent into the world.
The latter grew in piety, fame, and learning, and at the time the
former began his quarrel with the Republic there was none in
Venice so fit and prompt as Sarpi to stand forth in her defence. He
was at once taken into the service of St. Mark, and his clear, acute
mind fashioned the spiritual weapons of the Republic, and helped
to shape the secular measures taken to annul the interdict. As soon
as the bull of excommunication was issued, the Republic instructed her officers to stop every copy of it at the frontier, and it
was never read in any church in the Venetian dominions. The
Senate refused to receive it from the Papal Nuncio. All priests,
monks, and other servants of the Church, as well as all secular
persons, were commanded to disregard it; and refractory ecclesiastics were forced to open their churches on pain of death. The
Jesuits and Capuchins were banished; and clerical intriguers,
whom Rome sent in swarms to corrupt social and family relations,
by declaring an end of civil government in Venice, and preaching
among women disobedience to patriotic husbands and fathers,
were severely punished. With internal safety thus provided for, the
Republic intrusted her moral, religious, and political defence
entirely to Sarpi, who devoted himself to his trust with fidelity,
zeal, and power.

It might have been expected that the friend of Galileo, and the
most learned and enlightened man of his country, would have
taken the short and decisive method of discarding all allegiance to

Rome as the most logical resistance to the unjust interdict. But the
Venetians have ever been faithful Catholics,[1] and Sarpi was (or,
according to the Papal writers, seemed to be) a sincere and
obedient Servite friar, believing in the spiritual supremacy of the
Pope, and revering the religion of Rome. He therefore fought Paul
inside the Church, and his writings on the interdict remain the
monument of his polemical success. He was the heart and brain of
the Republic's whole resistance,—he supplied her with inexhaustible reasons and answers,—and, though tempted, accused, and
threatened, he never swerved from his fidelity to her.

As he was the means of her triumph,[2] he remained the object of
her love. He could never be persuaded to desert his cell in the
Minorite Convent for the apartments appointed him by the State;
and even when his busy days were spent in council at the Ducal
Palace, he returned each night to sleep in the cloister. After the

---

[1] It is convenient here to attest the truth of certain views of religious
sentiment in Italy, which Mr. Trollope, in his *Paul the Pope and Paul the
Friar*, quotes from an "Italian author, by no means friendly to Catholicism, and very well qualified to speak of the progress of opinions and
tendencies among his fellow-countrymen." This author is Bianchi Gio-
vini, who, speaking of modern Catholicism as the heir of the old
materialistic paganism, says: "The Italians have identified themselves
with this mode of religion. Cultivated men find in it the truth there is in
it, and the people find what is agreeable to them. But both the former and
the latter approve it as conformable to the national character. And
whatever may be the religious system which shall govern our descendants
twenty centuries hence, I venture to affirm that the exterior forms of it
will be pretty nearly the same as those which prevail at present, and
which did prevail twenty centuries ago." Mr. Trollope generously
dissents from the "*pessimism*" of these views. The views are discouraging
for some reasons; but, with considerable disposition and fair opportunity
to observe Italian character in this respect, I had arrived at precisely these
conclusions. I wish here to state that in my slight sketch of Sarpi and his
times I have availed myself freely of Mr. Trollope's delightful book—it is
near being too much of a good thing—named above.

[2] The triumph was such only so far as the successful resistance to the
interdict was concerned; for at the intercession of the Catholic powers the
Republic gave up the ecclesiastical prisoners, and allowed all the banished
priests except the Jesuits to return. The Venetians utterly refused to
perform any act of humiliation or penance. The interdict had been defied,
and it remained despised.

harmless interdict had been removed by Paul, and the unyielding Republic forgiven, the wrath of Rome remained kindled against the friar whose logic had been too keen for the last reason of Popes. He had been tried for heresy in his youth at Milan, and acquitted; and again, during the progress of St. Mark's quarrel with Rome, his orthodoxy had been questioned; and now that all was over, and Rome could turn her attention to one particular offender, he was entreated, coaxed, commanded to come to her, and put her heart at rest concerning these old accusations. But Sarpi was very well in Venice. He had been appointed Counsultor in Theology to the Republic, and had received free admission to the secret archives of the State,—a favor, till then, never bestowed on any. So he would not go to Rome, and Rome sent assassins to take his life. One evening, as he was returning from the Ducal Palace in company with a lay-brother of the convent and an old patrician, very infirm and helpless, he was attacked by these *nuncios* of the Papal court; one of them seized the lay-brother, and another the patrician, while a third dealt Sarpi innumerable dagger thrusts. He fell as if dead, and the ruffians made off in the confusion.

Sarpi had been fearfully wounded, but he recovered. The action of the Republic in this affair is a comforting refutation of the saying that Republics are ungrateful, and the common belief that Venice was particularly so. The most strenuous and unprecedented efforts were made to take the assassins, and the most terrific penalties were denounced against them. What was much better, new honors were showered upon Sarpi, and extraordinary and affectionate measures were taken to provide for his safety.

And, in fine, he lived in the service of the Republic, revered and beloved, till his seventieth year, when he died with zeal for her good shaping his last utterance: "I must go to St. Mark, for it is late and I have much to do."

Brave Sarpi, and brave Republic! Men cannot honor them enough. For though the terrors of the interdict were doubted to be harmless even at that time, it had remained for them to prove the interdict, then and forever, an instrument as obsolete as the catapult.

I was so curious as to make some inquiry among the workmen on the old convent ground whether any stone or other record commemorative of Sarpi had been found in the demolished cells. I hoped, not very confidently, to gather some trace of his presence there,—to have, perhaps, the spot on which he died shown me. To a man, they were utterly ignorant of Sarpi, while affecting in the Italian manner to be perfectly informed on the subject. I was passed, with my curiosity, from one to another, till I fell into the hands of a kind of foreman, to whom I put my questions anew. He was a man of Napoleonic beard, and such fair red-and-white complexion that he impressed me as having escaped from a show of wax-works, and I was not at all surprised to find him a wax figure in point of intelligence. He seemed to think my questions the greatest misfortunes which had ever befallen him, and to regard each suggestion of *Sarpi—tempo della Repubblica— scomunica di Paolo Quinto*—as an intolerable oppression. He could only tell me that on a certain spot (which he pointed out with his foot) in the demolished church there had been found a stone with Sarpi's name upon it. The padrone, who had the contract for building the new convent, had said, "Truly, I have heard speak of this Sarpi;" but the stone had been broken, and he did not know what had become of it.

And, in fact, the only thing that remembered Sarpi, on the site of the convent where he spent his life, died, and was buried, was the little tablet on the outside of the wall, of which the abbreviated Latin announced that he had been Theologue to the Republic, and that his dust was now removed to the island of San Michele. After this failure, I had no humor to make researches for the bridge on which the friar was attacked by his assassins. But, indeed, why should I look for it? Finding it, could I have kept in my mind the fine dramatic picture I now have, of Sarpi returning to his convent on a mild October evening, weary with his long walk from St. Mark's, and pacing with downcast eyes,—the old patrician and the lay-brother at his side, and the masked and stealthy assassins, with uplifted daggers, behind him? Nay, I fear I should have found the bridge with some scene of modern life upon it, and brought away in my remembrance an old woman with an oil-bottle, or a straggling boy with a tumbler, and a very little wine in it.

On our way home from the Servite Convent, we stopped again near the corner and bridge of Sior Antonio Rioba,—this time to go into the house of Tintoretto, which stands close at the right hand, on the same quay. The house, indeed, might make some pretensions to be called a palace: it is large, and has a carved and balconied front, in which are set a now illegible tablet describing it as the painter's dwelling, and a medallion portrait of Robusti. It would have been well if I had contented myself with this goodly outside; for penetrating, by a long, narrow passage and complicated stairway, to the interior of the house, I found that it had nothing to offer me but the usual number of commonplace rooms in the usual blighting state of restoration. I must say that the people of the house, considering they had nothing in the world to show me, were kind and patient under the intrusion, and answered with very polite affirmation my discouraged inquiry if this were really Tintoretto's house.

Their conduct was different from that of the present inmates of Titian's house, near the Fondamenta Nuove, in a little court at the left of the church of the Jesuits. These unreasonable persons think it an intolerable bore that the enlightened travelling public should break in upon their privacy. They put their heads out of the upper windows, and assure the strangers that the house is as utterly restored within as they behold it without (and it *is* extremely restored), that it merely occupies the site of the painter's dwelling, and that there is nothing whatever to see in it. I never myself had the heart to force an entrance after these protests; but an acquaintance of the more obdurate sex, whom I had the honor to accompany thither, once did so, and came out with a story of rafters of the original Titianic kitchen being still visible in the new one. After a lapse of two years I revisited the house, and found that, so far from having learned patience by frequent trial, the inmates had been apparently goaded into madness during the interval. They seemed to know of our approach by instinct, and thrust their heads out, ready for protest, before we were near enough to speak. The lazy, frowzy women, the worthless men, and idle, loafing boys of the neighborhood, gathered round to witness the encounter; but though repeatedly commanded to ring (I was again in company with ladies), and try to force the place, I refused decidedly to do so. The garrison were strengthening their position by plastering and renewed renovation, and I doubt that by this time the original rafters are no longer to be seen. A plasterer's boy, with a fine sense of humor, stood clapping his trowel on his board, inside the house, while we debated retreat, and derisively invited us to enter: "*Suoni pure, O signore! Questa e la famosa casa del gran pittore, l'immortale Tiziano,—suoni, signore!*" (Ring, by all means, sir. This is the famous house of the great painter, the immortal Titian. Ring!) *Da capo*. We retired amid the scorn of the populace. But indeed I could not blame the inhabitants of Titian's house; and were I condemned to live in a place so famous as to attract idle curiosity, flushed and insolent with travel, I should go to the verge of man-traps and shot-guns to protect myself.

This house, which is now hemmed in by larger buildings of later date, had in the painter's time an incomparably "lovely and delightful situation." Standing near the northern boundary of the city, it looked out over the lagoon—across the quiet isle of sepulchres, San Michele, across the smoking chimneys of the Murano glass-works, and the bell-towers of her churches, to the long line of the sea-shore on the right and to the main-land on the left; and beyond the nearer lagoon islands and the faintly pencilled outlines of Torcello and Burano in front to the sublime distance of the Alps, shining in silver and purple, and resting their snowy heads against the clouds. It had a pleasant garden of flowers and trees, into which the painter descended by an open stairway, and in which he is said to have studied the famous tree in The Death of Peter Martyr. Here he entertained the great and noble of his day, and here he feasted and made merry with the gentle sculptor Sansovino, and with their common friend, the rascal-poet Aretino. The painter's and the sculptor's wives knew each other, and

Sansovino's Paola was often in the house of Cecilia Vecellio;[1] and any one who is wise enough not to visit the place can easily think of those ladies there, talking at an open window that gives upon the pleasant garden, where their husbands walk up and down together in the purple evening light.

In the palace where Goldoni was born a servant showed me an entirely new room near the roof, in which he said the great dramatist had composed his immortal comedies. As I knew, however, that Goldoni had left the house when a child, I could scarcely believe what the cicerone said, though I was glad he said it, and that he knew anything at all of Goldoni. It is a fine old Gothic palace on a small canal near the Frari, and on the Calle dei Nomboli, just across from a shop of indigestible pastry. It is known by an inscription, and by the medallion of the dramatist above the land-door; and there is no harm in looking in at the court on the ground-floor, where you may be pleased with the picturesque old stairway, wandering upward I hardly know how high, and adorned with many little heads of lions.

Several palaces dispute the honor of being Bianca Cappello's birthplace, but Mutinelli awards the distinction to the palace at Sant' Appollinare near the Ponte Storto. One day a gondolier vaingloriously rowed us to the water-gate of the edifice, through a very narrow, damp, and uncleanly canal, pretending that there was a beautiful staircase in its court. At the moment of our arrival, however, Bianca happened to be hanging out clothes from a window, and shrilly disclaimed the staircase, attributing this merit to another Palazzo Cappello. We were less pleased with her appearance here than with that portrait of her which we saw on

---

[1] The wife of Titian's youth was, according to Ticozzi, named Lucia. It is in Mutinelli that I find allusion to Cecilia. The author of the *Annali Urbani*, speaking of the friendship and frequent meetings of Titian and Sansovino, says: "Vivevano . . . allora ambedue di un amore fatto sacro dalle leggi divine, essendo moglie di Tiziano una Cecilia." I would not advise the reader to place too fond a trust in anything concerning the house of Titian. Mutinelli refers to but one house of the painter, while Ticozzi makes him proprietor of two.

another occasion in the palace of a lady of her name and blood. This lady has since been married, and the name of Cappello is now extinct.

The Palazzo Mocenigo, in which Byron lived, is galvanized into ghastly newness by recent repairs, and as it is one of the ugliest palaces on the Grand Canal it has less claim than ever upon one's interest. The custodian shows people the rooms where the poet wrote, dined, and slept, and I suppose it was from the hideous basket-balcony over the main door that one of his mistresses threw herself into the canal. Another of these interesting relics is pointed out in the small butter-and-cheese shop which she keeps in the street leading from Campo Sant' Angelo to San Paterinan: she is a fat sinner, long past beauty, bald, and somewhat melancholy to behold. Indeed, Byron's memory is not a presence which I approach with pleasure, and I had most enjoyment in his palace when I thought of good-natured little Thomas Moore, who once visited his lordship there. Byron himself hated the recollection of his life in Venice, and I am sure no one else need like it. But he is become a *cosa di Venezia,* and you cannot pass his palace without having it pointed out to you by the gondoliers. Early after my arrival in the city I made the acquaintance of an old smooth-shaven, smooth-mannered Venetian, who said he had known Byron, and who told me that he once swam with him from the Port of San Nicolò to his palace-door. The distance is something over three miles; but if the swimmers came in with the sea, the feat was not so great as it seems, for the tide is as swift and strong as a mill-race. I think it would be impossible to make the distance against the tide.

CHAPTER XVI

COMMERCE

To make an annual report in September upon the Commercial Transactions of the port was an official duty to which I looked forward at Venice with a vague feeling of injury during a year of almost uninterrupted tranquillity. It was not because the preparation of the report was an affair of so great labor that I shrank from it, but because the material was wanting with which to make a respectable show among my consular peers in the large and handsomely misprinted volume of Commercial Relations annually issued by the enterprising Congressional publishers. It grieved me that upstart ports like Marseilles, Liverpool, and Bremen should occupy so much larger space in this important volume than my beloved Venice; and it was with a feeling of profound mortification that I used to post my meagre account of a commerce that once was greater than all the rest of the world's together. I sometimes desperately eked out the material furnished me in the statistics of the Venetian Chamber of Commerce by an agricultural essay on the disease of the grapes and its cure, or by a few wretched figures representative of a very slender mining interest in the province. But at last I determined to end these displeasures, and to make such researches into the history of her commerce as should furnish me forth material for a report worthy of the high place Venice held in my reverence.

Indeed, it seemed to be by a sort of anachronism that I had ever mentioned contemporary Venetian commerce; and I turned with exultation from the phantom transactions of the present to that solid and magnificent prosperity of the past, of which the long-enduring foundations were laid in the earliest Christian times. For the new cities formed by the fugitives from barbarian invasion of the main-land, during the fifth century, had hardly settled around a common democratic government on the islands of the lagoons, when they began to develop maritime energies and resources; and long before this government was finally established at Rialto (the ancient sea-port of Padua), or Venice had become the capital of the young Republic, the Veneti had thriftily begun to turn the wild invaders of the main-land to account, to traffic with them, and to make treaties of commerce with their rulers. Theodoric, the King of the Goths, had fixed his capital at Ravenna, in the sixth century, and would have been glad to introduce Italian civilization among his people; but this warlike race were not prepared to practise the useful arts, and although they inhabited one of the most fruitful parts of Italy, with ample borders of sea, they were neither sailors nor tillers of the ground. The Venetians supplied them (at a fine profit, no doubt) with the salt made in the lagoons, and with wines brought from Istria. The Goths viewed with especial amazement their skill in the management of their river-craft, by means of which the dauntless traders ascended the shallowest streams to penetrate the main-land, "running on the grass of the meadows and between the stalks of the harvest-field,"—just as in this day our own western steamers are known to run in a heavy dew.

The Venetians continued to extend and confirm their commerce with those helpless and hungry warriors, and were ready also to open a lucrative trade with the Longobards when they descended into Italy about the year 570. They had, in fact, abetted the Longobards in their war with the Greek Emperor Justinian (who had opposed their incursion), and in return the barbarians gave them the right to hold great free marts or fairs on the shores of the lagoons, whither the people resorted from every part of the Longobard kingdom to buy the salt of the lagoons, grain from Istria and Dalmatia, and slaves from every country.

The slave-trade, indeed, formed then one of the most lucrative branches of Venetian commerce, as now it forms the greatest stain upon the annals of that commerce. The islanders, however, were not alone guilty of this infamous trade in men; other Italian states made profit of it, and it may be said to have been all but universal. But the Venetians were the most deeply involved in it, they pursued it the most unscrupulously, and they relinquished it the last. The Pope forbade and execrated their commerce, and they sailed from the Papal ports with cargoes of slaves for the infidels in Africa. In spite of the prohibitions of their own government, they bought Christians of kidnappers throughout Europe, and purchased the captives of the pirates on the seas, to sell them again to the Saracens. Nay, being an ingenious people, they turned their honest penny over and over again: they sold the Christians to the Saracens, and then for certain sums ransomed them and restored them to their countries; they sold Saracens to the Christians, and plundered the infidels in similar transactions of ransom and restoration. It is not easy to fix the dates of the rise or fall of this slave-trade; but slavery continued in Venice as late as the fifteenth century, and in earlier ages was so common that every prosperous person had two or three slaves.[1] The corruption of the citizens at this time is properly attributed in part to the existence of slavery among them; and Mutinelli goes so far as to declare that the institution impressed permanent traits on the populace, rendering them idle and indisposed to honest labor by degrading labor and making it the office of bondmen.

While this hateful and enormous traffic in man was growing up, the Venetians enriched themselves by many other more blameless and legitimate forms of commerce, and gradually gathered into their grasp that whole trade of the East with Europe which passed through their hands for so many ages. After the dominion of the Franks was established in Italy in the eighth century, they began to supply that people, more luxurious than the Lombards, with the costly stuffs, the rich jewelry, and the perfumes of Byzantium; and held a great annual fair at the imperial city of Pavia, where they sold the Franks the manufactures of the polished and effeminate Greeks, and whence in return they carried back to the East the grain, wine, wool, iron, lumber, and excellent armor of Lombardy.

From the time when they had assisted the Longobards against the Greeks, the Venetians found it to their interest to cultivate the friendship of the latter, until, in the twelfth century, they mastered the people so long caressed, and took their capital, under Enrico Dandolo. The privileges conceded to the wily and thrifty republican traders by the Greek Emperors were extraordinary in their extent and value. Otho, the western Cæsar, having succeeded the Franks in the dominion of Italy, had already absolved the Venetians from the annual tribute paid the Italian kings for the liberty of traffic, and had declared their commerce free throughout the Peninsula. In the mean time they had attacked and beaten the pirates of Dalmatia, and the Greeks now recognized their rule all

---

[1] Mutinelli, *Del Costume Veneziano*. The present sketch of the history of Venetian commerce is based upon facts chiefly drawn from Mutinelli's delightful treatise, *Del Commercio dei Veneziani*.

over Dalmatia, thus securing to the Republic every port on the eastern shores of the Adriatic. Then, as they aided the Greeks to repel the aggressions of the Saracens and Normans, their commerce was declared free in all the ports of the empire, and they were allowed to trade without restriction in all the cities, and to build warehouses and *dépôts* throughout the dominions of the Greeks, wherever they chose. The harvest they reaped from the vast field thus opened to their enterprise must have more than compensated them for their losses in the barbarization of the Italian continent by the incessant civil wars which followed the disruption of the Lombard League, when trade and industry languished throughout Italy. When the Crusaders had taken the Holy Land, the King of Jerusalem bestowed upon the Venetians, in return for important services against the infidel, the same privileges conceded them by the Greek Emperor; and when finally, Constantinople fell into the hands of the Crusaders (whom they had skilfully diverted from the reconquest of Palestine to the siege of the Greek metropolis), nearly all the Greek islands fell to the share of Venice; and the Latin Emperors, who succeeded the Greeks in dominion, gave her such privileges as made her complete mistress of the commerce of the Levant.

From this opulent traffic the insatiable enterprise of the Republic turned, without relinquishing the old, to new gains in the farthest Orient. Against her trade the exasperated infidel had closed the Egyptian ports, but she did not scruple to coax the barbarous prince of the Scythian Tartars, newly descended upon the shores of the Black Sea; and having secured his friendship, she proceeded, without imparting her design to her Latin allies at Constantinople, to plant a commercial colony at the mouth of the Don, where the city of Azof stands. Through this *entrepôt,* thenceforward, Venetian energy, with Tartar favor, directed the entire commerce of Asia with Europe, and incredibly enriched the Republic. The vastness and importance of such a trade, even at that day, when the wants of men were far simpler and fewer than now, could hardly be overstated; and one nation then monopolized the traffic which is now free to the whole world. The

Venetians bought their wares at the great marts of Samarcand, and crossed the country of Tartary in caravans to the shores of the Caspian Sea, where they set sail and voyaged to the river Volga, which they ascended to the point of its closest proximity to the Don. Their goods were then transported overland to the Don, and were again carried by water down to their mercantile colony at its mouth. Their ships, having free access to the Black Sea, could, after receiving their cargoes, return direct to Venice. The products of every country of Asia were carried into Europe by these dauntless traffickers, who, enlightened and animated by the travels and discoveries of Matteo, Nicolò, and Marco Polo, penetrated the remotest regions, and brought away the treasures which the prevalent fears and superstitions of other nations would have deterred them from seeking, even if they had possessed the means of access to them.

The partial civilization of the age of chivalry had now reached its climax, and the class which had felt its refining effects was that best able to gratify the tastes still unknown to the great mass of the ignorant and impoverished people. It was a splendid time, and the robber counts and barons of the continent, newly tamed and christianized into knights, spent splendidly, as became magnificent cavaliers serving noble ladies. The Venetians, who seldom did merely heroic things, who turned the Crusades to their own account and made money out of the Holy Land, and whom one always fancies as having a half scorn of the noisy grandeur of chivalry, were very glad to supply the knights and ladies with the gorgeous stuffs, precious stones, and costly perfumes of the East; and they now also began to establish manufactories, and to practise the industrial arts at home. Their jewellers and workers in precious metals soon became famous throughout Europe; the glass-works of Murano rose into celebrity and importance which they have never since lost (for they still supply the world with beads); and they began to weave stuffs of gold tissue at Venice, and silks so exquisitely dyed that no cavalier or dame of perfect fashion was content with any other. Besides this they gilded leather for lining walls, wove carpets, and wrought miracles of ornament in wax,—a material that modern taste is apt to disdain,—while Venetian candles in chandeliers of Venetian glass lighted up the palaces of the whole civilized world.

The private enterprise of citizens was in every way protected and encouraged by the State, which did not, however, fail to make due and just profit out of it. The ships of the merchants always sailed to and from Venice in fleets, at stated seasons, seven fleets departing annually,—one for the Greek dominions, a second for Azof, a third for Trebizond, a fourth for Cyprus, a fifth for Armenia, a sixth for Spain, France, the Low Countries, and England, and a seventh for Africa. Each squadron of traders was accompanied and guarded from attacks of corsairs and other enemies by a certain number of the state galleys, let severally to the highest bidders for the voyage, at a price never less than about five hundred dollars of our money. The galleys were all manned and armed by the State, and the crew of each amounted to three hundred persons; including a captain, four supercargoes, eight pilots, two carpenters, two caulkers, a master of the oars, fifty cross-bowmen, three drummers, and two hundred rowers. The State also appointed a commandant of the whole squadron, with absolute authority to hear complaints, decide controversies, and punish offences.

While the Republic was thus careful in the protection and discipline of its citizens in their commerce upon the seas, it was no less zealous for their security and its own dignity in their traffic with the continent of Europe. In that rude day, neither the life nor the property of the merchant who visited the ultramontane countries was safe; for the sorry device which he practised, of taking with him a train of apes, buffoons, dancers, and singers, in order to divert his ferocious patrons from robbery and murder, was not always successful. The Venetians, therefore, were forbidden by the State to trade in those parts; and the Bohemians, Germans, and Hungarians, who wished to buy their wares, were obliged to come to the lagoons and buy them at the great marts which were held in different parts of the city and on the neighboring main-land. A triple purpose was thus served,—the Venetian merchants were protected in their lives and goods, the national honor was saved from insult, and many an honest *zecchino* was turned by the innkeepers and others who lodged and entertained the customers of the merchants.

Five of these great fairs were held every week, the chief market being at Rialto; and the transactions in trade were carefully supervised by the servants of the State. Among the magistracies especially appointed for the orderly conduct of the foreign and domestic commerce were the so-called Mercantile Consuls (*Uffficio dei Consoli dei Mercanti*), whose special duty it was to see that the traffic of the nation received no hurt from the schemes of any citizen or foreigner, and to punish offences of this kind with banishment and even graver penalties. They measured every ship about to depart, to learn if her cargo exceeded the lawful amount; they guarded creditors against debtors, and protected poor debtors against the rapacity of creditors, and they punished thefts sustained by the merchants. It is curious to find, contemporary with this beneficent magistracy, a charge of equal dignity exercised by the College of Reprisals. A citizen offended in his person or property abroad demanded justice of the government of the country in which the offence was committed. If the demand was refused, it was repeated by the Republic; if still refused, then the Republic, although at peace with the nation from which the offence came, seized any citizen of that country whom it could find, and, through its College of Reprisals, spoiled him of sufficient property to pay the damage done to its citizen. Finally, besides several other magistracies resident in Venice, the Republic appointed Consuls in its colonies and some foreign ports, to superintend the traffic of its citizens, and to compose their controversies. The Consuls were paid out of duties levied on the merchandise; they were usually nobles, and acted with the advice and consent of twelve other Venetian nobles or merchants.

At this time, and indeed throughout its existence, the great lucrative monopoly of the Republic was the salt manufactured in the lagoons, and forced into every market at rates that no other salt could compete with. Wherever alien enterprise attempted rivalry, it was instantly discouraged by Venice. There were troublesome salt mines, for example, in Croatia; and in 1381 the Republic caused them to be closed by paying the King of Hungary an annual pension of seven thousand crowns of gold. The exact income of the State, however, from the monopoly of salt, or from the various imposts and duties levied upon merchandise, it is now difficult to know, and it is impossible to compute accurately the value or extent of Venetian commerce at any one time. It reached the acme of its prosperity under Tommaso Mocenigo, who was Doge from 1414 to 1423. There were then three thousand and three hundred vessels of the mercantile marine, giving employment to thirty-three thousand seamen, and netting to their owners a profit of forty per cent. on the capital invested. How great has been the decline of this trade may be understood from the fact that in 1863 it amounted, according to the careful statistics of the Chamber of Commerce, to only $60,229,740, and that the number of vessels now owned in Venice is one hundred and fifty. As the total tonnage of these is but 26,000, it may be inferred that they are small craft, and in fact they are nearly all coasting vessels. They no longer bring to Venice the drugs and spices and silks of Samarcand, or carry her own rare manufactures to the ports of Western Europe; but they sail to and from her canals with humble freights of grain, lumber, and hemp. Almost as many Greek as Venetian ships now visit the old queen, who once levied a tax upon every foreign vessel in her Adriatic; and the shipping from the cities of the kingdom of Italy exceeds hers by ninety sail, while the tonnage of Great Britain is vastly greater. Her commerce has not only wasted to the shadow of its former magnitude, but it has also almost entirely lost its distinctive character. Glass of Murano is still exported to a value of about two millions of dollars annually; but in this industry, as in nearly all others of the lagoons, there is an annual decline. The trade of the port falls off from one to three millions of dollars yearly, and the manufacturing interests of the province have dwindled in the same proportion. So far as silk is concerned, there has been an immediate cause for the decrease in the disease which has afflicted the cocoons for several years past. Wine and oil are at present articles of import solely,—

the former because of a malady of the grape, the latter because of negligent cultivation of the olive.

A considerable number of persons are still employed in the manufacture of objects of taste and ornament; and in the Ruga Vecchia at Rialto they yet make the famous Venetian gold chain, which few visitors to the city can have failed to notice hanging in strands and wound upon spools in the shop windows of the Old Procuratie and the Bridge of Rialto. It is wrought of all degrees of fineness, and is always so flexile that it may be folded and wound in any shape. It is now no longer made in great quantity, and is chiefly worn by *contadine* (as a safe investment of their ready money)[1] and old-fashioned people of the city, who display the finer sort in skeins or strands. At Chioggia, I remember to have seen a babe, at its christening in church, literally manacled and shackled with Venetian chain; and the little girl who came to us one day, to show us the splendors in which she had appeared at a *disputa* (examination of children in doctrine), was loaded with it. Formerly, in the luxurious days of the Republic, it is said the chain was made as fine as sewing-silk, and worn embroidered on Genoa velvet by the patrician dames. It had then a cruel interest from the fact that its manufacture, after a time, cost the artisans their eyesight, so nice and subtle was the work. I could not help noticing that the workmen at the shops in the Ruga Vecchia still suffer in their eyes, even though the work is much coarser. I do not hope to describe the chain, except by saying that the links are horseshoe and oval shaped, and are connected by twos,—an oval being welded crosswise into a horseshoe, and so on, each two being linked loosely into the next.

An infintely more important art, in which Venice was distinguished a thousand years ago, has recently been revived there by

---

[1] Certain foreigners living in Venice were one day astonished to find their maid-servant in possession of a mass of this chain, and thought it their business to reprove her extravagance. "Signori," she explained paradoxically, "if I keep my money, I spend it; if I buy this chain, it is always money (*è sempre soldi*)."

Signor Salviati, an enthusiast in mosaic painting. His establishment is on the Grand Canal, not far from the Academy, and you might go by the old palace quite unsuspicious of the ancient art stirring with new life in its breast. "A. Salviati, Avvocato," is the legend of the bell-pull, and you do not by any means take this legal style for that of the restorer of a neglected art, and a possessor of forgotten secrets in gilded glass and "smalts," as they term the small, delicate rods of vitreous substance with which the wonders of the art are achieved. But inside of the palace are some two hundred artisans at work, cutting the smalts and glass into the minute fragments of which the mosaics are made, grinding and smoothing these fragments, polishing the completed works, and reproducing, with incredible patience and skill, the lights and shadows of the pictures to be copied.

You first enter the rooms of those whose talent distinguishes them as artists, and in whose work all the wonderful neatness and finish and long-suffering toil of the Byzantines are visible, as well as original life and inspiration alike impossible and profane to the elder mosaicists. Each artist has at hand a great variety of the slender stems of smalts already mentioned, and, breaking these into minute fragments as he proceeds, he inserts them in the bed of cement prepared to receive his picture, and thus counterfeits in enduring mineral the perishable work of the painter.

In other rooms artisans are at work upon various tasks of *marqueterie*,—table-tops, album-covers, paper-weights, brooches, pins, and the like,—and in others they are sawing the smalts and glass into strips, and grinding the edges. Passing through yet another room, where the finished mosaic-works—of course not the pictorial mosaics—are polished by machinery, we enter the store-room, where the crowded shelves display blocks of smalts and glass of endless variety of color. By far the greater number of these colors are discoveries of improvements of the venerable mosaicist Lorenzo Radi, who has found again the Byzantine secrets of counterfeiting, in vitreous paste, aventurine (gold stone), onyx, chalcedony, malachite, and other natural stones, and who has been praised by the Academy of Fine Arts in Venice for producing mosaics even more durable in tint and workmanship than those of the Byzantine artists.

In an upper story of the palace a room is set apart for the exhibition of the many beautiful and costly things which the art of the establishment produces. Here, besides pictures in mosaic, there are cunningly inlaid tables and cabinets, caskets, rich vases of chalcedony mounted in silver, and delicately wrought jewelry, while the floor is covered with a mosaic pavement ordered for the Viceroy of Egypt. There are here, moreover, to be seen the designs furnished by the Crown Princess of Prussia for the mosaics of the Queen's Chapel at Windsor. These, like all other pictures and decorations in mosaic, are completed in the establishment on the Grand Canal, and are afterward put up as wholes in the places intended for them.

In Venice nothing in decay is strange. But it is startling to find her in her old age nourishing into fresh life an art that, after feebly preserving the memory of painting for so many centuries, had decorated her prime only with the glories of its decline;—for Kugler ascribes the completion of the mosaics of the church of St. Cyprian in Murano to the year 882, and the earliest mosaics of St. Mark's to the tenth or eleventh centuries, when the Greek Church had already laid her ascetic hand on Byzantine art, and fixed its conventional forms, paralyzed its motives, and forbidden its inspirations.

I think, however, one would look about him in vain for other evidences of a returning prosperity in the lagoons. The old prosperity of Venice was based upon her monopoly of the most lucrative traffic in the world, as we have already seen,—upon her exclusive privileges in foreign countries, upon the enlightened zeal of her government, and upon men's imperfect knowledge of geography, and the barbarism of the rest of Europe, as well as upon the indefatigable industry and intelligent enterprise of her citizens. America was still undiscovered; the overland route to India was the only one known; the people of the continent outside of Italy were unthrifty serfs, ruled and ruined by unthrifty lords.

The whole world's ignorance, pride, and sloth were Venetian gain; and the religious superstitions of the day, which, gross as they were, embodied perhaps its noblest and most hopeful sentiment, were a source of incalculable profit to the sharp-witted mistress of the Adriatic. It was the age of penances, pilgrimages, and relic-hunting, and the wealth which she wrung from the devotion of others was exceedingly great. Her ships carried the pilgrims to and from the Holy Land; her adventurers ransacked Palestine and the whole Orient for the bones and memorials of the saints; and her merchants sold the precious relics throughout Europe at an immense advance upon first cost.

But the foundations of this prosperity were at last sapped by the tide of wealth which poured into Venice from every quarter of the world. Her citizens brought back the vices as well as the luxuries of the debauched Orient, and the city became that seat of splendid idleness and proud corruption which it continued till the Republic fell. It is needless here to rehearse the story of her magnificence and decay. At the time when the hardy, hungry people of other nations were opening paths to prosperity by land and sea, the Venetians, gorged with the spoils of ages, relinquished their old habits of daring enterprise, and dropped back into luxury and indolence. Their incessants wars with the Genoese began, and though they signally defeated the rival Republic in battle, Genoa finally excelled in commerce. A Greek prince had arisen to dispute the sovereignty of the Latin Emperors, whom the Venetians had helped to place upon the Byzantine throne; the Genoese, seeing the favorable fortunes of the Greek, threw the influence of their arms and intrigues in his favor, and the Latins were expelled from Constantinople in 1271. The new Greek Emperor had promised to give the sole navigation of the Black Sea to his allies, together with the church and palaces possessed by the Venetians in his capital, and he bestowed also upon the Genoese the city of Smyrna. It does not seem that he fulfilled literally all his promises, for the Venetians still continued to sail to and from their colony of Tana, at the head of the Sea of Azof, though it is certain that they had no longer the sovereignty of those waters; and the Genoese now planted on the shores of the Black Sea three large and important colonies to serve as *entrepôts* for the trade taken from their rivals. The oriental traffic of the latter was maintained through Tana, however, for nearly two centuries later, when, in 1410, the Mongol Tartars, under Tamerlane, fell upon the devoted colony, took, sacked, burnt, and utterly destroyed it. This was the first terrible blow to the most magnificent commerce which the world had ever seen, and which had endured for ages. No wonder that, on the day of Tana's fall, terrible portents of woe were seen at Venice,—that meteors appeared, that demons rode the air, that the winds and waters rose and blew down houses and swallowed ships! A thousand persons are said to have perished in the calamities which commemorated a stroke so mortally disastrous to the national grandeur. After that the Venetians humbly divided with their ancient foes the possession and maintenance of the Genoese colony of Caffa, and continued, with greatly diminished glory, their traffic in the Black Sea; till the Turks having taken Constantinople, and the Greeks having acquired under their alien masters a zeal for commerce unknown to them during the times of their native princes, the Venetians were finally, on the first pretext of war, expelled from those waters in which they had latterly maintained themselves only by payment of heavy tribute to the Turks.

In the mean time the industrial arts, in which Venice had heretofore excelled, began to be practised elsewhere, and the Florentines and the English took that lead in the manufactures of the world which the latter still retain. The league of the Hanseatic cities was established, and rose daily in importance. At London, at Bruges, at Bergen, and Novogorod banks were opened under the protection and special favor of the Hanseatic League; its ships were preferred to any other, and, the tide of commerce setting northward, the cities of the League persecuted the foreigners who would have traded in their ports. On the west, Barcelona began to dispute the preëminence of Venice in the Mediterranean, and Spanish salt was brought to Italy itself and sold by the enterprising Catalonians. Their corsairs vexed Venetian commerce everywhere; and in that day, as in our own, private English enterprise was employed in piratical depredations on the traffic of a friendly power.

The Portuguese also began to extend their commerce, once so important, and catching the rage for discovery then prevalent, infested every sea in search of unknown land. One of their navigators, sailing by a chart which a monk named Fra Mauro, in his convent on the island of San Michele, had put together from the stories of travellers, and his own guesses at geography, discovered the Cape of Good Hope, and the trade of India with Europe was turned in that direction, and the old overland traffic perished. The Venetian monopoly of this traffic had long been gone; had its recovery been possible, it would now have been useless to the declining prosperity of the Republic.

It remained for Christopher Columbus, born of that Genoese nation which had hated the Venetians so long and so bitterly, to make the discovery of America, and thus to give the death-blow to the supremacy of Venice. While all these discoveries were taking place, the old queen of the seas had been weighed down with many and unequal wars. Her naval power had been everywhere crippled; her revenues had been reduced; her possessions, one after one, had been lopped away; and at the time Columbus was on his way to America, half Europe, united in the League of Cambray, was attempting to crush the Republic of Venice.

The whole world was now changed. Commerce sought new channels; fortune smiled on other nations. How Venice dragged onward from the end of her commercial greatness, and tottered with a delusive splendor to her political death, is surely one of the saddest of stories, if not the sternest of lessons.

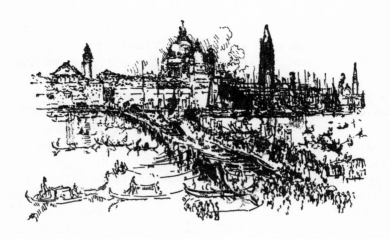

CHAPTER XVII

VENETIAN HOLIDAYS

THE national character of the Venetians was so largely influenced by the display and dissipation of the frequent festivals of the Republic that it cannot be fairly estimated without taking them into consideration, nor can the disuse of these holidays (of which I have heretofore spoken) be appreciated in all its import without particular allusion to their number and nature. They formed part of the aristocratic polity of the old commonwealth, which substituted popular indulgence for popular liberty, and gave the people costly pleasures in return for the priceless rights of which they had been robbed, set up national pride in the place of patriotism, and was as well satisfied with a drunken joy in its subjects as if they had possessed a true content.

Full notice of these holidays would be history[1] of Venice, for

---

[1] "Siccome," says the editor of Giustina Renier-Michiel's *Origine delle Feste Veneziane,*—"Siccome l'illustre Autrice ha voluto applicare al suo lavoro il modesto titolo di *Origine delle Feste Veneziane,* e siccome questo portrebbe porgere un'idea assai diversa dell' opera a chi non ne ha alcuna cognizione, da quello che è sostanzialmente, si espone questo Epitome, perchè ognun vegga almeno in parte, che quest' opera sarebbe

each one had its origin in some great event of her existence, and they were so numerous as to commemorate nearly every notable incident in her annals. Though, as has been before observed, they had nearly all a general religious character, the Church, as usual in Venice, only seemed to direct the ceremonies in its own honor, while it really ministered to the political glory of the oligarchy, which knew how to manage its priests as well as its prince and people. Nay, it happened in one case, at least, that a religious anniversary was selected by the Republic as the day on which to put to shame before the populace certain of the highest and reverendest dignitaries of the Church. In 1162, Ulrich, the Patriarch of Aquileja, seized, by a treacherous stratagem, the city of Grado, then subject to Venice. The Venetians immediately besieged and took the city, with the Patriarch and twelve of his canons in it, and carried them prisoners to the lagoons. The turbulent patriarchs of Aquileja had long been disturbers of the Republic's dominion, and the people now determined to make an end of these displeasures. They refused, therefore, to release the Patriarch, except on condition that he should bind himself to send them annually a bull and twelve fat hogs. It is not known what meaning the Patriarch attached to this singular ceremony; but with the Venetians the bull was typical of himself, and the swine of his canons, and they yearly suffered death in these animals, which were slaughtered during Shrovetide in the Piazza San Marco, amid a great concourse of the people, in the presence of the Doge and Signory. The locksmiths and other workers in iron had distinguished themselves in the recapture of Grado, and to their guild was allotted the honor of putting to death the bull and swine. Great art was shown in striking off the bull's head at one blow, without suffering the sword to touch the ground after

---

del titolo di *storia* condegna, giacchè essa non è che una costante descrizione degli avvenimenti più importanti e luminosi della Repubblica di Venezia." The work in question is one of much research and small philosophy, like most books which Venetians have written upon Venice; but it has admirably served my purpose, and I am indebted to it for most of the information contained in this chapter.

passing through the animal's neck; the swine were slain with lances. Athletic games among the people succeeded, and the Doge and his Senators attacked and destroyed, with staves, several lightly built wooden castles, to symbolize the abasement of the feudal power before the Republic. As the centuries advanced, this part of the ceremony, together with the slaughter of the swine, was disused; in which fact Mr. Ruskin sees evidence of a corrupt disdain of simple and healthy allegory on the part of the proud Doges, but in which I think most people will discern only a natural wish to discontinue in more civilized times a puerile barbarity. Mr. Ruskin himself finds no evidence of "state pride" in the abolition of the slaughter of the swine. The festival was very popular and continued a long time, though I believe not till the fall of the Republic.

Another tribute, equally humiliating to those who paid it, was imposed upon the Paduans for an insult offered to St. Mark, and gave occasion for a national holiday, some fifty years after the Patriarch of Aquileja began atonement for his outrage. In the year 1214, the citizens of Treviso made an entertainment, to which they invited the noble youth of the surrounding cities. In the chief piazza of the town a castle of wood, exquisitely decorated, was held against all comers by a garrison of the fairest Trevisan damsels. The weapons of defence were flowers, fruits, bonbons, and the bright eyes of the besieged; while the missiles of attack were much the same, with whatever added virtue might lie in tender prayers and sugared supplications. Padua, Vicenza, Bassano, and Venice sent their gallantest youths, under their municipal banners, to take part in this famous enterprise; and the attack was carried on by the leagued forces with great vigor, but with no effect on the castle of Love, as it was called, till the Venetians made a breach at a weak point. These young men were better skilled in the arts of war than their allies; they were richer, and had come to Treviso decked in the spoils of the recent sack of Constantinople, and at the moment they neared the castle it is reported that they corrupted the besieged by throwing handfuls of gold into the tower. Whether this be true or not, it is certain the

the conduct of the Venetians in some manner roused the Paduans to insult, and that the hot youths came to blows. In an instant the standard of St. Mark was thrown down and trampled under the feet of the furious Paduans; blood flowed, and the indignant Trevisans drove the combatants out of their city. The spark of war spreading to the rival cities, the Paduans were soon worsted, and three hundred of their number were made prisoners. These they would willingly have ransomed at any price, but their enemies would not release them except on the payment of two white pullets for each warrior. The shameful ransom was paid in the Piazza, to the inextinguishable delight of the Venetians, who, never wanting in sharp and biting wit, abandoned themselves to sarcastic exultation. They demanded that the Paduans should, like the Patriarch, repeat the tribute annually; but the prudent Doge Ziani judged the single humiliation sufficient, and refused to establish a yearly celebration of the feast.

One of the most famous occasional festivals of Venice is described by Petrarch in a Latin letter to his friend Pietro Bolognese. It was in celebration of the reduction of the Greeks of Candia, an island which in 1361 had recently been ceded to the Republic. The Candiotes rose in general rebellion, but were so promptly subdued that the news of the outbreak scarcely anticipated the announcement of its suppression in Venice. Petrarch was at this time the guest of the Republic, and from his seat at the right of the Doge on the gallery of St. Mark's Church, in front of the bronze horses, he witnessed the chivalric shows given in the Piazza below, which was then unpaved, and admirably adapted for equestrian feats of arms. It is curious to read the poet's account of these in a city where there is now no four-footed beast larger than a dog. But in the age of chivalry even the Venetians were mounted, and rode up and down their narrow streets, and jousted in their great campos.

Speaking of twenty-four noble and handsome youths, whose feats formed a chief part of a show of which he "does not know if in the whole world there has been seen the equal," Petrarch says: "It was a gentle sight to see so many youths decked in purple and gold, as they ruled with the rein and urged with the spur their coursers, moving in glittering harness, with iron-shod feet which scarcely seemed to touch the ground." And it must have been a noble sight, indeed, to behold all this before the "golden façade of the temple," in a place so packed with spectators "that a grain of barley could not have fallen to the ground. The great piazza, the church itself, the towers, the roofs, the arcades, the windows, all were—I will not say full, but running over, walled and paved with people." At the right of the church was built a great platform, on which sat "four hundred honestest gentlewomen, chosen from the flower of the nobility, and distinguished in their dress and bearing, who, amid the continual homage offered them morning, noon, and night, presented the image of a celestial congress." Some noblemen, come hither by chance, "from the part of Britain, comrades and kinsmen of their king, were present," and attracted the notice of the poet. The feasts lasted many days, but on the third day Petrarch excused himself to the Doge, pleading, he says, his "ordinary occupations, already known to all."

Among remoter feasts in honor of national triumphs was one on the Day of Annunciation, commemorative of the removal of the capital of the Venetian isles to Rialto from Malamocco, after King Pepin had burnt the latter city, and when, advancing on Venice, he was met in the lagoons and beaten by the islanders and the tides: these by their recession stranding his boats in the mud, and those falling upon his helpless host with the fury of an insulted and imperilled people. The Doge annually assisted at mass in St. Mark's in honor of the victory, but not long afterward the celebration of it ceased, as did that of a precisely similar defeat of the Hungarians, who had just descended from Asia into Europe. In 1339 there were great rejoicings in the Piazza for the peace with Mastino della Scala, who, beaten by the Republic, ceded his city of Treviso to her.

Doubtless the most splendid of all the occasional festivals was that held for the Venetian share of the great Christian victory at Lepanto over the Turks. All orders of the State took part in it; but the most remarkable feature of the celebration was the roofing of

the Merceria, all the way from St. Mark's to Rialto, with fine blue
cloth, studded with golden stars to represent the firmament, as the
shopkeepers imagined it. The pictures of the famous painters of
that day, Titian, Tintoretto, Palma, and the rest, were exposed
under this canopy, at the end near Rialto. Later, the Venetian
victories over the Turks at the Dardanelles were celebrated by a
regatta, in 1658; and Morosini's brilliant reconquest of the
Morea, in 1688, was the occasion of other magnificent shows.

The whole world has now adopted, with various modifications,
the picturesque and exciting pastime of the regatta, which,
according to Mutinelli,[2] originated among the lagoons at a very
early period, from a peculiar feature in the military discipline of
the Republic. A target for practice with the bow and cross-bow
was set up every week on the beach at the Lido, and nobles and
plebeians rowed thither in barges of thirty oars, vying with each
other in the speed and skill with which the boats were driven. To
divert the popular discontent that followed the Serrar del Consiglio and the suppression of Bajamonte Tiepolo's conspiracy
early in the fourteenth century, the proficiency arising from this
rivalry was turned to account, and the spectacle of the regatta was
instituted. Agreeably, however, to the aristocratic spirit of the
newly established oligarchy, the patricians withdrew from the
lists, and the regatta became the affair exclusively of the gondoliers. In other Italian cities, where horse and donkey races were the
favorite amusement, the riders were of both sexes; and now at
Venice women also entered into the rivalry of the regatta. But in
gallant deference to their weakness, they were permitted to begin
the course at the mouth of the Grand Canal before the Doganna
di Mare, while the men were obliged to start from the Public
Gardens. They followed the Grand Canal to its opposite extremity, beyond the present railway station, and there doubling a pole
planted in the water near the Ponte della Croce, returned to the
common goal before the Palazzo Foscari. Here was erected an
ornate scaffolding to which the different prizes were attached. The

---

[2] *Annali Urbani di Venezia.*

first boat carried off a red banner; the next received a green flag; the third, a blue; and the fourth, a yellow one. With each of these was given a purse, and with the last was added, by way of gibe, a live pig, a picture of which was painted on the yellow banner. Every regatta included five courses, in which single and double oared boats and single and double oared gondolas successively competed,—the fifth contest being that in which the women participated with two-oared boats. Four prizes like those described were awarded to the winners in each course.

The regatta was celebrated with all the pomp which the superb city could assume. As soon as the government announced that it was to take place, the preparations of the champions began. "From that time the gondolier ceased to be a servant; he became almost an adoptive son;"[3] his master giving him every possible assistance and encouragement in the daily exercises by which he trained himself for the contest, and his parish priest visiting him in his own house, to bless his person, his boat, and the image of the Madonna or other saint attached to the gondola. When the great day arrived, the Canalazzo swarmed with boats of every kind. "All the trades and callings," says Giustina Renier-Michiel,[4] with that pride in the Venetian past which does not always pass from verbosity to eloquence, "had each its boats appropriately mounted and adorned; and private societies filled an hundred more. The chief families among the nobility appeared in their boats, on which they had lavished their taste and wealth." The rowers were dressed with the most profuse and elaborate luxury, and the barges were made to represent historical and mythological conceptions. "To this end the builders employed carving and sculpture, together with all manner of costly stuffs of silk and velvet, gorgeous fringes and tassels of silver and gold, flowers, fruits, shrubs, mirrors, furs, and plumage of rare birds. . . . Young patricians, in fleet and narrow craft, propelled by swift rowers, preceded the champions and cleared the way for them, obliging

---

[3] *Feste Veneziane.*
[4] *Feste Veneziane.*

the spectators to withdraw on either side. . . . They knelt on
sumptuous cushions in the prows of their gondolas, cross-bow in
hand, and launched little pellets of plaster at the directors of such
obstinate boats as failed to obey their orders to retire. . . .

"To augment the brilliancy of the regatta the nature of the place
concurred. Let us imagine that superb canal, flanked on either side
by a long line of edifices of every sort; with great numbers of
marble palaces,—nearly all of noble and majestic structure, some
admirable for an antique and Gothic taste, some for the richest
Greek and Roman architecture,—their windows and balconies
decked with damasks, stuffs of the Levant, tapestries and velvets,
the vivid colors of which were animated still more by borders and
fringes of gold, and on which leaned beautiful women richly
dressed and wearing tremulous and glittering jewels in their hair.
Wherever the eye turned, it beheld a vast multitude at doorways,
on the rivas, and even on the roofs. Some of the spectators
occupied scaffoldings erected at favorable points along the sides of
the canal; and the patrician ladies did not disdain to leave their
palaces, and, entering their gondolas, lose themselves among the
infinite number of the boats. . . .

"The cannons give the signal of departure. The boats dart over
the water with the rapidity of lightning. . . . They advance and fall
behind alternately. One champion who seems to yield the way to
a rival suddenly leaves him in the rear. The shouts of his friends
and kinsmen hail his advantage, while others, already passing
him, force him to redouble his efforts. Some weaker ones succumb
midway, exhausted. . . . They withdraw, and the kindly venetian
populace will not aggravate their shame with jeers; the spectators
glance at them compassionately, and turn again to those still in the
lists. Here and there they encourage them by waving handker-
chiefs, and the women toss their shawls in the air. Each patrician,
following close upon his gondolier's boat, incites him with his
voice, salutes him by name, and flatters his pride and spirit. . . .
The water foams under the repeated strokes of the oars; it leaps up
in spray and falls in showers on the backs of the rowers already

dripping with their own sweat. . . . At last behold the dauntless mortal who seizes the red banner! His rival had almost clutched it, but one mighty stroke of the oar gave him the victory. . . . The air reverberates with a clapping of hands so loud that at the remotest point on the canal the moment of triumph is known. The victors plant on their agile boat the conquered flag, and instead of thinking to rest their weary arms take up the oars again and retrace their course, to receive congratulations and applause."

The regattas were by no means of frequent occurrence, for only forty-one took place during some five centuries. The first was given in 1315, and the last in 1857, in honor of the luckless Archduke Maximilian's marriage with Princess Charlotte of Belgium. The most sumptuous and magnificent regatta of all was that given to the city in the year 1686, by Duke Ernest of Brunswick. This excellent prince, having sold a great part of his subjects to the Republic for use in its wars against the Turk, generously spent their price in the costly and edifying entertainments of which Venice had already become the scene. The Judgment of Paris and the Triumph of the Marine Goddesses had been represented at his expense on the Grand Canal, with great acceptance, and now the Triumph of Neptune formed a principal feature in the gayeties of his regatta. Nearly the whole of the salt-water mythology was employed in the ceremony. An immense wooden whale supporting a structure of dolphins and Tritons, surmounted by a statue of Neptune, and drawn by sea-horses, moved from the Piazzetta to the Palazzo Foscari, where numbers of sirens sported about in every direction till the regatta began. The whole company of the deities, very splendidly arrayed, then joined them as spectators, and behaved in the manner affected by gods and goddesses on these occasions. Mutinelli[5] recounts the story with many sighs and sneers and great exactness; but it is not interesting.

The miraculous recovery of the body of St. Mark, in 1094, after it had been lost for nearly two centuries, created a festive

---

[5] *Annali Urbani.*

anniversary which was celebrated for a while with great religious pomp; but the rejoicings were not separately continued in after years. The festival was consolidated (if one may so speak) with two others in honor of the same saint, and the triple occasions were commemorated by a single holiday. The holidays annually distinguished by civil or ecclesiastical displays were twenty-five in number, of which only eleven were of religious origin, though all were of partly religious observance.

One of the most curious and interesting of the former was of the earliest date, and was continued till the last years of the Republic. In 596, Narses, the general of the Greek Emperor, was furnished by the Venetians with means of transport by sea from Aquileja to Ravenna for the army which he was leading against the Ostrogoths; and he made a vow that, if successful in his campaign, he would requite their generosity by erecting two churches in Venice. Accordingly, when he had beaten the Ostrogoths, he caused two votive churches to be built,—one to St. Theodore, on the site of the present St. Mark's Church, and another to San Geminiano, on the opposite bank of the canal which then flowed there. In lapse of time the citizens, desiring to enlarge their Piazza, removed the church of San Geminiano back as far as the present Fabbrica Nuova, which Napoleon built on the site of the demolished temple, between the western ends of the New and Old Procuratie. The removal was effected without the Pope's leave, which had been asked, but was refused in these words: "The Holy Father cannot sanction the commission of a sacrilege, though he can pardon it afterwards." The pontiff, therefore, imposed on the Venetians for penance that the Doge should pay an annual visit forever to the church. On the occasion of this visit the parish priest met him at the door, and offered the holy water to him; and then the Doge, having assisted at mass, marched with his Signory and the clergy of the church to its original site, where the clergy demanded that it should be rebuilt, and the Doge replied with the promise, "Next year." A red stone was set in the pavement to mark the spot where the Doge renewed this never-fulfilled promise.[6] The old church was destroyed by fire, and Sansovino built, in 1506, the temple thrown down by Napoleon to make room for his palace.

The 31st of January, on which day in 828 the body of St. Mark was brought from Alexandria to Venice, is still observed, though the festival has lost all the splendor which it received from civil intervention. For a thousand years the day was hallowed by a solemn mass in St. Mark's, at which the Doge and his Signory assisted.

The chief of the State annually paid a number of festive visits, which were made the occasion of as many holidays. To the convent of San Zaccaria he went in commemoration of the visit paid to that retreat by Pope Benedict III., in 855, when the pontiff was so charmed by the piety and goodness of the fair nuns that, after his return to Rome, he sent them great store of relics and indulgences. It thus became one of the most popular of the holidays, and the people repaired in great multitude with their Doge to the convent, on each recurrence of the day, that they might see the relics and buy the indulgences. The nuns were of the richest and noblest families of the city, and on the Doge's first visit they presented him with that bonnet which became the symbol of his sovereignty. It was wrought of pure gold, and set with precious stones of marvelous great beauty and value; and in order that the State might never seem forgetful of the munificence which bestowed the gift, the bonnet was annually taken from the treasury and shown by the Doge himself to the Sisters of San Zaccaria. The Doge Pietro Tradonico, to whom the bonnet was given, was killed in a popular tumult on this holiday, while going to the convent.

---

[6] As the author of the *Feste Veneziane* tells this story, it is less dramatic and characteristic. The clergy, she says, reminded the Doge of the occasion of his visit, and his obligation to renew it the following year, which he promised to do. I cling to the version in the text, for it seems to me that the Doge's perpetual promise to rebuild the church was a return in kind for the Pope's astute answer to the petition asking him to allow its removal. So good a thing ought to be history.

There was likewise a vast concourse of people and traffic in indulgences at the church of Santa Maria della Carità (now the Academy of Fine Arts), on the anniversary of the day when Pope Alexander III., in 1177, flying from the Emperor Barbarossa, found refuge in that monastery.[7] He bestowed great privileges upon it, and the Venetians honored the event to the end of their national existence.

One of the rare occasions during the year when the Doge appeared officially in public after nightfall was on St. Stephen's Day. He then repaired at dusk in his gilded barge, with splendid attendance of nobles and citizens, to the island church of San Giorgio Maggiore, whither, in 1009, the body of St. Stephen was brought from Constantinople. On the first of May the Doge visited the Convent of the Virgins (the convent building now forms part of the Arsenal), where the abbess presented him with a bouquet, and graceful and pleasing ceremonies took place in commemoration of the erection and endowment of the church. The head of the State also annually assisted at mass in St. Mark's, to celebrate the arrival in Venice of St. Isidore's body, which the Doge Domenico Michiel brought with him from the East, at the end of twenty-six years' war against the infidels; and, finally, after the year 1485, when the Venetians stole the bones of San Rocco from the Milanese, and deposited them in the newly finished Scuola di San Rocco, a ducal visit was annually paid to that edifice.

Two only of the national religious festivals yet survive the Republic,—that of the church of the Redentore on the Giudecca, and that of the church of the Salute on the Grand Canal, both votive churches, built in commemoration of the city's deliverances from the pest in 1578 and 1630. In their general features the celebrations of the two holidays are much alike; but that of the Salute is the less important of the two, and is more entirely religious in its character. A bridge of boats is annually thrown

---

[7] Selvatico and Lazari, in their admirable *Guida Artistica e Storica di Venezia*, say that the Pope merely lodged in the monastery on the day when he signed the treaty of peace with Barbarossa.

across the Canalazzo, and on the day of the Purification the people throng to the Virgin's shrine to express their gratitude for her favor. This gratitude was so strong immediately after the cessation of the pest in 1630 that the Senate, while the architects were preparing their designs for the present church, caused a wooden one to be built on its site, and consecrated with ceremonies of singular splendor. On the Festa del Redentore (the third Sunday of July) a bridge of boats crosses the great canal of the Giudecca, and vast throngs constantly pass it, day and night. But though the small tradesmen who deal in fried cakes, and in apples, peaches, pears, and other fruits, make intolerable uproar behind their booths on the long quay before the church; though the venders of mulberries (for which the gardens of the Giudecca are famous) fill the air with their sweet jargoning (for their cries are like the shrill notes of so many singing-birds); though thousands of people pace up and down, and come and go upon the bridge, yet the Festa del Redentore has now none of the old-time gayety it wore when the Venetians thronged the gardens, and feasted, sang, danced, and flirted the night away, and at dawn went in their fleets of many-lanterned boats, covering the lagoon with fairy light, to behold the sunrise on the Adriatic Sea.

Besides the religious festivals mentioned, there were five banquets annually given by the State on the several days of St. Mark, St. Vitus, St. Jerome, and St. Stephen, and the Day of the Ascension, all of which were attended with religious observances. Good Friday was especially hallowed by church processions in each of the campos; and St. Martha's Day was occasion for junketings on the Giudecca Canal, when a favorite fish, being in season, was devotionally eaten.

The civil and political holidays which lasted till the fall of the Republic were eleven. One of the earliest was the anniversary of the recapture of the Venetian Brides, who were snatched from their bridegrooms at the altar of San Pietro di Castello, by Triestine pirates. The class of citizens most distinguished in the punishment of the abductors was the trade of carpenters, who lived chiefly in the parish of Santa Maria Formosa; and when the

Doge, in his gratitude, bade them demand any reasonable grace, the trade asked that he should pay their quarter an annual visit. "But if it rains?" said the Doge. "We will give you a hat to cover you," answered the carpenters. "And if I am hungry?" "We will give you to eat and drink." So when the Doge made his visit on the day of the Virgin's Purification, he was given a hat of gilded straw, a bottle of wine, and loaves of bread. On this occasion the State bestowed dowers upon twelve young girls among the fairest and best of Venice (chosen two from each of the six sections of the city), who marched in procession to the church of Santa Maria Formosa. But as time passed the custom lost its simplicity and purity: pretty girls were said to make eyes at handsome youths in the crowd, and scandals occurred in public. Twelve wooden figures were then substituted, but the procession in which they were carried was followed by a disgusted and hooting populace, and assailed with a shower of turnips. The festivities, which used to last eight days, with incredible magnificence, fell into discredit, and were finally abolished during the war when the Genoese took Chioggia and threatened Venice, under Doria. This was the famous Festa delle Marie.

In 997 the Venetians beat the Narentines at sea, and annexed all Istria, as far as Dalmatia, to the Republic. On the day of the Ascension, of the same year, the Doge, for the first time, celebrated the dominion of Venice over the Adriatic, though it was not till some two hundred years later that the Pope Alexander III. blessed the famous espousals and confirmed the Republic in the possession of the sea forever. "What," cries Giustina Renier-Michiel, turning to speak of the holiday thus established, and destined to be the proudest in the Venetian calendar,—"what shall I say of the greatest of all our solemnities, that of the Ascension? Alas! I myself saw Frenchmen and Venetians, full of derision and insult, combine to dismantle the Bucintoro and burn it for the gold upon it!"[8] . . . (This was the nuptial-ship in which the Doge went to

---

[8] That which follows is a translation of the report given by Cesare Cantù, in his *Grande Illustrazione del Lombardo-Veneto*, of a conversation with

wed the sea, and the patriotic lady tells us concerning the Bucintoro of her day): "It was in the form of a galley, and two hundred feet long, with two decks. The first of these was occupied by an hundred and sixty rowers, the handsomest and strongest of the fleet, who sat four men to each oar, and there awaited their orders; forty other sailors completed the crew. The upper deck was divided lengthwise by a partition, pierced with arched doorways, ornamented with gilded figures, and covered with a roof supported by caryatides,—the whole surmounted by a canopy of crimson velvet embroidered with gold. Under this were ninety seats, and at the stern a still richer chamber for the Doge's throne, over which drooped the banner of St. Mark. The prow was double-beaked, and the sides of the vessel were enriched with figures of Justice, Peace, Sea, Land, and other allegories and ornaments.

"Let me imagine those times,—it is the habit of the old. At midday, having heard mass in the chapel of the Collegio, the Doge descends the Giant's Stairs, issues from the Porta della Carta,[9] and passes the booths of the mercers and glass-venders erected for the fair beginning that evening. He is preceded by eight standard-bearers with the flags of the Republic,—red, blue, white, and purple,—given by Alexander III. to the Doge Ziani. Six trumpets of silver, borne by as many boys, mix their notes with the clangor of the bells of the city. Behind come the retinues of the ambassadors in sumptuous liveries, and the fifty Comandadori in their flowing blue robes and red caps; then follow musicians, and the squires of the Doge in black velvet; then the guards of the Doge,

---

the author of *Feste Veneziane*. It is not necessary to remind readers of Venetian history that Renier and Michiel were of the foremost names in the Golden Book. She who bore them both was born before the fall of the Republic which she so much loved and lamented, and no doubt felt more than the grief she expresses for the fate of the last Bucintoro. It was destroyed, as she described, in 1796, by the French Republicans and Venetian Democrats, after the abdication of the oligarchy; but a fragment of its mast yet remains, and is to be seen in the museum of the Arsenal.
[9] The gate of the Ducal Palace which opens upon the Piazzetta next St. Mark's.

two chancellors, the secretary of the Pregadi, a deacon clad in purple and bearing a wax taper, six canons, three parish priests in their sacerdotal robes, and the Doge's chaplain dressed in crimson. The grand chancellor is known by his crimson vesture. Two squires bear the Doge's chair and the cushion of cloth of gold. And the Doge—the representative, and not the master of his country; the executor, and not the maker of the laws; citizen and prince, revered and guarded, sovereign of individuals, servant of the State—comes clad in a long mantle of ermine, cassock of blue, and vest and hose of *tocca d'oro*,[10] with the golden bonnet on his head, under the umbrella borne by a squire, and surrounded by the foreign ambassadors and the papal nuncio, while his drawn sword is carried by a patrician recently destined for some government of land or sea, and soon to depart upon his mission. In the rear comes a throng of personages,—the grand captain of the city, the judges, the three chiefs of the Forty, the Avogodori, the three chiefs of the Council of Ten, the three censors, and the sixty of the Senate with the sixty of the Aggiunta, all in robes of crimson silk.

"On the Bucintoro, each takes the post assigned him, and the prince ascends the throne. The Admiral of the Arsenal and the Lido stands in front as pilot; at the helm is the Admiral of Malamocco, and around him the ship-carpenters of the Arsenal. The Bucintoro, amid redoubled clamor of bells and roar of cannon, quits the *riva* and majestically ploughs the lagoon, surrounded by innumerable boats of every form and size.

"The Patriarch, who had already sent several vases of flowers to do courtesy to the company in the Bucintoro, joins them at the island of Sant' Elena, and sprinkles their course with holy water. So they reach the port of Lido, whence they formerly issued out upon the open sea; but in my time they paused there, turning the stern of the vessel to the sea. Then the Doge, amid the thunders of the artillery of the fort, took the ring blessed by the Patriarch,— who now emptied a cup of holy water into the sea,—and, advancing into a little gallery behind his throne, threw the ring

---

[10] A gauze of gold and silk.

into the waves, pronouncing the words, *Desponsamus te, mare, in signum veri perpetuique dominii.* Proceeding then to the church of San Nicoletto, they listened to a solemn mass, and returned to Venice, where the dignitaries were entertained at a banquet, while the multitude peacefully dispersed among the labyrinths of the booths erected for the fair."[11]

This fair, which was established as early as 1180, was an industrial exhibition of the arts and trades peculiar to Venice, and was repeated annually, with increasing ostentation, till the end, in 1796. Indeed, the feasts of the Republic at last grew so numerous that it became necessary, as we have seen before, to make a single holiday pay a double or triple debt of rejoicing. When the Venetians recovered Chioggia after the terrible war of 1380, the Senate refused to yield them another *festa*, and merely ordered that St. Mark's Day should be thereafter observed with some added ceremony: there was already one festival commemorative of a triumph over the Genoese (that of San Giovanni Decollato, on whose day, in 1358, the Venetians beat the Genoese at Negroponte), and the Senate declared that this was sufficient. A curious custom, however, on the Sunday after Ascension, celebrated a remoter victory over the same enemies, to which it is hard to

---

[11] One of the sops thrown to the populace on this occasion, as we learn from Mutinelli, was the admission to the train of gilded barges following the Bucintoro of a boat bearing the chief of the Nicolotti, one of the factions into which from time immemorial the lower classes of Venice had been divided. The distinction between the two parties seems to have been purely geographical; for there is no apparent reason why a man should have belonged to the Castellani except that he lived in the eastern quarter of the city, or to the Nicolotti except that he lived in the western quarter. The government encouraged a rivalry not dangerous to itself, and for a long time the champions of the two sections met annually and beat each other with rods. The form of contest was afterwards modified, and became a struggle for the possession of certain bridges, in which the defeated were merely thrown into the canals. I often passed the scene of the fiercest of these curious battles at San Barnaba, where the Ponte de Pugni is adorned with four feet of stone let into the pavement, and defying each other from the four corners of the bridge. Finally, even these contests were given up, and the Castellani and Nicolotti spent their rivalry in marvellous acrobatic feats.

attach any historic probability. It is not known exactly when the
Genoese in immense force penetrated to Poveglia (one of the small
islands of the lagoons), nor why, being there, they stopped to ask
the islanders the best way of getting to Venice. But tradition says
that the sly Povegliesi persuaded these silly Genoese that the best
method of navigating the lagoons was by means of rafts, which
they constructed for them, and on which they sent them afloat.
About the time the Venetians came out to meet the armada, the
withes binding the members of the rafts gave way, and the
Genoese who were not drowned in the tides stuck in the mud, and
were cut in pieces like so many melons. No one will be surprised
to learn that not a soul of them escaped, and that only the
Povegliesi lived to tell the tale. Special and considerable privileges
were conferred on them for their part in this exploit, and were
annually confirmed by the Doge, when a deputation of the
islanders called on him in his palace, and hugged and kissed the
devoted prince.

People who *will* sentimentalize over the pigeons of St. Mark's
may like to know that they have been settled in the city ever since
877. After the religious services on Palm Sunday, it was anciently
the custom of the sacristans of St. Mark's to release doves fettered
with fragments of paper, and thus partly disabled from flight, for
the people to scramble for in the Piazza. The people fatted such of
the birds as they caught, and ate them at Easter, but those pigeons
which escaped took refuge in the roof of the church, where they
gradually assumed a certain sacredness of character, and increased
to enormous numbers. They were fed by provision of the Republic,
and being neglected at the time of its fall many of them were
starved. But they now flourish on a bequest left by a pious lady for
their maintenance, and on the largess of grain and *polenta*
constantly bestowed by strangers.

Besides the holidays mentioned, the 6th of December was
religiously observed in honor of the taking of Constantinople, the
Doge assisting at mass in the ducal chapel of St. Nicholas. He also
annually visited, with his Signory in the state barges, and with
great concourse of people, the church of San Vito on the 15th of

June, in memory of the change of the government from a democracy to an oligarchy, and of the suppression of Bajamonte Tiepolo's conspiracy. On St. Isidore's Day he went with his Signory, and the religious confraternities, in torchlight procession, to hear mass at St. Mark's in celebration of the failure of Marin Falier's plot. On the 17th of January he visited by water the hospital erected for invalid soldiers and sailors, and thus commemorated the famous defence of Scutari against the Turks, in 1413. For the peace of 1516, concluded after the dissolution of the League of Cambray, he went in his barge to the church of Santa Marina, who had potently exerted her influence for the preservation of the Republic against allied France, Austria, Spain, and Rome. On St. Jerome's Day, when the newly-elected members of the Council of Ten took their seats, the Doge entertained them with a banquet, and there were great popular rejoicings over an affair in which the people had no interest.

It is by a singular caprice of fortune that, while not only all the Venetian holidays in anywise connected with the glory of the Republic, but also those which peculiarly signalized her piety and gratitude, have ceased to be, a festival common to the whole Catholic world should still be observed in Venice with extraordinary display. On the day of Corpus Christi there is a superb ecclesiastical procession in the Piazza.

The great splendor of the solemnization is said to date from the times when Enrico Dandolo and his fellow-crusaders so far forgot their purpose of taking Palestine from the infidels as to take Constantinople from the schismatics. Up to that period the day of Corpus Christi was honored by a procession from what was then the Cathedral of San Pietro di Castello; but now all the thirty parishes of the city, with their hundred churches, have part in the procession, which is of such great length as to take some two hours in its progress round the Piazza.

Several days before the holiday workmen begin to build, within the Place of St. Mark, the colonnade through which the procession is to pass; they roof it with blue cotton cloth, and adorn it with rolls of pasteboard representing garlands of palm. At last, on the

festive morning, the dwellers on the Grand Canal are drawn to
their balconies by the apparition of boat-loads of *facchini*,
gorgeous in scarlet robes, and bearing banners, painted candles,
and other movable elements of devotion, with which they pass to
the Piazzetta, and thence into St. Mark's. They reappear presently,
and, with a guard of Austrian troops to clear the way before them,
begin their march under the canopy of the colonnade.

When you have seen the Place of St. Mark by night your eye has
tasted its most delicate delight. But then it is the delight given by
a memory only, and it touches you with sadness. You must see the
Piazza today,—every window fluttering with rich stuffs and vivid
colors; the three great flagstaffs[12] hanging their heavy flags; the
brilliant square alive with a holiday population, with respendent
uniforms, with Italian gesture and movement, and that long,
glittering procession, bearing slowly on the august paraphernalia
of the Church,—you must see all this before you can enter into the
old heart of Venetian magnificence, and feel its life about you.

To-day, the ancient church of San Pietro di Castello comes first
in the procession, and, with a proud humility, the Basilica San
Marco last. Before each parochial division goes a banner display-
ing the picture or distinctive device of its titular saint, under the
shadow of which chants a priest; there are the hosts of the
different churches, and the gorgeous canopies under which they
are elevated; then come *facchini* dressed in scarlet and bearing the
painted candles, or the long carved and gilded candlesticks; and
again *facchini* delicately robed in vestments of the purest white
linen, with caps of azure, green, and purple, and shod with sandals
or white shoes, carrying other apparatus of worship. Each banner
and candlestick has a fluttering leaf of tinsel paper attached to it,
and the procession makes a soft rustling as it passes. The
matter-of-fact character of the external Church walks between
those symbolists, the candle-bearers, in the form of persons who
gather the dropping fatness of the candles, and deposit it in a vase
carried for that purpose. Citizens march in the procession with

---

[12] Once bearing the standards of Cyprus, Candia, and Venice.

candles; and there are charity schools which also take part, and
sing in the harsh, shrill manner of which I think only little boys
who have their heads closely shorn are capable.

On all this we looked down from a window of the Old
Procuratie,—of course with that calm sense of superiority which
people are apt to have in regarding the solemnities of a religion
different from their own. But that did not altogether prevent us
from enjoying what was really beautiful and charming in the
scene. I thought most of the priests very good and gentle
looking,—and in all respects they were much pleasanter to the eye
than the monks of the Carmelite order, who, in shaving their
heads to simulate the Saviour's crown of thorns, produce a
hideous burlesque of the divine humiliation. Yet many even of
these had earnest and sincere faces, and I could not think so much
as I ought, perhaps, of their idle life, and the fleas in their coarse
brown cloaks. I confess, indeed, I felt rather a sadness than an
indignation at all that self-sacrifice to an end of which I could but
dimly see the usefulness. With some things in this grand spectacle
we were wholly charmed, and doubtless had most delight in the
little child who personated John the Baptist, and who was quite
naked, but for a fleece folded about him: he bore the cross-headed
staff in one small hand, and led with the other a lamb much tied
up with blue ribbon. Here and there in the procession little girls,
exquisitely dressed, and gifted by fond mothers with wings and
aureoles, walked, scattering flowers. I likewise greatly relished the
lively holiday air of a company of airy old men, the pensioners of
some charity, who, in their white linen trousers and blue coats,
formed a prominent feature of the display. Far from being puffed
up with their consequence, they gossiped cheerfully with the
spectators in the pauses of the march, and made jests to each other
in that light-hearted, careless way observable in old men taken
care of, and with nothing before them to do worth speaking of but
to die. I must own that the honest *facchini* who bore the candles
were equally affable, and even freer with their jokes. But in this
they formed a fine contrast to here and there a closely hooded
devotee, who, with hidden face and silent lips, was carrying a

taper for religion, and not, like them, for money. I liked the great good-natured crowd, so orderly and amiable; and I enjoyed even that old citizen in the procession who, when the Patriarch gave his blessing, found it inconvenient to kneel, and compromised by stretching one leg a great way out behind him. These things, indeed, quite took my mind off of the splendors; and I let the canopy of the Scuola di San Rocco (worth 40,000 ducats) go by with scarce a glance, and did not bestow much more attention upon the brilliant liveries of the Patriarch's servants,—though the appearance of these ecclesiastical flunkies is far more impressive than that of any of their secular brethren. They went gorgeously before the Patriarch, who was surrounded by the richly dressed clergy of St. Mark's, and by clouds of incense rising from the smoking censers. He walked under the canopy in his cardinal's robes, and with his eye fixed upon the Host.

All at once the procession halted, and the Patriarch blessed the crowd, which knelt in a profound silence. Then the military band before him struck up an air from Un Ballo in Maschera; the procession moved on to the cathedral, and the crowd melted away.

The once magnificent day of the Ascension the Venetians now honor by closing all shop-doors behind them and putting all thought of labor out of their minds, and going forth to enjoy themselves in the mild, inexplosive fashion which seems to satisfy Italian nature. It is the same on all the feast days: then the city sinks into profounder quiet; only bells are noisy, and where their clangor is so common as in Venice it seems at last to make friends with the general stillness, and disturbs none but people of untranquil minds. We always go to the Piazza San Marco when we seek pleasure, and now, for eight days only of all the year, we have there the great spectacle of the Adoration of the Magi, performed every hour by automata within the little golden-railed gallery on the façade of the Giant's Clock Tower. There the Virgin sits above the azure circle of the zodiac, all heavily gilded, and holding the Child, equally splendid. Through the doors on either side, usually occupied by the illuminated figures of the hours, appears the procession, and disappears. The stately giant on the summit of the tower, at the hither side of the great bell, solemnly strikes the hour—as a giant should who has struck it for centuries—with a grand, whole-arm movement, and a slow, muscular pride. We look up,—we tourists of the red-backed books; we peasant-girls radiant with converging darts of silver piercing the masses of our thick black hair; we Austrian soldiers in white coats and blue tights; we voiceful sellers of the cherries of Padua; and we calm loafers about the many-pillared base of the church,—we look up and see the Adoration. First the trumpeter, blowing the world news of the act; then the first king, turning softly to the Virgin, and bowing; then the second, that enthusiastic devotee,—the second, who lifts his crown quite from his head; last the Ethiopian prince, gorgeous in green and gold, who, I am sorry to say, burlesques the whole solemnity. His devotion may be equally heart-felt, but it is more jerky than that of the others. He bows well and adequately, but recovers his balance with a prodigious start, altogether too suggestive of springs and wheels. Perhaps there is a touch of the pathetic in this grotesque fatality of the black king, whose suffering race has always held mankind between laughter and tears, and has seldom done a fine thing without leaving somewhere the neutralizing absurdity; but if there is, the sentimental may find it, not I. When the procession has disappeared, we wait till the other giant has struck the hour, and then we disperse.

If it is six o'clock, and the sea has begun to breathe cool across the Basin of St. Mark, we find our account in strolling upon the long Riva degli Schiavoni towards the Public Gardens. One would suppose, at first thought, that here, on this magnificent quay, with its glorious lookout over the lagoons, the patricians would have built their finest palaces; whereas there is hardly anything but architectural shabbiness from the Ponte della Paglia at one end to the Ponte Santa Marina at the other. But there need be nothing surprising in the fact, after all. The feudal wealth and nobility of other cities kept the base as a respectful distance by means of lofty stone walls, and so shut in their palaces and gardens. Here equal seclusion could only be achieved by building flush upon the water, and therefore all the finest palaces rise sheer from the canals; and *caffè*, shops, barracks, and puppet-shows occupy the Riva degli Schiavoni. Nevertheless, it is the favorite promenade of the Venetians for the winter sunshine, and at such times in the summer as when the sun's rage is tempered. There is always variety in the throng on the Riva, but the fashionable part of it is the least interesting: here and there a magnificent Greek flashes through the crowd, in dazzling white petticoats and gold-embroidered leggings and jacket; now and then a tall Dalmat or a solemn Turk; even the fishermen and the peasants, and the lower orders of the people, are picturesque; but polite Venice is hopelessly given to the pride of the eyes, and commits all the excesses of the French modes. The Venetian dandy, when dressed to his own satisfaction, is the worst dressed man in the world. His hat curls outrageously in brim and sides; his coat-sleeves are extremely full, and the garment pinches him at the waist; his pantaloons flow forth from the hips, and contract narrowly at the boot, which is square-toed and made too long. The whole effect is something not to be seen elsewhere, and is well calculated to move the beholder to desperation.[13] The Venetian fine lady, also, is prone to be superfine. Her dress is as full of color as a Paolo Veronese; in these narrow streets, where it is hard to expand an umbrella, she exaggerates hoops to the utmost; and she fatally hides her ankles in pantalets.

In the wide thoroughfare leading from the last bridge of the Riva to the gate of the gardens there is always a clapping of wooden shoes on the stones, a braying of hand-organs, a shrieking of people who sell fish and fruit, at once insufferable and indescribable. The street is a *rio terrà*,—a filled-up canal,—and, as always happens with *rii terrai*, is abandoned to the poorest classes, who manifest themselves, as the poorest classes are apt to do always, in groups of frowzy women, small girls carrying large

---

[13] These exaggerations of the fashions of 1862 have been succeeded by equal travesties of the present modes.

babies, beggars, of course, and soldiers. I spoke of fruit-sellers; but in this quarter the traffic in pumpkin-seeds is the most popular,— the people finding these an inexpensive and pleasant excess, when taken with a glass of water flavored with anise.

The Gardens were made by Napoleon, who demolished to that end some monasteries cumbering the ground. They are pleasant enough, and are not gardens at all, but a park of formally-planted trees,—sycamores, chiefly. I do not remember to have seen here any Venetians of the better class, except on the Mondays-of-the-Garden, in September. Usually the promenaders are fishermen, Austrian corporals, loutish youth of low degree, and women too old and too poor to have anything to do. Strangers go there, and the German visitors even drink the exceptionable beer which is sold in the wooden cottage on the little hillock at the end of the Gardens. There is also a stable, where are the only horses in Venice. They are let at a florin an hour, and I do not know why the riders are always persons of the Hebrew faith. In a word nothing can be drearier than the company in the Gardens, and nothing lovelier than the view they command,—from the sunset on the dome of the church of the Salute, all round the broad sweep of lagoon, to the tower at the port of San Nicolò, where you catch a glimpse of the Adriatic.

The company is commonly stupid, but one evening, as we strolled idly through the walks, we came upon an interesting group—forty or fifty sailors, soldiers, youth of the people, gray-haired fishermen, and *contadini*—sitting and lying on the grass, and listening with rapt attention to an old man reclining against a tree. I never saw a manner of sweeter or easier dignity than the speaker's. Nature is so lavish of her grace to these people that grow near her heart—the sun! Infinite study could not have taught one Northern-born the charm of oratory as this old man displayed it. I listened, and heard that he was speaking Tuscan. Do you guess with what he was enchanting his simple auditors? Nothing less than Orlando Furioso. They listened with the hungriest delight, and when Ariosto's interpreter raised his finger and said,

"Disse l'imperatore," or, "Orlando disse, Carlomano mio," they hardly breathed.

On the *Lunedì dei Giardini,* already mentioned, all orders of the people flock thither, and promenade, and banquet on the grass. The trees get back the voices of their dryads, and the children fill the aisles with glancing movement and graceful sport.

Of course, the hand-organ seeks here its proper element, the populace,—but here it brays to a peculiarly beautiful purpose. For no sooner does it sound than the young girls of the people wreathe themselves into dances, and improvise the poetry of motion. Over the grass they whirl, and up and down the broad avenues, and no one of all the gentle and peaceable crowd molests or makes them afraid. It is a scene to make you believe in Miriam dancing with Donatello there in that old garden at Rome, and reveals a simple beauty in the nature of the Italian poor, which shall one day, I hope, be counted in their favor when they are called to answer for lying and swindling.

CHAPTER XVIII

CHRISTMAS HOLIDAYS

I T often happens, even after the cold has announced itself in
Venice, that the hesitating winter lingers in the Tyrol, and a
mellow Indian-summer weather has possession of the first weeks
of December. There was nothing in the December weather of
1863 to remind us Northerners that Christmas was coming. The
skies were as blue as those of June, the sun was warm, and the air
was bland, with only now and then a trenchant breath from

the Alps, coming like a delicate sarcasm from loveliness unwilling to be thought insipidly amiable. But if there was no warning in the weather, there were other signs of Christmas-time not to be mistaken: a certain foolish leaping of the heart in one's own breast, as if the dead raptures of childhood were stirred in their graves by the return of the happy season; and in Venice, in weary, forlorn Venice, there was the half-unconscious tumult, the expectant bustle which cities feel at the approach of holidays. The little shops put on their gayest airs; there was a great clapping and hammering on the stalls and booths which were building in the campos; the street-cries were more shrill and resonant than ever, and the air was shaken with the continual clangor of the church bells.

All this note of preparation is rather bewildering to strangers, and is apt to disorder the best disciplined intentions of seeing Christmas as the Venetians keep it. The public observance of the holiday in the churches and on the streets is evident and accessible to the most transient sojourner; but it is curious proof of the difficulty of knowledge concerning the in-door life and usages of the Italians that I had already spent two Christmases in Venice without learning anything of their home celebration of the day. Perhaps a degree of like difficulty attends like inquiry everywhere, for the happiness of Christmas contracts the family circle more exclusively than ever around the home hearth, or the domestic *scaldino*, as the case may be. But, at any rate, I was quite ready to say that the observance of Christmas in Venice was altogether public, when I thought it a measure of far-sighted prudence to consult my barber.

In all Latin countries the barber is a source of information, which, skilfully tapped, pours forth in a stream of endless gossip and local intelligence. Every man talks with his barber; and perhaps a lingering dignity clings to this artist from his former profession of surgeon: it is certain the barber here prattles on with a freedom and importance perfectly admitted and respected by the interlocutory count under his razor.

Those who care to know how things passed in an Italian barber

shop three hundred years ago may read it in Miss Evans's
Romola; those who are willing to see Nello alive and carrying on
his art in Venice at this day must go to be shaved at his shop in the
Frezzaria. Here there is a continual exchange of gossip, and I have
often listened with profit to the sage and piquant remarks of the
head barber and chief *ciarlone* on the different events of human
life brought to his notice. His shop is well known as a centre of
scandal, and I have heard a fair Venetian declare that she had cut
from her list all acquaintance who go there, as persons likely to
become infected with the worst habits of gossip.

To this Nello, however, I used to go only when in the most
brilliant humor for listening, and my authority on Christmas
observances is another and humbler barber, but not less a babbler,
than the first. By birth, I believe, he is a Mantuan, and he prides
himself on speaking Italian instead of Venetian. He has a defective
eye, which obliges him to tack before bringing his razor to bear,
but which is all the more favorable to conversation. On the whole,
he is flattered to be asked about Christmas in Venice, and he first
tells me that it is one of the chief holidays of the year:—

"It is then, Signore, that the Venetians have the custom to make
three sorts of peculiar presents: Mustard, Fish, and Mandorlato.
You must have seen the mustard in the shop windows: it is a thick
conserve of fruits, flavored with mustard; and the mandorlato is a
candy made of honey, and filled with almonds. Well, they buy fish,
as many as they will, and a vase of mustard, and a box of mandorlato, and make presents of them, one family to another, the day
before Christmas. It is not too much for a rich family to present a
hundred boxes of mandorlato and as many pots of mustard. These
are exchanged between friends in the city, and Venetians also send
them to acquaintance in the country, whence the gift is returned in
cakes and eggs at Easter. Christmas Eve people invite each other to
great dinners, and eat and drink, and make merry; but there are only
fish and vegetables, for it is a meagre day, and meats are forbidden.
This dinner lasts so long that, when it is over, it is almost time to
go to midnight mass, which all must attend, or else hear three
masses on the morrow; and no doubt it was some delinquent who

made our saying, 'Long as a Christmas mass.' On Christmas Day people dine at home, keeping the day with family reunions. But the day after! Ah-heigh! That is the first of Carnival, and all the theatres are opened, and there is no end to the amusements,—or was not, in the old time. Now, they never begin. A week later comes the day of the Lord's Circumcision, and then the next holiday is Easter. The Nativity, the Circumcision, and the Resurrection—behold! these are the three mysteries of the Christian faith. Of what religion are the Americans, Signore?"

I think I was justified in answering that we were Christians. My barber was politely surprised. "But there are so many different religions," he said, in excuse.

On the afternoon before Christmas I walked through the thronged Merceria to the Rialto Bridge, where the tumultuous mart which opens at Piazza San Marco culminates in a deafening uproar of bargains. At this time the Merceria, or street of the shops, presents the aspect of a fair, and is arranged with a tastefulness and a cunning ability to make the most of everything which are seldom applied to the abundance of our fairs at home. The shops in Venice are all very small, and the streets of lofty houses are so narrow and dark that whatever goods are not exposed in the shop-windows are brought to the door to be clamored over by purchasers; so that the Merceria is roused by unusual effort to produce a more pronounced effect of traffic and noise than it always wears; but now the effort had been made and the effect produced. The street was choked with the throngs, through which all sorts of peddlers battled their way and cried their wares. In Campo San Bartolomeo, into which the Merceria expands, at the foot of Rialto Bridge, holiday traffic had built enormous barricades of stalls, and entrenched itself behind booths, whence purchasers were assailed with challenges to buy bargains. More than half the campo was paved with crockery from Rovigo and glassware from Murano; clothing of every sort, and all kinds of small household wares, were offered for sale; and among the other booths, in the proportion of two to one, were stalls of the inevitable Christmas mustard and mandorlato.

But I cared rather for the crowd than what the crowd cared for. I had been long ago obliged to throw aside my preconceived notions of the Italian character, though they were not, I believe, more absurd than the impressions of others who have never studied Italian character in Italy. I hardly know what of bacchantic joyousness I had not attributed to them on their holidays: a people living in a mild climate under such a lovely sky, with wine cheap and abundant, might not unreasonably have been expected to put on a show of the greatest jollity when enjoying themselves. Venetian crowds are always perfectly gentle and kindly, but they are also as a whole usually serious; and this Christmas procession, moving up and down the Merceria, and to and from between the markets of Rialto, was in the fullest sense a solemnity. It is true that the scene was dramatic, but the drama was not consciously comic. Whether these people bought or sold, or talked together, or walked up and down in silence, they were all equally in earnest. The crowd, in spite of its noisy bustle and passionate uproar, did not seem to me a blithe or light-hearted crowd. Its sole activity was that of traffic, for, far more dearly than any Yankee, a Venetian loves a bargain, and puts his whole heart into upholding and beating down demands.

Across the Bridge began the vegetable and fruit market, where whole Hollands of cabbage and Spains of onions opened on the view, with every other succulent and toothsome growth; and beyond this we entered the glory of Rialto, the fish-market, which is now more lavishly supplied than at any other season. It was picturesque and full of gorgeous color, for the fish of Venice seem all to catch the rainbow hues of the lagoon. There is a certain kind of red mullet, called *triglia,*which is as rich and tender in its dyes as if it had never swam in water less glorious than that which crimsons under October sunsets. But a fish-market, even at Rialto, with fishermen in scarlet caps and *triglie* in sunset splendors, is only a fish-market, after all: it is wet and slimy under foot, and the innumerable gigantic eels, writhing everywhere, set the soul asquirm, and soon-sated curiosity slides willingly away.

We had an appointment with a young Venetian lady to attend

midnight mass at the church of San Moisè, and thither about half past eleven we went to welcome in Christmas. The church of San Moisè is in the highest style of the Renaissance art, which is, I believe, the lowest style of any other. The richly sculptured façade is divided into stories; the fluted columns are stilted upon pedestals, and their lines are broken by the bands which encircle them like broad barrel-hoops. At every possible point theatrical saints and angels, only sustained from falling to the ground by iron bars let into their backs, start from the niches and cling to the sculpture. The outside of the church is in every way detestable, and the inside is consistently bad. All the side-altars have broken arches, and the high altar is built of rough blocks of marble to represent Mount Sinai, on which a melodramatic statue of Moses receives the tables of the law from God the Father, with frescoed seraphim in the background. For the same reason, I suppose, that the devout prefer a hideous Bambino and a Madonna in crinoline to the most graceful artistic conception of those sacred personages, San Moisè is the most popular church for the midnight mass in Venice, and there is no mass at all in St. Mark's, where its magnificence would be so peculiarly impressive.

On Christmas Eve, then, this church was crowded, and the doorways were constantly thronged with people passing in and out. I was puzzled to see so many young men present, for Young Italy is not usually in great number at church; but a friend explained the anomaly: "After the guests at our Christmas Eve dinners have well eaten and drunken, they all go to mass in at least one church, and the younger offer a multiplied devotion by going to all. It is a good thing in some ways, for by this means they manage to see every pretty face in the city, which that night has specially prepared itself to be seen." And from this slender text my friend began to discourse at large about these Christmas Eve dinners, and chiefly how jollily the priests fared, ending with the devout wish, "Would God had made me nephew of a canonico!" The great dinners of the priests are a favorite theme with Italian talkers; but I doubt it is after all only a habit of speech. The priests are too numerous to feed sumptuously in most cases.

We had a good place to see and hear, sitting in the middle of the main aisle, directly over the dust of John Law, who alighted in Venice when his great Mississippi bubble burst, and died here, and now sleeps peacefully under a marble tablet in the ugly church of San Moisè. The thought of that busy, ambitious life, come to this unscheming repose under our feet,—so far from the scene of its hopes, successes, and defeats,—gave its own touch of solemnity to the time and place, and helped the offended sense of propriety through the bursts of operatic music which interspersed the mass. but on the whole, the music was good and the function sufficiently impressive,—what with the gloom of the temple everywhere starred with tapers, and the grand altar lighted to the mountain-top. The singing of the priests also was here much better than I had found it elsewhere in Venice.

The equality of all classes in church is a noticeable thing always in Italy, but on this Christmas Eve it was unusually evident. The rags of the beggar brushed the silks of luxury, as the wearers knelt side by side on the marble floor; and on the night when God was born to poverty on earth, the rich seemed to feel that they drew nearer Him in the neighborhood of the poor. In these costly temples of the eldest Christianity, the poor seem to enter upon their inheritance of the future, for it is they who frequent them most and possess them with the deepest sense of ownership. The withered old woman, who creeps into St. Mark's with her *scaldino* in her hand, takes visible possession of its magnificence as God's and hers, and Catholic wealth and rank would hardly, if challenged, dispute her claim.

Even the longest mass comes to an end at last, and those of our party who could credit themselves with no gain of masses against the morrow received the benediction at San Moisè with peculiar unction. We all issued forth, and passing through the lines of young men who draw themselves up on either side of the doors of public places in Venice, to look at the young ladies as they come out, we entered the Place of St. Mark. The Piazza was more gloriously beautiful than ever I saw it before, and the church had a saintly loveliness. The moon was full, and snowed down the mellowest light on the gray domes, which, in their soft, elusive outlines and strange effect of far withdrawal, rhymed like faint-heard refrains to the bright and vivid arches of the façade. And if the bronze horses had been minded to quit their station before the great window over the central arch, they might have paced around the night's whole half-world, and found no fairer resting-place.

As for Christmas Day in Venice, it amounted to very little; everything was closed, and whatever merry-making went on was all within doors. Although the shops and the places of amusement were opened the day following, the city entered very sparingly on the pleasures of Carnival, and Christmas week passed off in every-day fashion. It will be remembered that on St. Stephen's Day—the first of Carnival—one of the five annual banquets took place at the Ducal Palace in the time of the Republic. A certain number of patricians received invitations to the dinner, and those for whom there was no room were presented with fish and poultry by the Doge. The populace were admitted to look on during the first course, and then, having sated their appetites with this savory observance, were invited to withdraw. The patriotic Giustina Renier-Michiel of course makes much of the courtesy thus extended to the people by the State, but I cannot help thinking it must have been hard to bear. The banquet, however, has passed away with the Republic which gave it, and the only savor of dinner which Venetian poverty now inhales on St. Stephen's Day is that which arises from its own proper pot of broth.

New Year's is the carnival of the beggars in Venice. Their business is carried on briskly throughout the year, but on this day it is pursued with an unusual degree of perseverance, and an enterprise worthy of all disinterested admiration. At every corner, on every bridge, under every doorway, hideous shapes of poverty, mutilation, and deformity stand waiting, and thrust out palms, plates, and pans, and advance good wishes and blessings to all who pass. It is an immemorial custom, and it is one in which all but the quite comfortable classes participate. The *facchini* in every square take up their collections; the gondoliers have their plates prepared for contribution at every ferry; at every *caffè* and restaurant begging-boxes appeal to charity. Whoever has lifted hand in your service in an way during the past year expects a reward on New Year's for the complaisance, and in some cases the shop-keepers send to wish you a *bel capo d'anno,* with the same practical end in view. On New Year's Eve and morning bands of *facchini* and gondoliers go about howling *vivas* under charitable windows till they open and drop alms. The Piazza is invaded by the legions of beggary, and held in overpowering numbers against all comers; and to traverse it is like a progress through a lazar-house.

Beyond encouraging so gross an abuse as this, I do not know that Venice celebrates New Year's in a peculiar manner. It is a *festa,* and there are masses, of course. Presents are exchanged, which consist chiefly of books, printed for the season, and brilliant outside and dull within, like all annuals.

CHAPTER XIX

LOVE-MAKING AND MARRYING; BAPTISMS AND BURIALS

THE Venetians have had a practical and strictly business-like way of arranging marriages from the earliest times. The shrewdest provision has always been made for the dower and for the good of the State; private and public interest being consulted, the small matters of affections have been left to the chances of association; and it does not seem that Venetian society has ever dealt severely with husbands or wives whom incompatibilities forced to seek consolation outside of matrimony. Herodotus relates that the Illyrian Veneti sold their daughters at auction to the highest bidder; and the fair being thus comfortably placed in life, the hard-favored were given to whomsoever would take them, with such dower as might be considered a reasonable compensation. The auction was discontinued in Christian times, but marriage contracts still partook of the form of a public and a half-mercantile transaction. At a comparatively late period Venetian fathers went with their daughters to a great annual matrimonial fair at San Pietro di Castello Olivolo, and the youth of the lagoons repaired thither to choose wives from the number of the maidens. These were all dressed in white, with hair loose about the neck, and each bore her dower in a little box, slung over her shoulder by a ribbon. It is to be supposed that there was commonly a previous understanding between each damsel and some youth in the crowd: as soon as all had paired off, the bishop gave them a sermon and his benediction, and the young men gathered up their brides and boxes, and went away wedded. It was on one of these occasions, in the year 944, that the Triestine pirates stole the Brides of Venice with their dowers, and gave occasion to the Festa delle Marie, already described, and to Rogers's poem, which everybody pretends to have read.

This going to San Pietro's, selecting a wife and marrying her on the spot, out of hand, could only have been the contrivance of a straightforward, practical race. Among the common people betrothals were managed with even greater ease and dispatch, till a very late day in history; and in the record of a certain trial which took place in 1443 there is an account of one of these brief and unceremonious courtships. Donna Catarussa, who gives evidence, and whom I take to have been a worthless, idle gossip, was one day sitting at her door, when Piero di Trento passed, selling brooms, and said to her, "Madonna, find me some nice girl." To which Donna Catarussa replied, "Ugly foot! do you take me for a go-between?" "No," said Piero, "not that; I mean a girl to be my wife." And as Donna Catarussa thought at once of a suitable match, she said, "In faith of God, I know one for you. Come again to-morrow." So they both met next day, and the woman chosen by Donna Catarussa being asked, "Wouldst thou like to have Piero for thy husband, as God commands and Holy Church?" she answered, "Yes." And Peter being asked the like question answered, "Why, yes, certainly." And they went off and had the wedding feast. A number of these betrothals takes place in the last scene of Goldoni's Baruffe Chiozzotte, where the belligerent women and their lovers take hands in the public streets, and, saluting each other as man and wife, are affianced, and get married as quickly as possible:—

"*Checa* (to Tofolo). Take my hand.
"*Tofolo*. Wife!
"*Checa*. Husband!
"*Tofolo*. Hurra!"

The betrothals of the Venetian nobles were celebrated with as much pomp and ceremony as could possibly distinguish them from those of the people, and there was much more polite indifference to the inclinations of the parties immediately concerned. The contract was often concluded before the betrothed had seen each other, by means of a third person, when the amount of the dower was fixed. The bridegroom elect, having verbally agreed with the parents of the bride, repaired at an early day to the court-yard of the Ducal Palace, where the match was published, and where he shook hands with his kinsmen and friends. On the day fixed for signing the contract the bride's father invited to his house the bridegroom and all his friends, and hither came the high officers of state to compliment the future husband. He, with the father of his betrothed, met the guests at the door of the palace, and conducted them to the grand saloon, which no woman was allowed (*si figuri!*) at this time to enter. When the company was seated, the bride, clad in white, was led from her rooms and presented. She wore a crown of pearls and brilliants on her head, and her hair, mixed with long threads of gold, fell loose about her shoulders, as you may see it in Carpaccio's pictures of the Espousals of St. Ursula. Her ear-rings were pendants of three pearls set in gold; her neck and throat were bare but for a collar of lace and gems, from which slid a fine jewelled chain into her bosom. Over her breast she wore a stomacher of cloth of gold, to which were attached her sleeves, open from the elbow to the hand.

The formal words of espousal being pronounced, the bride paced slowly round the hall to the music of fifes and trumpets, and made a gentle inclination to each of the guests; and then returned to her chamber, from which she issued again on the arrival of any tardy friend, and repeated the ceremony. After all this, she descended to the court-yard, where she was received by gentlewomen, her friends, and placed on a raised seat (which was covered with rich stuffs) in an open gondola, and thus, followed by a fleet of attendant gondolas, went to visit all the convents in which there were kinspeople of herself or her betrothed. The excessive publicity of these ceremonies was supposed to strengthen the validity of the marriage contract. At an early day after the espousals the betrothed, preceded by musicians and followed by relatives and friends, went at dawn to be married in the church,—the bridegroom wearing a toga, and the bride a dress of white silk or crimson velvet, with jewels in her hair, and pearls embroidered on her robes. Visits of congratulation followed, and on the same day a public feast was given in honor of the wedding, to which at least three hundred persons were always invited, and at which the number, quality, and cost of the dishes were carefully regulated by the Republic's laws. On this occasion, one or more persons were chosen as governors of the feast, and after the tables were removed a mock-heroic character appeared, and recounted with absurd exaggeration the deeds of the ancestors of the bride and groom. The next morning *ristorativi* of sweetmeats and confectionery were presented to the happy couple, by whom the presents were returned in kind.

A splendor so exceptional, even in the most splendid age of the most splendid city, as that which marked the nuptial feasts of the unhappy Jacopo Foscari could not be left unnoticed in this place. He espoused Lucrezia, daughter of Lionardo Contarini, a noble as rich and magnificent as Jacopo's own father, the Doge; and, on the 29th of January, 1441, the noble Eustachio Balbi being chosen lord of the feasts, the bridegroom, the bride's brother, and eighteen other patrician youths assembled in the Palazzo Balbi, whence they went on horseback to conduct Lucrezia to the Ducal

Palace. They were all sumptuously dressed in crimson velvet and silver brocade of Alexandia, and rode chargers superbly caparisoned. Other noble friends attended them; musicians went before; a troop of soldiers brought up the rear. They thus proceeded to the court-yard of the Ducal Palace, and then, returning, traversed the Piazza, and threading the devious little streets to the Campo San Samuele, there crossed the Grand Canal upon a bridge of boats to San Barnaba opposite, where the Contarini lived. On their arrival at this place the bride, supported by two Procuratori di San Marco and attended by sixty ladies, descended to the church and heard mass, after which an oration was delivered in Campo San Barnaba before the Doge, the ambassadors, and a multitude of nobles and people, in praise of the spouses and their families. The bride then returned to her father's house, and jousts took place in the campos of Santa Maria Formosa and San Paolo (the largest in the city), and in the Piazza San Marco. The Doge gave a great banquet, and at its close one hundred and fifty ladies proceeded to the bride's palace in the Bucintoro, where one hundred other ladies joined them, together with Lucrezia, who, seated between Francesco Sforza (then general-in-chief of the Republic's armies) and the Florentine ambassador, was conducted, amid the shouts of the people and the sound of trumpets, to the Ducal Palace. The Doge received her at the *riva* of the Piazzetta, and, with Sforza and Balbi, led her to the foot of the palace stairs, where the Dogaressa, with sixty ladies, welcomed her. A state supper ended this day's rejoicings, and on the following day a tournament took place in the Piazza, for a prize of cloth of gold, which was offered by Sforza. Forty knights contested the prize, and supped afterward with the Doge. On the next day there were processions of boats, with music, on the Grand Canal; on the fourth and last day there were other jousts for prizes offered by the jewellers and Florentine merchants; and every night there were dancing and feasting in the Ducal Palace. The Doge was himself the giver of the last tournament, and with this the festivities came to an end.

I have read an account by an old-fashioned English traveller of a Venetian marriage which he saw, sixty or seventy years ago, at

the church of San Giorgio Maggiore: "After a crowd of nobles,"
he says, "in their usual black robes, had been some time in
attendance, the gondolas, appearing, exhibited a fine show,
though all of them were painted of a sable hue, in consequence of
a sumptuary law, which is very necessary in this place, to prevent
an expense which many who could not bear it would incur;
nevertheless, the *barcarioli,* or boatmen, were dressed in handsome liveries; the gondolas followed one another in a line, each
carrying two ladies, who were likewise dressed in black. As they
landed they arranged themselves in order, forming a line from the
gate to the great altar. At length the bride, arrayed in white as the
symbol of innocence, led by the bridesman, ascended the stairs of
the landing-place. There she received the compliments of the
bridegroom, in his black toga, who walked at her right hand to the
altar, where they and all the company kneeled. I was often afraid
the poor young creature would have sunk upon the ground before
she arrived, for she trembled with great agitation, while she made
her low courtesies from side to side: however, the ceremony was
no sooner performed than she seemd to recover her spirits, and
looked matrimony in the face with a determined smile. Indeed, in
all appearance she had nothing to fear from her husband, whose
age and aspect were not at all formidable; accordingly she tripped
back to the gondola with great activity and resolution, and the
procession ended as it began. Though there was something
attractive in this aquatic parade, the black hue of the boats and the
company presented to a stranger, like me, the idea of a funeral
rather than a wedding. My expectation was raised too high by the
previous description of the Italians, who are much given to
hyperbole, who gave me to understand that this procession would
far exceed anything I had ever seen. When I reflect upon this
rhodomontade," disdainfully adds Mr. Drummond, "I cannot
help comparing, in my memory, the paltry procession of the
Venetian marriage with a very august occurrence of which I was
eye-witness in Sweden," and which being the reception of their
Swedish Majesties by the British fleet, I am sure the reader will not
ask me to quote.

With change of government, changes of civilization following the revolutions, and the decay of wealth among the Venetian nobles, almost all their splendid customs have passed away, and the habit of making wedding presents of sweetmeats and confectionery is perhaps the only relic which has descended from the picturesque past to the present time. These gifts are still exchanged not only by nobles, but by all commoners according to their means, and are sometimes a source of very profuse outlay. It is the habit to send the candies in the elegant and costly paper caskets which the confectioners sell, and the sum of a thousand florins scarcely suffices to pass the courtesy round a moderately large circle of friends.

With the nobility and with the richest commoners marriage is still greatly a matter of contract, and is arranged without much reference to the principals, though it is now scarcely probable in any case that they have not seen each other But with all other classes, except the poorest, who cannot and do not seclude the youth of either sex from each other, and with whom, consequently, romantic contrivance and subterfuge would be superfluous, love is made to-day in Venice as in the *capa y espada* comedies of the Spaniards, and the business is carried on with all the cumbrous machinery of confidants, billets-doux, and stolen interviews.

Let us take our nominal friends, Marco and Todaro, and attend them in their solemn promenade under the arcades of the Procuratie, or upon the Molo, whither they go every evening to taste the air and to look at the ladies, while the Austrians and the other foreigners listen to the military music in the Piazza. They are both young, our friends; they have both glossy silk hats; they have both light canes and an innocent swagger. Inconceivably mild are these youth, and in their talk indescribably small and commonplace.

They look at the ladies, and suddenly Todaro feels the consuming ardors of love.

Todaro (to Marco). Here, dear! Behold this beautiful blonde here! Beautiful as an angel! But what loveliness!

Marco. But where?

Todaro. It is enough. Let us go. I follow her.

Such is the force of the passion in southern hearts. They follow that beautiful blonde, who, marching demurely in front of the gray-mustached papa and the fat mamma, after the fashion in Venice, is electrically conscious of pursuit. They follow her during the whole evening, and, at a distance, softly follow her home, where the burning Todaro photographs the number of the house upon the sensitized tablets of his soul.

This is the first great step in love: he has seen his adored one, and he knows that he loves her with an inextinguishable ardor. The next advance is to be decided between himself and the faithful Marco, and is to be debated over many cups of black coffee, not to name glasses of sugar-and-water and the like exciting beverages. The friends may now find out the *caffè* which the Biondina frequents with her parents, and to which Todaro may go every evening and feast his eyes upon her loveliness, never making his regard known by any word, till some night, when he has followed her home, he steals speech with her as he stands in the street under her balcony,—and looks sufficiently sheepish as people detect him on their late return from the theatre.[1] Or, if the friends do not take this course in their courtship (for they are both engaged in the wooing), they decide that Todaro, after walking back and forth a sufficient number of times in the street where the Biondina lives, shall write her a tender letter, to demand if she be disposed to correspond his love. This billet must always be conveyed to her by her serving-maid, who must be bribed by Marco for the purpose. At every juncture Marco must be consulted, and acquainted with every step of progress; and no doubt the Biondina has some lively Moretta for her friend, to whom she confides her part of the love-affair in all its intricacy.

It may likewise happen that Todaro shall go to see the Biondina in church, whither, but for her presence, he would hardly go, and that there, though he may not have speech with her, he shall still

---

[1] The love-making scenes in Goldoni's comedy of *Il Bugiardo* are photographically faithful to present usage in Venice.

fan the ardors of her curiosity and pity by persistent sighs. It must be confessed that if the Biondina is not pleased with his looks, his devotion must assume the character of an intolerable bore to her, and that to see him everywhere at her heels; to behold him leaning against the pillar near which she kneels at church, the head of his stick in his mouth, and his attitude carefully taken with a view to captivation; to be always in deadly fear lest she shall meet him in promenade, or, turning round at the *caffè,* encounter his pleading gaze,—that all this must drive the Biondina to a state bordering upon blasphemy and finger-nails. *Ma, come si fa? Ci vuol pazienza!* This is the sole course open to ingenuous youth in Venice, where confessed and unashamed acquaintance between young people is extremely difficult; and so this blind pursuit must go on, till the Biondina's inclinations are at last laboriously ascertained.

Suppose the Biondina consents to be loved? Then Todaro has just and proper inquiries to make concerning her dower, and if her fortune is as pleasing as herself, he has only to remind her in marriage of her father, and after that to make her acquaintance.

One day a Venetian friend of mine, who spoke a little English, came to me with a joyous air, and said:—

"I am in lofe."

The recipient of repeated confidences of this kind from the same person, I listened with tempered effusion.

"It is a blonde again?"

"Yes, you have right; blonde again."

"And pretty?"

"Oh, but beautiful. I lofe her—*come si dice!—immensamente.*"

"And where did you see her? Where did you make her acquaintance?"

"I have not make the acquaintance. I see her pass with his fazer every night on Rialto Bridge. We did not spoke yet—only with the eyes. The lady is not of Venice. She has four thousand florins. It is not much—no. But!"

Is not this love at first sight almost idyllic? Is it not also a sublime prudence to know the lady's fortune better than herself, before herself? These passionate, headlong Italians look well to the main chance before they leap into matrimony, and you may be sure Todaro knows, in black and white, what the Biondina has to her fortune before he weds her. After that may come the marriage, and the sonnet written by the next of friendship, and printed to hang up in all the shop-windows, celebrating the auspicious event. If he be rich, or can write *nobile* after his Christian name, perhaps some abbate, elegantly addicted to verses and alive to grateful consequences, may publish a poem, elegantly printed by the matchless printers at Rovigo, and send it to all the bridegroom's friends. It is not the only event which the facile Venetian Muse shall sing for him. If his child is brought happily through the measles by Dottor Cavasangue, the Nine shall celebrate the fact. If he takes any public honor or scholastic degree, it is equal occasion for verses; and when he dies the mortuary rhyme shall follow him. Indeed, almost every occurrence—a boy's success at school, an advocate's triumphal passage of the perils of examination at Padua, a priest's first mass, a nun's novitiate, a birth, an amputation—is the subject of tuneful effusion, and no less the occasion of a visit from the *facchini* of the neighboring campo, who assemble with blare of trumpets and tumult of voices around the victim's door, and proclaim his skill or good fortune, and break into *vivas* that never end till he bribes their enthusiasm into silence. The naive commonplaceness of feeling in all matrimonial transactions, in spite of the gloss which the operatic methods of courtship threw about them, was a source of endless amusement, as it stole out in different ways. "You know my friend Marco?" asked an acquaintance one day. "Well, we are looking out a wife for him. He does n't want to marry, but his father insists; and he has begged us to find somebody. There are three of us on the lookout. But he hates women, and is very hard to suit. *Ben! Ci vuol pazienza!*"

It rarely happens now that the religious part of the marriage ceremony is not performed in church, though it may be performed at the house of the bride. In this case, it usually takes place in the evening, and the spouses attend five o'clock mass next morning.

But if the marriage takes place at the church, it must be between five and eleven in the morning, and the blessing is commonly pronounced about six o'clock. Civil marriage is still unknown among the Venetians. It is entirely the affair of the Church, in which the bans are published beforehand, and which exacts from the candidates a preliminary visit to their parish priest, for examination in their catechism, and for instruction in religion when they are defective in knowledge of the kind. There is no longer any civil publication of the betrothals, and the hand-shaking in the court of the Ducal Palace has long been disused. I cannot help thinking that the ceremony must have been a great affliction, and that in the Republican times at Venice a bride-groom must have fared nearly as hard as a President elect in our times at home.

There was a curious display on occasion of births among the nobility in former times. The room of the young mother was decorated with a profusion of paintings, sculpture, and jewelry; and, while yet in bed, she received the congratulations of her friends, and regaled them with sweetmeats served in vases of gold and silver.

The child of noble parents had always at least two godfathers, and sometimes as many as a hundred and fifty; but in order that the relationship of godfather (which is the same, according to the canonical law, as a tie of consanguinity) should not prevent desirable matrimony between nobles, no patrician was allowed to be godfather to another's child. Consequently the *compare* was usually a client of the noble parent, and was not expected to make any present to the godchild, whose father, on the day following the baptism, sent him a piece of marchpane, in acknowledgment of their relationship. No women were present at the baptism except those who had charge of the babe. After the fall of the Republic, the French custom of baptism in the parents' house was introduced, as well as the custom, on the godfather's part, of giving a present,—usually of sugar-plums and silver toys. But I think that most baptisms still take place in church, if I may judge from the numbers of tight little glass cases I have noticed,—half bed and half coffin,—containing little eight-day-old Venetians, closely swathed in mummy-like bandages, and borne to and from the churches by mysterious old women. The ceremony of baptism itself does not apparently differ from that in other Catholic countries, and is performed, like all religious services in Italy, without a ray of religious feeling or solemnity of any kind.

For many centuries funeral services in Venice hve been conducted by the Scuole del Sacramento, instituted for that purpose. To one of these societies the friends of the defunct pay a certain sum, and the association engages to inter the dead and bear all the expenses of the ceremony, the dignity of which is regulated by the priest of the parish in which the deceased lived. The rite is now most generally undertaken by the Scuola di San Rocco. The funeral train is of ten or twenty *facchini,* wearing tunics of white, with caps and capes of red, and bearing the society's lone, gilded candlesticks of wood, with lighted tapers. Priests follow them, chanting prayers, and then comes the bier, with a gilt crown lying on the coffin, if the dead be a babe, to indicate the triumph of innocence. Formerly hired mourners attended, and a candle weighing a pound was given to any one who chose to carry it in the procession.

Anciently there was great show of mourning in Venice for the dead, when, according to Mutinelli, the friends and kinsmen of the deceased, having seen his body deposited in the church, "fell to weeping and howling, tore their hair and rent their clothes, and withdrew forever from that church, thenceforth become for them a place of abomination." Decenter customs prevailed in aftertimes, and there was a pathetic dignity in the ceremony of condolence among patricians: the mourners, on the day following the interment, repaired to the porticos of Rialto and the court of the Ducal Palace, and their friends came, one after one, and expressed their sympathy by a mute pressure of the hand.

Death, however, is hushed up as much as possible in modern Venice. The corpse is hurried from the house of mourning to the parish church, where the friends, after the funeral service, take leave of it. Then it is placed in a boat and carried to the burial-ground, where it is quickly interred. I was fortunate, therefore, in witnessing a cheerful funeral, at which I one day casually assisted, at San Michele. There was a church on this island as early as the tenth century, and in the thirteenth century it fell into the possession of the Comandulensen Friars. They built a monastery on it, which became famous as a seat of learning, and gave much erudite scholarship to the world. In later times Pope Gregory XVI. carried his profound learning from San Michele to the Vatican. The present church is in the Renaissance style, but not very offensively so, and has some indifferent paintings. The arcades and the courts around which it is built contain funeral monuments as unutterably ugly and tasteless as anything of the kind I ever saw at home; but the dead, for the most part, lie in graves marked merely by little iron crosses in the narrow and roofless space walled in from the lagoon, which laps sluggishly at the foot of the masonry with the impulses of the tide. The old monastery was abolished in 1810, and there is now a convent of Reformed Benedictines on the island, who perform the last service for the dead.

On the day of which I speak, I was taking a friend to see the objects of interest at San Michele, which I had seen before, and the funeral procession touched at the *riva* of the church just as we arrived. The procession was of one gondola only, and the pall-bearers were four pleasant ruffians in scarlet robes of cotton, hooded, and girdled at the waist. They were accompanied by a priest of a broad and jolly countenance, two grinning boys, and finally the corpse itself, severely habited in an under-dress of black box, but wearing an outer garment of red velvet, bordered and tasselled gayly. The pleasant ruffians (who all wore smoking-caps with some other name) placed this holiday corpse upon a bier, and after a lively dispute with our gondolier, in which the compliments of the day were passed in the usual terms of Venetian chaff, lifted the bier on shore and set it down. The priest followed with the two boys, whom he rebuked for levity, simultaneously tripping over the Latin of a prayer, with his eyes fixed on our harmless little party as if we were a funeral, and the dead in the black box an indifferent spectator. Then he popped down upon his knees and made us a lively little supplication, while a blind beggar scuffled for a lost soldo about his feet, and the gondoliers quarrelled volubly. After which he threw off his surplice with the air of one who should say his day's work was done, and preceded the coffin into the church.

We had hardly deposited the bier upon the floor in the centre of the nave, when two pale young friars appeared, throwing off their hooded cloaks of coarse brown, as they passed to the sacristy, and reappearing in their rope-girdled gowns. One of them bore a lighted taper in his right hand and a book in his left; the other had also a taper, but a pot of holy water instead of the book.

They are very handsome young men, these monks, with heavy, sad eyes and graceful, slender figures, which their monastic life will presently overload with gross humanity full of coarse appetites. They go and stand beside the bier, giving a curious touch of solemnity to a scene composed of the four pleasant ruffians in the loaferish postures which they have learned as *facchini* waiting for jobs, of the two boys with inattentive grins, and of the priest with wandering eyes, kneeling behind them.

A weak, thin-voiced organ pipes huskily from its damp loft; the monk hurries rapidly over the Latin text of the service, while

"His breath to heaven like vapor goes"

on the chilly, humid air; and the other monk makes the responses, giving and taking the sprinkler, which his chief shakes vaguely in the direction of the coffin. They both bow their heads,—shaven down to the temples, to simulate His crown of thorns. Silence. The organ is still; the priest has vanished; the tapers are blown out; the pall-bearers lay hold of the bier, and raise it to their shoulders; the boys slouch into procession behind them; the monks glide softly and dispiritedly away. The soul is prepared for eternal life, and the body for the grave.

The ruffians are expansively gay on reaching the open air again. They laugh, they call "Ciò!"[2] continually, and banter each other as they trot to the grave.

The boys follow them, gambolling among the little iron crosses, and trying if here and there one of them may not be overthrown.

We two strangers follow the boys.

But here the pall-bearers become puzzled: on the right is an open trench, on the left is an open trench.

"Presence of the Devil! To which grave does this dead belong?" They discuss, they dispute, they quarrel.

From the side of the wall, as if he rose from the sea, appears the grave-digger, with his shovel on his shoulder,—slouching toward us.

"Ah heigh! *Ciò*, the grave-digger! Where does this dead belong?"

"Body of Bacchus, what potatoes! Here, in this trench to the right."

They set down the bier there, gladly. They strip away the coffin's gay upper garment; they leave but the under-dress of black box, painted to that favor with pitch. They shove it into the grave-digger's arms, where he stands in the trench, in the soft earth, rich with bones. He lets it slide swiftly to the ground— thump! *Ecco fatto!*

The two boys pick up the empty bier, and dance merrily away with it to the *riva* gate, feigning a little play after the manner of children,—"Oh, what a beautiful dead!"

---

[2] Literally, *That* in Italian, and meaning in Venetian, *You! Heigh!* To talk in *Ciò ciappa* is to assume insolent familiarity or unbounded good fellowship with the person addressed. A Venetian says *Ciò* a thousand times in a day, and hails every one but his superior in that way. I think it is hardly the Italian pronoun, but rather a contraction of *Veccio* (vecchio), *Old fellow!* It is common with all classes of the people: parents use it in speaking to their children, and brothers and sisters call one another *Ciò*. It is a salutation between friends, who cry out *Ciò!* as they pass in the street. Acquaintances, men who meet after separation, rush together with "*Ah Ciò!*" Then they kiss on the right cheek, "*Ciò!*" on the left, "*Ciò!*" on the lips, "*Ciò! Bon dì Ciò!*"

The eldest of the pleasant ruffians is all the pleasanter for *sci-ampagnin*, and can hardly be persuaded to go out at the right gate.

We strangers stay behind a little, to consult with another spectator,—Venetian, this.

"Who is the dead man, signore?"

"It is a woman, poor little thing! Dead in childbed. The baby is in there with her."

It has been a cheerful funeral, and yet we are not in great spirits as we go back to the city.

For my part, I do not think the cry of sea-gulls on a gloomy day is a joyous sound; and the sight of those theatrical angels, with their shameless, unfinished backs, flying off the top of the rococo façade of the church of the Jesuits, has always been a spectacle to fill me with despondency and foreboding.

CHAPTER XX

VENETIAN TRAITS AND CHARACTERS

O N a small canal, not far from the railroad station, the gondoliers show you a house, by no means notable (except for the noble statue of a knight, occupying a niche in one corner), as the house of Othello. It was once the palace of the patrician family Moro, a name well known in the annals of the Republic, and one which, it has been suggested, misled Shakespeare into the invention of Moor of Venice. Whether this is possibly the fact, or whether there is any tradition of a tragic incident in the history of the Moro family similar to that upon which the play is founded, I do not know; but it is certain that the story of Othello, very nearly as Shakespeare tells it, is popularly known in Venice; and the gondoliers have fixed upon the Casa Moro in question as the edifice best calculated to give satisfaction to strangers in search of the True and the Memorable. The statue is happily darkened by time, and thus serves admirably to represent Othello's complexion, and to place beyond the shadow of a doubt the fact of his residence in the house. Indeed, what can you say to the gondolier, who, in answer to your cavils, points to the knight, with the convincing argument, "There is his statue!"

One day I was taken to see this house, in company with some friends, and when it had been victoriously pointed out, as usual, we asked meekly, "Who was Othello?"

"Othello, Signori," answered the gondolier, "was a general of the Republic, in the old times. He was an African, and black; but nevertheless the State valued him, and he beat the Turks in many battles. Well, Signori, this General Othello had a very young and beautiful wife, and his wife's cousin (*sic!*) Cassio was his major-domo, or, as some say, his lieutenant. But after a while happens along (*capita*) another soldier of Othello, who wants Cassio's employment, and so accuses him to the general of corrupting his wife. Very well, Signori! Without thinking an instant, Othello, being made so, flew into a passion (*si riscaldò la tèsta*), and killed his wife; and then when her innocence came out, he killed himself and that liar; and the State confiscated his goods, he being a very rich man. There has been a tragedy written about all this, you know."

"But how is it called? Who wrote it?"

"Oh! in regard to that, then, I don't know. Some Englishman."

"Shakespeare?"

"I don't know, Signori. But if you doubt what I tell you, go to any bookseller, and say, 'Favor me with the tragedy of Othello.' He will give it you, and there you will find it all written out just as I tell it."

This gondolier confirmed the authenticity of his story by showing us the house of Cassio near the Rialto Bridge, and I have no doubt he would also have pointed out that of Iago if we had wished it.

But as a general thing, the lore of the gondoliers is not rich nor very great. They are a loquacious and a gossiping race, but they love better to have a quiet chat at the tops of their voices, as they loaf idly at the ferries, or to scream repartees across the Grand Canal, than to tell stories. In all history that relates to localities they are sufficiently versed to find the notable places for strangers, but beyond this they trouble themselves as little with the past as with the future. Three tragic legends, however, they know, and will tell with the most amusing effect, namely: Biasio, *luganegher,* the Innocent Baker-Boy, and Veneranda Porta.

The first of these legends is that of a sausage-maker who flourished in Venice some centuries ago, and who improved the quality of the broth which the *luganegheri* make of their scraps and sell to the gondoliers, by cutting up into it now and then a child of some neighbor. He was finally detected by a gondolier who discovered a little finger in his broth, and being brought to justice was dragged through the city at the heels of a wild horse. This most uncomfortable character appears to be the first hero in the romance of the gondoliers, and he certainly deserves to rank with that long line of imaginary personages who have made childhood so wretched and tractable. The second is the Innocent Baker-Boy already named, who was put to death on suspicion of having murdered a noble, because in the dead man's heart was found a dagger fitting a sheath which the baker had picked up in the street, on the morning of the murder, and kept in his possession. Many years afterwards, a malefactor who died in Padua confessed the murder, and thereupon two lamps were lighted before a shrine in the southern façade of St. Mark's Church,—one for the murdered nobleman's soul, and the other for that of the innocent boy. Such is the gondoliers' story, and the lamps still burn every night before the shrine from dark till dawn in witness of its truth. The fact of the murder and its guiltless expiation is an incident of Venetian history, and it is said that the Council of the Ten never pronounced a sentence of death there-

after till they had been solemnly warned by one of their number
with "*Ricordatevi del povero Fornaretto!*" (Remember the poor
Baker-Boy!) The poet Dall 'Ongaro has woven the story into a
beautiful and touching tragedy; but I believe the poet is still to be
born who shall take from the gondoliers their Veneranda Porta,
and place her historic figure in dramatic literature. Veneranda
Porta was a lady of the days of the Republic, between whom and
her husband existed an incompatibility. This was increased by the
course of Signora Porta in taking a lover, and it at last led to the
assassination of the husband by the paramours. The head of the
murdered man was found in one of the canals, and being exposed,
as the old custom was, upon the granite pedestal at the corner of
St. Mark's Church, it was recognized by his brother, who found
among the papers on which the long hair was curled fragments of
a letter he had written to the deceased. The crime was traced to the
paramours, and, being brought before the Ten, they were both
condemned to be hanged between the columns of the Piazzetta.
The gondoliers relate that when the sentence was pronounced
Veneranda said to the Chief of the Ten, "But as for me this
sentence will never be carried out. You cannot hang a woman.
Consider the impropriety!" The Venetian rulers were wise men in
their generation, and far from being balked by this question of
delicacy, the Chief replied, solving it, "My dear, you shall be
hanged in my breeches."

   It is very coarse salt which keeps one of these stories; another is
remembered because it concerns one of the people; and another
for its abomination and horror. The incidents of Venetian history
which take the fancy and touch the sensibility of the world seem
hardly known to the gondoliers, the most intelligent and quick-
witted of the populace, and themselves the very stuff that some
romantic dreams of Venice are made of. However sad the fact, it
is undeniable that the stories of the sausage-maker whose broth
was flavored with murder, and the baker-boy who suffered
guiltlessly, and that savage jest at the expense of the murderess,
interest these people more than the high, well-born sorrows of the
Foscari, the tragic fate of Carmagnola, or the story of Falier,—

which last they know partly, however, because of the scandal about Falier's wife. Yet after all, though the gondoliers are not the gondoliers of imaginative literature, they have qualities which recommended them to my liking, and I look back upon my acquaintance with two or three of them in a very friendly spirit. Compared with the truculent hackmen, who prey upon the travelling public in all other cities of the civilized world, they are eminently intelligent and amiable. Rogues they are, of course, for small dishonesties are the breath in the nostrils of common carriers by land or water, everywhere; but the trickery of the gondoliers is so good-natured and simple that it can hardly offend. A very ordinary jocular sagacity defeats their profoundest purposes of swindling, and no one enjoys their exposure half so much as themselves, while a faint prospect of future employment purifies them of every trait of dishonesty. I had only one troublesome experience with them, and that was in the case of the old gondolier who taught me to row. He, when I had no longer need of his services, plunged into drunkenness, and came and dismissed me one day with every mark of ignominy. But he afterwards forgave me, and saluted me kindly when we met.

The immediate goal of every gondolier's ambition is to serve, no matter for how short a time, an Inglese, by which generic title nearly all foreigners except Germans are known to him. The Inglese, whether he be English or American, is apt to make the tour of the whole city in a gondola, and to give handsome drink money at the end; whereas your Tedesco frugally walks to every place accessible by land, or when, in a party of six or eight, he takes a gondola, plants himself upon the letter of the tariff, and will give no more than the rate fixed by law. The gondolier is therefore flowingly polite to the Inglese, and he is even civil to the Tedesco; but he is not at all bound in courtesy to that provincial Italian who comes from the country to Venice, bargains furiously for his boat, and commonly pays under the tariff. The Venetian who does not himself keep a gondola seldom hires one, and even on this rare occasion makes no lavish demand such as, "How much do you want for taking me to the railway station?" Lest the fervid imagination of the gondolier rise to zwanzigers and florins, and a tedious dispute ensue, he asks, "How many centissimi do you want?" and the contract is made for a number of soldi.

The number of private gondolas owned in Venice is not very great. The custom is rather to hire a gondolier with his boat. The exclusive use of the gondola is thus secured, and the gondolier gives his services as a domestic when off his special duty. He waits at table, goes marketing, takes the children to school, and serves the ladies as footman, for five francs a day, himself paying the proprietor of the gondola about a franc daily for the boat. In former times, when Venice was rich and prosperous, many noble families kept six of seven gondolas; and what with this service, and the numerous gala-days of the Republic, when the whole city took boat for the Lido, or the Giudecca, or Murano, and the gondoliers were allowed to exact any pay they could, they were a numerous and prosperous class. But these times have passed from Venice forever, and though the gondoliers are still, counting the boatmen of Giudecca and Lido, some thousands in number, there are comparatively few young men among them, and their gains are meagre.

In the little city of Venice, where the dialect spoken at Canareggio or Castello is a different tongue from that heard under the Procuratie of St. Mark's Place, the boatmen of the several quarters of the city of course vary greatly in character and appearance; and the gondolier who lounges at the base of the columns of the Piazzetta, and airily invites the Inglesi to tours of the Grand Canal, is of quite a different type from the weather-beaten *barcaiuolo* who croaks "*Barca!*" at the promenaders on the Zattere. But all, as I say, are simple and harmless enough, and however loudly they quarrel among themselves, they never pass from the defamation of their female relatives to blows. As for the game of knives, as it is said to be played at Naples, and as About describes it at Rome, I doubt if it is much known to the populace of Venice. Only the doctors let blood there,—though from their lancets it flows pretty freely and constantly.

It is true that the gondolier loves best of everything a clamorous quarrel, carried on with the canal between him and his antagonist; but next to this he loves to spend his leisure at the ferry in talking of eating and of money, and he does not differ from many of his fellow-citizens in choice of topics. I have seldom caught a casual expression from passers in the streets of Venice which did not relate in some way to gold Napoleons, zwanzigers, florins, or soldi, or else to wine and *polenta*. I note this trait in the Venetians, which Goldoni observed in the Milanese a hundred years ago, and which I incline to believe is common to all Italians. The gondoliers talk a great deal in figure and hyperbole, and their jocose chaff is quite inscrutable, even to some classes of Venetians. With foreigners, to whom the silence and easy progress of the gondola gives them the opportunity to talk, they are fond of using a word or two of French. They are quick at repartee, and have a clever answer ready for most occasions. I was one day bargaining for a boat to the Lido, whither I refused to be taken in a shabby gondola, or at a rate higher than seventy-five soldi for the trip. At last the patience of the gondoliers was exhausted, and one of them called out, "Somebody fetch the Bucintoro, and take this gentleman to the Lido for seventy-five soldi!" (The Bucintoro being the magnificent barge in which the Doge went to wed the Adriatic.)

The skill with which the gondoliers manage their graceful craft is always admired by strangers, and is certainly remarkable. The gondola is very long and slender, and rises high from the water at either end. Both bow and stern are sharp, the former being ornamented with the deeply serrated blade of steel which it is the pride of the gondolier to keep bright as silver, and the poop having a small platform not far behind the cabin, on which he stands when he rows. The danger of collision has always obliged Venetian boatmen to face the bow, and the stroke with the oar (for the gondolier uses only a single oar) is made by pushing, and not by pulling. No small degree of art (as I learnt from experience) is thus required to keep the gondola's head straight,—all the strokes being made on one side,—and the sculling return of the oar-blade preparatory for each new stroke is extremely difficult to effect. Under the hands of the gondolier, however, the gondola seems a living thing, full of grace and winning movement. The wood-work of the little cabin is elaborately carved, and it is usually furnished with mirrors and seats luxuriously cushioned. The sensation of the gondola's progress felt by the occupant of the cabin, as he falls back upon these cushions, may be described, to the female apprehension at least, as "*too* divine." The cabin is removable at pleasure, and is generally taken off and replaced by awnings in summer. But in the evening, when the fair Venetians go out in their gondolas to take the air, even this awning is dispensed with, and the long, slender boat glides darkly down the Grand Canal, bearing its dazzling freight of white *tulle,* pale-faced, black-eyed beauty, and flashing jewels, in full view.

As for the singing of the gondoliers, they are the only class of Venetians who have not good voices, and I am scarcely inclined to regret the silence which long ago fell upon them. I am quite satisfied with the peculiar note of warning which they utter as they approach the corner of a canal, and which, meaning simply, "To the Right," or "To the Left," is the most pathetic and melancholy sound in the world. If, putting aside my own comfort, I have sometimes wished, for the sake of a dear, sentimental old friend at home, who loves such idle illusions with an ardor unbecoming his years, that I might hear the voice

> "of Adria's gondolier,
> By distance mellowed, o'er the waters sweep,"

I must still confess that I never did hear it under similar circumstances, except in conversation across half a mile of lagoon, when, as usual, the burden of the lay was *polenta* or soldi.

A recent Venetian writer, describing the character of the lower classes of Venice, says: "No one can deny that our populace is loquacious and quick-witted; but, on the other hand, no one can deny that it is regardless of improvement. Venice, a city exceptional in its construction, its customs, and its habits, has also an exceptional populace. It still feels, although sixty-eight years have passed, the influence of the system of the fallen Republic, of that oligarchic government, which, affording almost every day some amusement to the people, left them no time to think of their offended rights. . . . Since 1859 Venice has resembled a sepulchre of the living,—squalor and beggary gaining ground with each day, and commerce, with few exceptions, converted into monopoly; yet the populace remains attached to its old habits, and will have its pleasure. If the earnings are little, what then? Must one die of *ennui?* The *caffè* is depopulated: not so the drinking-house. The last day before the drawing of the lottery, the offices are thronged with fathers and mothers of families, who stint their children of bread to buy dearly a few hours of golden illusion. . . . At the worst, there is the Monte di Pietà, as a last resort."

It is true, as this writer says, that the pleasure-loving populace looks back fondly to the old Republican times of feasting and holidays; but there is certainly no truth any more in the old idea that any part of Italy is a place where people may be "idle with impunity," or make amusement the serious business of life. I can remember that the book from which I received my first impressions of geography was illuminated with a picture professing to represent Italian customs. The spirit of inquiry had long before caused me to doubt the exact fidelity of this representation; but it cost me a pang to learn that the picture was utterly delusive. It has been no part of my experience in Venice to see an Italian sitting upon the ground, and strumming the guitar, while two gayly dressed peasants danced to the music. Indeed, the indolence of Venetians is listless and silent, not playful or joyous; and as I learned to know their life more intimately, I came to understand that in many cases they are idle from despair of finding work, and that indolence is as much their fate as their fault. Any diligence of theirs is surprising to us of northern and free lands, because their climate subdues and enervates us, and because we can see before them no career open to intelligent industry. With the poorest, work is necessarily a hand-to-hand struggle against hunger; with those who would not absolutely starve without it, work is an inexplicable passion.

Partly because the ways of these people are so childlike and simple in many things, and partly from one's own swindling tendency to take one's self in (a tendency really fatal to all sincerity of judgment, and incalculably mischievous to such downfallen peoples as have felt the baleful effects of the world's sentimental, impotent sympathy), there is something pathetic in the patient content with which Italians work. They have naturally so large a capacity for enjoyment that the degree of self-denial involved in labor seems exorbitant, and one feels that these children, so loved of Nature, and so gifted by her, are harshly dealt with by their stepmother Circumstance. No doubt there ought to be truth in the silly old picture, if there is none, and I would willingly make-believe to credit it, if I could. I am glad that they at least work in old-world, awkward, picturesque ways, and not in commonplace, handy, modern fashion. Neither the habits nor the implements of labor are changed since the progress of the Republic ceased, and her heart began to die within her. All sorts of mechanics' tools are clumsy and inconvenient: the turner's lathe moves by broken impulses; door-hinges are made to order, and lift the door from the ground as it opens upon them; all nails and tacks are hand-made; window-sashes are contrived to be glazed without putty, and the panes are put in from the top, so that to repair a broken glass, the whole sash is taken apart; cooking-stoves are unknown to the native cooks, who work at an open fire, with crane and dangling pot-hooks; furniture is put together with wooden pegs instead of screws; you do not buy a door-lock at a hardware store,—you get a *fabbro* to make it, and he comes with a leathern satchel full of tools to fit and finish it on the door. The wheelbarrow of this civilization is peculiarly wonderful in construction, with a prodigious wooden wheel, and a ponderous, incapable body. The canals are dredged with scoops mounted on long poles, and manned each by three of four Chiozzotti. There never was a pile-driving machine known in Venice; nor a steam-tug in all the channels of the lagoons, through which the largest craft are towed to and from the ports by row-boats. In the model of the sea-going vessels there has apparently been little change from the first. Yet in spite of all this backwardness in invention, the city is full of beautiful workmanship in every branch of artificing, and the Venetians are still the best sailors in the Adriatic.

I do not offer the idea as a contribution to statistics, but it seems to me that the most active branch of industry in Venice is plucking fowls. In summer the people all work on their thresholds, and in their windows, and as nearly out-of-doors as the narrowness of the streets will let them; and it is hard to pass through any part of the city without coming to a poulterer's shop, in the door of which inevitably sits a boy, tugging at the plumage of some wretched bird. He is seldom to be seen except in that crisis of plucking when he seems to have all but finished; yet he seems never to accomplish the fact perfectly. Perhaps it is part of his hard fate that the feathers shall grow again under his hand as fast as he plucks them away: at the restaurants, I know, the quantity of plumage one devours in consuming roast chicken is surprising—at first. The birds are always very lean, too, and have but a languid and weary look, in spite of the ardent manner in which the boy clasps them while at work. It may be that the Venetians do not like fat poultry. Their turkeys, especially, are of that emaciation which is attributed among ourselves only to the turkey of Job; and as for the geese and ducks, they can only interest anatomists. It is as if the long ages of incursion and oppression which have impoverished and devastated Italy had at last taken effect upon the poultry, and made it as poor as the population.

I do not want to give too exclusive an impression of Venetian industry, however, for now I remember the Venetian *lasagnoni,* whom I never saw doing anything, and who certainly abound in respectable numbers.

The *lasagnone* is a loafer, as an Italian can be a loafer, without the admixture of ruffianism, which blemishes most loafers of northern race. He may be quite worthless, and even impertinent, but he cannot be a rowdy,—that pleasing blossom on the nose of our fast, high-fed, thick-blooded civilization. In Venice he must not be confounded with other loiterers at the *caffè;* not with the natty people who talk politics interminably over little cups of black coffee; not with those old *habitués,* who sit forever under the Procuratie, their hands folded upon the tops of their sticks, and staring at the ladies who pass with a curious steadfastness and knowing skepticism of gaze not pleasing in the dim eyes of age; certainly, the last persons who bear any likeness to the *lasagnone* are the Germans, with their honest, heavy faces comically anglicized by leg-of-mutton whiskers. The truth is, the *lasagnone* does not flourish in the best *caffè;* he comes to perfection in cheaper resorts, for he is commonly not rich. It often happens that a glass of water, flavored with a little anisette, is the order over which he sits a whole evening. He knows the waiter intimately, and does not call him "Shop!" (*Bottega*) as less familiar people do, but Gigi, or Beppi, as the waiter is pretty sure to be named. "Behold!" he says, when the servant places his modest drink before him, "who is that loveliest blonde there?" Or to his fellow-*lasagnone:* "She regards me! I have broken her the heart!" This is his sole business and mission, the cruel *lasagnone,*—to break ladies the heart. He spares no condition,—neither rank nor wealth is any defence against him. I often wonder what is in that note he continually shows to his friend. The confession of some broken heart, I think. When he has folded it, and put it away, he chuckles "*Ah, cara!*" and sucks at his long, slender Virginia cigar. It is unlighted, for fire consumes cigars. I never see him read the papers,—neither the Italian papers nor the Parisian journals, though if he can get Galignani he is glad, and he likes to pretend to a knowledge of English, uttering upon occasion, with great relish, such distinctively English words as "Yes" and "Not," and to the waiter, "A-little-fire-if-you-please." He sits very late in the *caffè,* and he touches his hat—his curly French hat—to the company as he goes out with a mild swagger, his cane held lightly in his left hand, his coat cut snugly to show his hips, and genteelly swaying with the motion of his body. He is a dandy, of course,—all Italians are dandies,—but his vanity is perfectly harmless, and his heart is not bad. He would go half an hour out of his way to put you in the direction of the Piazza. A little thing can make him happy: to stand in the pit at the opera, and gaze at the ladies in the lower boxes; to attend the Marionette, or the Malibran Theatre, and imperil the peace of pretty seamstresses and *contadinas;* to stand at the church doors and ogle the fair saints as they pass out. Go, harmless *lasagnone,* to thy lodging in some mysterious height, and break hearts if thou wilt. They are quickly mended.

Of other vagabonds in Venice, if I had my choice, I think I must select a certain ruffian who deals in dog-flesh, as the nearest my ideal of what a vagabond should be in all respects. He stands habitually under the Old Procuratie, beside a basket of small puppies in that snuffling and quivering state which appears to be the favorite condition of very young dogs, and occupies himself in conversation with an adjacent dealer in grapes and peaches, or sometimes fastidiously engages in trimming the hair upon the closely shaven bodies of the dogs; for in Venice it is the ambition of every dog to look as much like the Lion of St. Mark as the nature of the case will permit. My vagabond at times makes expeditions to the groups of travellers always seated in summer before the Caffè Florian, appearing at such times with a very small puppy,—neatly poised upon the palm of his hand, and winking pensively,—which he advertises to the company as a "Beautiful Beast," or a "Lovely Babe," according to the inspiration of his light and pleasant fancy. I think the latter term is used generally as a means of ingratiation with the ladies, to whom my vagabond always shows a demeanor of agreeable gallantry. I never saw him sell any of these dogs, nor ever in the least cast down by his failure to do so. His air is grave, but not severe; there is even, at times, a certain playfulness in his manner, possibly attributable to *sciampagnin.* His curling black locks, together with his velveteen jacket and pantaloons, are oiled and glossy, and his beard is cut in the French imperial mode. His personal presence is unwholesome, and it is chiefly his moral perfection as a vagabond that makes him fascinating. One is so confident, however, of his fitness for his position and business, and of his entire contentment with it, that it is impossible not to exult in him.

He is not without self-respect. I doubt, it would be hard to find any Venetian of any vocation, however base, who forgets that he too is a man and a brother. There is enough servility in the language,—it is the fashion of the Italian tongue, with its *Tu* for inferiors, *Voi* for intimates and friendly equals, and *Lei* for superiors,—but in the manner there is none, and there is a sense of equality in the ordinary intercourse of the Venetians, at once apparent to foreigners.

All ranks are orderly; the spirit of aggression seems not to exist among them, and the very boys and dogs in Venice are so well behaved that I have never seen the slightest disposition in them to quarrel. Of course, it is of the street-boy—the *biricchino*, the boy in his natural, unreclaimed state—that I speak. This state is here, in winter, marked by a clouded countenance, bare head, tatters, and wooden-soled shoes open at the heels; in summer by a preternatural purity of person, by abandon to the amphibious pleasure of leaping off the bridges into the canals, and by an insatiable appetite for *polenta*, fried minnows, and watermelons.

When one of these boys takes to beggary, as a great many of them do, out of a spirit of adventure and wish to pass the time, he carries out the enterprise with splendid daring. A favorite artifice is to approach Charity with a slice of *polenta* in one hand, and, with the other extended, implore a soldo to buy cheese to eat with the *polenta*. The street-boys also often perform the duties of the *gransieri*, who draw your gondola to shore, and keep it firm with a hook. To this order of beggar I usually gave; but one day at the railway station I had no soldi, and as I did not wish to render my friend discontented with future alms by giving silver, I deliberately apologized, praying him to excuse me, and promising him for another time. I cannot forget the lofty courtesy with which he returned, "*S'accomodi pur, Signor!*" They have sometimes a sense of humor, these poor swindlers, and can enjoy the exposure of their own enormities. An amiable rogue drew our gondola to land one evening when we went too late to see the church of San Giorgio Maggiore. The sacristan made us free of a perfectly dark church, and we rewarded him as if it had been noonday. On our return to the gondola, the same beggar whom we had just fed held out his hat for another alms. "But we have just paid you," we cried in an agony of grief and desperation. "*Sì, Signori!*" he admitted, with an air of argument, "*è vero. Ma, la chiesa!*" (Yes, gentlemen, it is true. But the church!) he added, with confidential insinuation and a patronizing wave of the hand toward the edifice, as if he had been San Giorgio himself, and held the church as a source of revenue. This was too much, and we laughed him to scorn; at which, beholding the amusing abomination of his conduct, he himself joined in our laugh with a cheerfulness that won our hearts.

Beggary is attended by no disgrace in Italy, and it therefore comes that no mendicant is without a proper degree of the self-respect common to all classes. Indeed, the habit of taking gifts of money is so general and shameless that the street beggars must be diffident souls indeed if they hesitated to ask for it. A perfectly well-dressed and well-mannered man will take ten soldi from you for a trifling service, and not consider himself in the least abased. The detestable custom of largess, instead of wages, still obtains in so great degree in Venice that a physician, when asked for his account, replies: "What you please to give." Knowing these customs, I hope I have never acted discourteously to the street beggars of Venice, even when I gave them nothing, and I know that only one of them ever so far forgot himself as to curse me for not giving. Him, however, I think to have been out of his right mind at the time.

There were two mad beggars in the parish of San Stefano whom I should be sorry to leave unmentioned here. One, who presided chiefly over the Campo San Stefano, professed to be also a *facchino,* but I never saw him employed, except in addressing select circles of idlers whom a brawling noise always draws together in Venice. He had been a soldier, and he sometimes put himself at the head of a file of Croats passing through the campo, and gave them the word of command, to the great amusement of those swarthy barbarians. He was a good deal in drink, and when in this state was proud to go before any ladies who might be passing, and clear away the boys and idlers, to make room for them. When not occupied in any of these ways, he commonly slept in the arcades of the old convent.

But the mad beggar of Campo Sant' Angelo seemed to have a

finer sense of what became him as a madman and a beggar, and never made himself obnoxious by his noise. He was, in fact, very fat and amiable, and in the summer lay asleep, for the most part, at a certain street corner which belonged to him. When awake he was a man of extremely complaisant presence, and suffered no lady to go by without a compliment to her complexion, her blonde hair, or her beautiful eyes, whichever it might be. He got money for these attentions, and people paid him for any sort of witticism. One day he said to the richest young dandy of the city, "Pah! you stomach me with your perfumes and fine airs," for which he received half a florin. His remarks to gentlemen had usually this sarcastic flavor. I am sorry to say that so excellent a madman was often drunk and unable to fulfil his duties to society.

There are, of course, laws against mendicancy in Venice, and they are, of course, never enforced. Beggars abound everywhere, and nobody molests them. There was long a troop of weird sisters in Campo San Stefano, who picked up a livelihood from the foreigners passing to and from the Academy of Fine Arts. They addressed people with the title of Count, and no doubt gained something by this sort of heraldry, though there are counts in Venice almost as poor as themselves, and titles are not distinctions. The Venetian seldom gives to beggars; he says deliberately, "*No go*" (I have nothing), or "*Quando ritornerò*" (when I return), and never comes back that way. I noticed that professional hunger and cold took this sort of denial very patiently, as they did every other; but I confess I had never the heart to practise it. In my walks to the Public Gardens there was a venerable old man, with the beard and bearing of a patriarch, whom I encountered on the last bridge of the Riva, and who there asked alms of me. When I gave him a soldo, he returned me a blessing which I would be ashamed to take in the United States for half a dollar; and when the soldo was in some inaccessible pocket, and I begged him to await my coming back, he said sweetly, "Very well, Signor, I will be here." And I must say, to his credit, that he never broke his promise, nor suffered me, for shame's sake, to break mine. He was quite a treasure to me in this respect, and assisted me to form habits of punctuality.

That exuberance of manner which one notes, the first thing, in his intercourse with Venetians characterizes all classes, but is most excessive and relishing in the poor. There is a vast deal of ceremony with every order, and one hardly knows what to do with the numbers of compliments it is necessary to respond to. A Venetian does not come to see you, he comes to revere you; he not only asks if you be well when he meets you, but he bids you remain well at parting, and desires you to salute for him all common friends; he reverences you at leave-taking; he will sometimes consent to incommode you with a visit; he will relieve you of the disturbance when he rises to go. All spontaneous wishes which must, with us, take original forms, for lack of the complimentary phrase, are formally expressed by him: good appetite to you, when you go to dinner; much enjoyment, when you go to the theatre; a pleasant walk, if you meet in promenade. He is your servant at meeting and parting; he begs to be commanded when he has misunderstood you. But courtesy takes its highest flights, as I hinted, from the poorest company. Acquaintances of this sort, when not on the *Ciò ciappa* footing, or that of the familiar thee and thou, always address each other in *Lei* (lordship), or *Elo*, as the Venetians have it; and their compliment-making at encounter and separation is endless: I salute you! Remain well! Master! Mistress! (*Paron! Parona!*) being repeated as long as the polite persons are within hearing.

One day, as we passed through the crowded Merceria, an old Venetian friend of mine, who trod upon the dress of a young person before us, called out, *"Scusate, bella giovane!"* (Pardon, beautiful girl!) She was not so fair nor so young as I have seen women; but she half turned her face with a forgiving smile, and seemed pleased with the accident that had won her the amiable apology. The waiter of the *caffè* frequented by the people says to the ladies for whom he places seats, "Take this place, beautiful blonde;" or, "Sit here, lovely brunette," as it happens.

A Venetian who enters or leaves any place of public resort touches his hat to the company, and one day at the restaurant some ladies, who had been dining there, said *"Complimenti!"* on

going out, with a grace that went near to make the beefsteak
tender. It is this uncostly gentleness of bearing which gives a
winning impression of the whole people, whatever selfishness or
real discourtesy lie beneath it. At home it sometimes seems that we
are in such haste to live and be done with it, we have no time to
be polite. Or is popular politeness merely a vice of servile peoples?
And is it altogether better to be rude? I wish it were not. If you are
lost in his city (and you are pretty sure to be lost there,
continually), a Venetian will go with you wherever you wish. And
he will do this amiable little service out of what one may say old
civilization has established in place of goodness of heart, but
which is perhaps not so different from it.

You hear people in the streets bless each other in the most
dramatic fashion. I once caught these parting words between an
old man and a young girl:—

Giovanetta. Revered sir! (*Patron riverito!*)

Vecchio. (With that peculiar backward wave and beneficent
wag of the hand, only possible to Italians.) Blessed child! (*Benedetta!*)

It was in a crowd, but no one turned round at the utterance of
terms which Anglo-Saxons would scarcely use in their most
emotional moments. The old gentleman who sells boxes for the
theatre in the Old Procuratie always gave me his benediction when
I took a box.

There is equal exuberance of invective, and I have heard many
fine maledictions on the Venetian streets, but I recollect none more
elaborate than that of a gondolier who, after listening peacefully
to a quarrel between two other boatmen, suddenly took part
against one of them, and saluted him with, "Ah! baptized son of
a dog! And if I had been present at thy baptism, I would have
dashed thy brains out against the baptismal font!"

All the theatrical forms of passion were visible in a scene I
witnessed in a little street near San Samuele, where I found the
neighborhood assembled at doors and windows in honor of a
wordy battle between two poor women. One of these had been
forced in-doors by her prudent husband, and the other upbraided

her across the marital barrier. The assailant was washing, and twenty times she left her tub to revile the besieged, who thrust her long arms over those of her husband, and turned each reproach back upon her who uttered it, thus:—

Assailant. Beast!

Besieged. Thou!

A. Fool!

B. Thou!

A. Liar!

B. Thou!

E via in seguito! At last the assailant, beating her breast with both hands, and tempestuously swaying her person back and forth, wreaked her scorn in one wild outburst of vituperation, and returned finally to her tub, wisely saying, on the purple verge of asphyxiation, "*O, non discorro più con gente.*"

I returned half an hour later, and she was laughing and playing sweetly with her babe.

It suits the passionate nature of the Italians to have incredible ado about buying and selling, and a day's shopping is a sort of campaign, from which the shopper returns plundered and discomfited, or laden with the spoil of vanquished shopmen.

The embattled commercial transaction is conducted in this wise:—

The shopper enters, and prices a given article. The shopman names a sum of which only the fervid imagination of the South could conceive as corresponding to the value of the goods.

The purchaser instantly starts back with a wail of horror and indignation, and the shopman throws himself forward over the counter with a protest that, far from being dear, the article is ruinously cheap at the price stated, though they may nevertheless agree for something less.

What, then, is the very most ultimate price?

Properly, the very most ultimate price is so much. (Say, the smallest trifle under the price first asked.)

The purchaser moves toward the door. He comes back, and offers one third of the very most ultimate price.

The shopman, with a gentle desperation, declares that the thing cost him as much. He cannot really take the offer. He regrets, but he cannot. That the gentleman would say something more! So much, for example. That he regard the stuff, its quality, fashion, beauty.

The gentleman laughs him to scorn. Ah, heigh! and, coming forward, he picks up the article and reviles it. Out of the mode, old, fragile, ugly of its kind.

The shopman defends his wares. There is not such quantity and quality elsewhere in Venice. But if the gentleman will give even so much (still something preposterous), he may have it, though truly its sale for that money is utter ruin.

The shopper walks straight to the door. The shopman calls him back from the threshold, or sends his boy to call him back from the street.

Let him accommodate himself,—which is to say, take the thing at his own price.

He takes it.

The shopman says cheerfully, "*Servo suo!*"

The purchaser responds, "*Bon dì! Patron!*" (Good day! my Master!)

Thus, as I said, every bargain is a battle, and every purchase a triumph or a defeat. The whole thing is understood; the opposing forces know perfectly well all this is to be done beforehand, and retire after the contest, like the captured knights in Morgante Maggiore, "calm as oil," however furious and deadly their struggle may have appeared to strangers.

Foreigners sood discern, however, that there is no bloodshed in such encounters, and enter into them with a zeal as great as that of natives, though with less skill. I knew one American who prided himself on such matters, and who haughtily closed a certain bargain without words, as he called it. The shopman offered several articles, for which he demanded prices amounting in all to ninety-three francs. His wary customer rapidly computed the total, and replied, "Without words, now, I'll give you a hundred francs for the lot." With a pensive elevation of the eyebrows and a reluctant shrug of the shoulders, the shopman suffered him to take them.

Your Venetian is *simpatico*, if he is anything. He is always ready to feel and to express the deepest concern, and I rather think he likes to have his sensibilities appealed to, as a pleasant and healthful exercise for them. His sympathy begins at home, and he generously pities himself as the victim of a combination of misfortunes which leave him citizen of a country without liberty, without commerce, without money, without hope. He next pities his fellow-citizens, who are as desperately situated as himself. Then he pities the degradtion, corruption, and despair into which the city has fallen. And I think his compassion is the most hopeless thing in his character. That alone is touched; that alone is moved; and when its impulse ceases he and everything about him remain just as before.

With the poor, this sensibility is amusingly mischievous. They never speak of one of their own class without adding some such ejaculation as "Poor fellow!" or, "Poor little creature!" They pity all wretchedness, no matter from what cause, and the greatest rogue has their compassion when under a cloud. It is all but impossible to punish thieves in Venice, where they are very bold and numerous; for the police are too much occupied with political surveillance to give due attention to mere cutpurses and house-breakers, and even when they make an arrest people can hardly be got to bear witness against their unhappy prisoner. *Povareto anca lu!* There is no work and no money: people must do something; so they steal. *Ci vuol pazienza!* Bear witness against an ill-fated fellow-sufferer? God forbid! Stop a thief? I think a burglar might run from Rialto to San Marco, and not one compassionate soul in the Merceria would do aught to arrest him—*povareto!* Thieves came to the house of a friend of mine at noonday, when his servant was out. They tied their boat to his landing, entered his house, filled their boat with plunder from it, and rowed out into the canal. The neighbors on the floor above saw them, and cried, "Thieves! thieves!" It was in the most frequented part of the Grand Canal, where scores of boats passed and repassed; but no one molested the thieves, and these *povareti* escaped with their booty.[1]

One night, in a little street through which we passed to our ferry, there came a wild rush before us, of a woman screaming for help, and pursued by her husband with a knife in his hand; their children, shrieking piteously, came after them. The street was crowded with people and soldiers, but no one put out his hand; and the man presently overtook his wife and stabbed her in the back. We only knew of the rush, but what it all meant we could not tell till we saw the woman bleeding from the stab, which, happily, was slight. Inquiry of the bystanders developed the facts, but, singularly enough, scarcely a word of pity. It was entirely a family affair, it seemed: the man, poor little fellow, had a mistress, and his wife had maddened him with reproaches. *Come si fa?* He had to stab her. The woman's case was not one that appealed to popular compassion, and the only words of pity for her which I heard were expressed by the wife of a fruiterer, whom her husband angrily silenced.

---

[1] The rogues, it must be confessed, are often very polite. This same friend of mine one day found a man in the act of getting down into a boat with his favorite singing bird in its cage. "What are you doing with that bird?" he thought himself authorized to inquire. The thief looked about him a moment, and, perceiving himself detected, handed back the cage with a cool "*La scusi!*" (Beg pardon!) as if its removal had been a trifling inadvertence.

CHAPTER XXI

SOCIETY

IT was natural that the Venetians, whose State lay upon the borders of the Greek Empire, and whose greatest commerce was with the Orient, should be influenced by the Constantinopolitan civilization. Mutinelli records that in the twelfth century they had many religious offices and observances in common with the Greeks, especially the homily, or sermon, which formed a very prominent part of the service of worship. At this time, also, when

265

the rupture of the Lombard League had left other Italian cities to
fall back into incessant local wars, and barbarized their customs,
the people of Venice dressed richly and delicately, after the Greek
fashion. They combed and dressed their hair, and wore the long,
pointed Greek beard;[1] and though these Byzantine modes fell, for
the most part, into disuse, in aftertime, there is still a peculiarity
of dress among the women of the Venetian poor which is said to
have been inherited from the oriental costumes of Constantinople;
namely, that high-heeled, sharp-toed slipper, or sandal, which
covers the front of the foot, and drops from the heel at every step,
requiring no slight art in the wearer to keep it on at all.

The philosophic vision, accustomed to relate trifling particulars
to important generalities, may perhaps see another relic of
Byzantine civilization among the Venetians in that jealous re-
straint which they put upon all the social movements of young
girls, and the great liberty which they allow to married women. It
is true that their damsels are now no longer imprisoned under the
parental roof, as they were in times when they never left its shelter
but to go, closely veiled, to communion in the church, on
Christmas and Easter; but it is still quite impossible that any
young lady should go out alone. Indeed, she would scarcely be
secure from insult in broad day, if she did so. She goes out with
her governess, and, even with this protection, she cannot be too
guarded and circumspect in her bearing; for in Venice a woman
has to encounter upon the public street a rude license of glance,
from men of all ages and conditions, which falls little short of
outrage. They stare at her as she approaches; and I have seen them
turn and contemplate ladies as they passed them, keeping a few
paces in advance, with a leisurely sidelong gait. Something of this
insolence might be forgiven to thoughtless, hot-blooded youth;
but the gross and knowing leer that the elders of the Piazza and
the *caffè* put on at the approach of a pretty girl is an ordeal which
few women, not as thoroughly inured to it as the Venetians,
would care to encounter. However, as I never heard the trial

---

[1] A Foscarini, in 1687, was the last patrician who wore the beard.

complained of by any but foreigners, I suppose it is not regarded by Italians as intolerable; and it is certain that an audible compliment, upon the street, to a pretty girl of the poor is by no means an affront.

The arts of pleasing and of coquetry come by nature to the gentler sex; and if in Italy they add to them a habit of intrigue, I wonder how much they are to blame, never being in any wise trusted? They do not differ from persons of any age or sex in that country, if the world has been as justly, as it has always been firmly, persuaded that the people of Italy are effete in point of good faith. I have seen much to justify this opinion, and something also to confute it; and as long as Garibaldi lives, I shall not let myself believe that a race which could produce a man so signally truthful and single-hearted is a race of liars and cheats. I think the student of their character should also be slow to upbraid Italians for their duplicity, without admitting, in palliation of the fault, facts of long ages of alien and domestic oppression, in politics and religion, which must account for a vast deal of every kind of evil in Italy. Yet after exception and palliation has been duly made, it must be confessed that in Italy it does not seem to be thought shameful to tell lies, and that there the standard of sincerity, compared with that of the English or American, is low, as the Italian standard of morality in other respects is also comparatively low.

With the women, bred in idleness and ignorance, the imputed national untruthfulness takes the form naturally to be expected, and contributes to a state of things which must be examined with the greatest caution and reservation by every one but the Italians themselves. Goethe says that there is no society so corrupt that a man may not live virtuously in it; and I think the immorality of any people will not be directly and wholly seen by the stranger who does not seek it. Certainly, the experience and acquaintance of a foreigner in Italy must have been most unfortunate, if they confirm all the stories of corruption told by Italians themselves. A little generous distrust is best in matters of this kind; but while I strengthen my incredulity concerning the utter depravation of

Venetian society in one respect, I am not disposed to deal so leniently with it in others. The state of things is bad in Venice, not because all women in society are impure, but because the Italian theory of morals does not admit the existence of opportunity without sin. It is by rare chance that a young girl makes acquaintance with young men in society; she seldom talks with them at the parties to which she is sometimes taken by her mother, and they do not call upon her at her home; while for her to walk alone with a young man would be vastly more scandalous than much worse things, and is, consequently, unheard of. The Italians say freely they cannot trust their women as northern women are trusted; and some Italian women frankly confess that their sex would be worse if it were trusted more. But the truth does not appear in this shallow suspicion and this shallow self-conviction; and one who cares to have a just estimate of this matter must by no means believe all the evil he hears. There may be much corruption in society, but there is infinitely more wrong in the habits of idle gossip and guilty scandal, which eat all sense of shame and pity out of the heart of Venice. There is no parallel to the prying, tattling, backbiting littleness of the place elsewhere in the world. A small country village in America or England has its meddlesomeness, but not its worldly, wicked sharpness. Figure the meanness of a chimney-corner gossip added to the bitter shrewdness and witty penetration of a gifted *roué*, and you have some idea of Venetian scandal. In that city, where all the nobler organs of expression are closed by political conditions, the viler channels run continual filth and poison, and the people, shut out from public and free discussion of religious and political themes, occupy themselves with private slander, and rend each other in their abject desperation. As it is part of the existing political demonstration to avoid the opera and theatre, the Venetians are deprived of these harmless distractions; balls and evening parties, at which people, in other countries, do nothing worse than bore each other, are almost unknown, for the same reason; and when persons meet in society, it is too often to retail personalities, or Italian politics made as unintelligible and as like local gossip as possible. The talk which is small and noxious in private circles is the same thing at the *caffè*, when the dread of spies does not reduce the talkers to a dreary silence. Not permitted to feel the currents of literature and the great world's thought in religion freshly and directly, they seldom speak of these things, except in that tone of obsolete superiority which Italians are still prone to affect, as the monopolists of culture. As to Art, the Venetians are insensible to it and ignorant of it, here in the very atmosphere of Art, to a degree absolutely amusing. I would as soon think of asking a fish's opinion of water as of asking a Venetian's notion of architecture or painting, unless he were himself a professed artist or critic.

Admitting, however, that a great part of the corruption of society is imputed, there still remains, no doubt, a great deal of real immorality to be accounted for. This, I think, is often to be attributed to the bad system of female education, and the habits of idleness in which women are bred. Indeed, to Americans, the whole system of Italian education seems calculated to reduce women to a state of imbecile captivity before marriage; and I have no fault to find with the Italians that they are jealous in guarding those whom they have unfitted to protect themselves, but have rather to blame them that, after marriage, their women are thrown at once upon society, when worse than helpless against its temptations. Except with those people who attempt to maintain a certain appearance in public upon insufficient means (and there are too many of these in Venice, as everywhere else), and who spare in every other way that they may spend on dress, it does not often happen that Venetian ladies are housekeepers. Servants are cheap and numerous, as they are uncleanly and untrustworthy, and the Venetians prefer to keep them[2] rather than take part in housewifely duties, and, since they must lavish upon dress and show, to suffer from cold and hunger in their fireless houses and

---

[2] A clerk or employé with a salary of fifty cents a day keeps a maid-servant, that his wife may fulfil to society the important duty of doing nothing.

at their meagre boards. In this way the young girls, kept imprisoned from the world, instead of learning cookery and other domestic arts, have the grievous burden of idleness added to that of their solitary confinement, not only among the rich and noble, but among that large class which is neither and wishes to appear both.[3] Their idle thoughts, not drilled by study nor occupied with work, run upon the freedom which marriage shall bring them, and form a distorted image of the world, of which they know as little as of their own undisciplined selves. Denied the just and wholesome amusements of society during their girlhood, it is scarcely a matter of surprise that they should throw themselves into the giddiest whirl of its excitement when marriage sets them free to do so.

I have said I do not think Venetians who give each other bad names are always to be credited, and I have no doubt that many a reputation in Venice is stained while the victim remains without guilt. A questioned reputation is, however, no great social calamity. It forms no bar to society, and few people are so cruel as to blame it, though all discuss it. And it is here that the harshness of American and English society toward the erring woman (harshness which is not injustice, but half-justice only) contrasts visibly to our advantage over the bad *naïveté* and lenity of the Italians. The carefully secluded Italian girl is accustomed to hear of things

---

[3] The poet Gray, genteelly making the grand tour in 1740, wrote to his father from Florence: "The only thing the Italians shine in is their reception of strangers. At such times everything is magnificence: the more remarkable as in their ordinary course of life they are parsimonious to a degree of nastiness. I saw in one of the vastest palaces of Rome (that of the Prince Pamfilio), the apartment which he himself inhabited, a bed that most servants in England would disdain to die in, and furniture much like that of a soph at Cambridge. This man is worth 30,000*l.* a year." Italian nature has changed so little in a century that all this would hold admirably true of Italian life at this time. The goodly outside in religion, in morals, in everything, is too much the ambition of Italy; this achieved, she is content to endure any pang of self-denial, and sell what little comfort she knows—it is mostly imported, like the word, from England— to strangers at fabulous prices. In Italy the luxuries of life are cheap, and the conveniences unknown or excessively dear.

and speak of things which, with us, parents strive in every way to keep from their daughters' knowledge; and while her sense of delicacy is thus early blunted, while she is thus used to know good and evil, she hears her father and mother comment on the sinful errors of a friend or neighbor who visits them and meets them every day in society. How can the impunity of the guilt which she believes to exist around her but sometimes have its effect, and ripen, with opportunity, into wrong? Nay, if the girl reveres her parents at all, how can she think the sin which they caress in the sinner is so very bad? If, however, she escape all these early influences of depravation; if her idleness and solitude and precocious knowledge leave her unvitiated; if, when she goes into society, it is by marriage with a man who is neither a dotard nor a fortune-seeker, and who remains constant and does not tempt her, by neglect, to forebode offence and to inflict anticipative reprisals, yet her purity goes uncredited, as her guilt would go unpunished; scandal makes haste to blacken her name to the prevailing hue; and whether she has sin or not, those with sin will cast, not the stone that breaks and kills, but the filth that sticks and stinks. The wife must continue the long social exile of her girlhood if she would not be the prey of scandal. The *cavaliere servente* no longer exists, but gossip now attributes often more than one lover in his place, and society has the cruel clemency to wink at the license. Nothing is in worse taste than jealousy, and, consequently, though intrigue sometimes causes stabbing, and the like, among low people, it is rarely noticed by persons of good breeding. It seems to me that in Venetian society the reform must begin, not with dissolute life, but with the social toleration of the impure, and with the wanton habits of scandal, which make all other life incredible, and deny to virtue the triumph of fair fame.

I confess that what I saw of the innocent amusements of this society was not enough to convince me of their brilliancy and attractiveness; but I doubt if a foreigner can be a trustworthy judge of these things, and perhaps a sketch drawn by an alien hand, in the best faith, might have an air of caricature. I would not, therefore, like to trust my own impression of social diversions.

They were, very probably, much more lively and brilliant than I thought them. But Italians assembled anywhere, except at the theatre or the *caffè*, have a certain stiffness, all the more surprising because tradition has always led one to expect exactly the reverse of them. I have seen nothing equal to the formality of this people, who deride colder nations for inflexible manners; and I have certainly never seen society in any small town in America so ill at ease as I have seen society in Venice, writhing under self-imposed restraints. At a musical *soirée,* attended by the class of people who at home would have been chatty and sociable, given to making acquaintance and to keeping up acquaintance,—the young men harmlessly talking and walking with the young ladies, and the old people listening together, while constant movement and inter-course kept life in the assembly, and there was some real pleasure felt amidst a good deal of unavoidable suffering,—I say, I found such a *soirée* in Venice to be a spectacle of ladies planted in formal rows of low-necks and white dresses around the four sides of one room, and of gentlemen restively imprisoned in dress-coats and white gloves in another. During the music all these devoted people listened attentively, and at the end the ladies lapsed back into their chairs and fanned themselves, while the gentlemen walked up and down the floor of their cell, and stopped, two by two, at the door of the ladies' room, glanced mournfully athwart the moral barrier which divided them, and sadly and dejectedly turned away. Amazed at this singular species of special enjoyment, I inquired afterward, of a Venetian lady, if evening parties in Venice were usually such ordeals, and was discouraged to learn that what I had seen was scarcely an exaggeration of prevailing torments. Commonly people do not know each other, and it is difficult for the younger to procure introductions; and when there is previous acquaintance, the presence of some commanding spirit is necessary to break the ice of propriety, and substitute enjoyment for correctness of behavior. Even at dancing parties, where it would seem that the poetry of motion might do something to soften the rigid bosom of Venetian deportment, the poor young people separate after each dance, and take each sex its appointed prison, till the next quadrille offers them a temporary liberation. For my own part, I cannot wonder that young men fly these virtuous scenes, and throng the rooms of those pleasant women of the *demimonde,* who only exact from them that they shall be natural and agreeable; I cannot wonder that their fair partners in wretchedness seize the first opportunity to revenge themselves upon the propriety which has so cruelly used them. It is said that the assemblies of the Jews, while quite as unexceptionable in character, are far more sociable and lively than those of the Christians. The young Hebrews are frequently intelligent, well-bred, and witty, with a *savoir faire* which their Christian brethren lack. But, indeed, the young Venetian is, at that age when all men are owlish, ignorant, and vapid, the most owlish, ignorant, and vapid man in the world. He talks, not milk-and-water, but warm water alone, a little sweetened; and, until he has grown wicked, has very little good in him.

Most ladies of fashion receive calls on a certain day of each week, when it is made a matter of pride to receive as many calls as possible. The number sometimes reaches three hundred, when nobody sits down, and few exchange more than a word with the hostess. In winter, the stove is heated on these reception days, and little cups of black coffee are passed round to the company; in summer lemonade is substituted for the coffee; but in all seasons a thin, waferish slice of toasted rusk (the Venetian *baicolo*) is offered to each guest with the drink. At receptions where the sparsity of the company permits the lady of the house to be seen, she is commonly visible on a sofa, surrounded by visitors in a half circle. Nobody stays more than ten or fifteen minutes, and I have sometimes found even this brief time of much greater apparent length, and apt to produce a low state of nerves, from which one seldom recoveres before dinner. Gentlemen, however, do not much frequent these receptions; and I assert again the diffidence I should feel in offering this glance at Venetian social enjoyment as conveying a just and full idea of it. There is no doubt that the Venetians find delight in their assemblies, where a stranger seeks it in vain. I dare say they would not think our own reunions brilliant, and that, looking obliquely (as a foreigner must) on the most sensible faces at one of our evening parties, they might mistake the look of pathetic dejection visible in them as the expression of people rather bored by their pleasure than otherwise.

The *conversazioni* are of all sorts, from the *conversazioni* of the rigid proprietarians, where people sit down to a kind of hopeless whist, at a soldo the point, and say nothing, to the *conversazioni* of the *demi-monde* where they say anything. There are persons in Venice, as well as everywhere else, of new-fashioned modes of thinking, and these strive to give a greater life and ease to their assemblies by attracting as many young men as possible; and in their families gentlemen are welcome to visit, and to talk with the young ladies in the presence of their mothers. But though such people are no more accused of impropriety than the straitest of the old-fashioned, they are not regarded with the greatest esteem, and their daughters do not so readily find husbands. The Italians are fickle, the women say; they get soon tired of their wives after marriage, and when they see much of ladies before marriage they get tired of them then, and never make them their wives. So it is much better to see nothing of a possible husband till you actually have him. I do not think *conversazioni* of any kind are popular with young men, however; they like better to go to the *caffè*, and the people you meet at private houses are none the less interesting for being old or middle-aged. A great many of the best families, at present, receive no company at all, and see their friends only in the most private manner; though there are still cultivated circles to which proper introduction gives the stranger (who has no Austrian acquaintance) access. But unless he have thorough knowledge of Italian politics localized to apply to Venice, an interest in the affairs, fortunes, and misfortunes of his neighbors, and an acquaintance with the Venetian dialect, I doubt if he will be able to enjoy himself in the places so cautiously opened to him. Even in the most cultivated society, the dialect is habitually spoken; and if Italian is used, it is only in compliment to some foreigner present, for whose sake, also, topics of general interest are sometimes chosen.

The best society is now composed of the families of professional men, such as the advocates, the physicians, and the richer sort of merchants. The shopkeepers, master-artisans, and others, whom industry and thrift distinguish from the populace, seem not to have any social life, in the American sense. They are wholly devoted to affairs, and partly from choice, and partly from necessity, are sordid and grasping. It is their class which has to fight hardest for life in Europe, and they give no quarter to those above or below them. The shop is their sole thought and interest, and they never, never sink it. But, since they have habits of diligence, and, as far as they are permitted, of enterprise, they seem to be in great part the stuff from which a prosperous State is to be rebuilt in Venice, if ever the fallen edifice rise again. They have sometimes a certain independence of character which a better condition of things and further education would perhaps lift into honesty; though as yet they seem not to scruple to take any unfair advantage, and not to know that commercial success can never rest permanently on a system of bad faith. Below this class is the populace, between which and the patrician order a relation something like Roman clientage existed, contributing greatly to the maintenance of exclusively aristocratic power in the State. The greatest conspiracy (that of Marin Falier) which the commons ever moved against the oligarchy was revealed to one of the nobility by his plebeian creature, or client; and the government rewarded by every species of indulgence a class in which it had extinguished even the desire of popular liberty. The heirs of the servile baseness which such a system as this must create are not yet extinct. There is still a helplessness in many of the servant class, and a disposition to look for largess as well as wages, which are the traits naturally resulting from a state of voluntary submission to others. The nobles, as the government, enervated and de- bauched the character of the poor by public shows and countless holidays; as individuals, they taught them to depend upon patri- cian favor, and not upon their own plebeian industry, for support. The lesson was an evil one, hard to be unlearned, and it is yet to be forgotten in Venice. Certain traits of soft and familiar dependence give great charm to the populace; but their existence makes the student doubtful of a future to which the plebeians themselves look forward with perfect hope and confidence. It may be that they are right, and will really rise to the dignity of men, when free government shall have taught them that the laborer is worthy of his hire—after he has earned it. This has been the result, to some degree, in the kingdom of Italy, where the people have found that freedom, like happiness, means work.

Undoubtedly the best people in the best society of Venice are the advocates, an order of consequence even in the times of the Republic, though then shut out from participation in public affairs by a native government, as now by a foreign one. Acquaintance with several members of this profession impressed me with a sense of its liberality of thought and feeling, where all liberal thinking and feeling must be done by stealth, and where the common intelligence of the world sheds its light through multiplied barriers. Daniele Manin, the President of the Republic of 1848, was of this class, which, by virtue of its learning, enlightenment, and talent, occupies a place in the esteem and regard of the Venetian people far above that held by the effete aristocracy. The better part of the nobility, indeed, is merged in the professional class, and some of the most historic names are now preceded by the learned titles of Doctor and Advocate, rather than the cheap dignity of Count, offered by the Austrian government to all the patricians who chose to ask for it, when Austrian rule was extended over their country.

The physicians rank next to the advocates, and are usually men learned in their profession, however erroneous and old-fashioned some of their theories of practice may be. Like the advocates, they are often men of letters: they write for the journals, and publish little pamphlets on those topics of local history which it is so much the fashion to treat in Venice. No one makes a profession of authorship. The returns of an author's work would be too uncertain, and its restrictions and penalties would be too vexatious and serious; and so literary topics are only occasionally treated by those whose main energies are bent in another direction.

The doctors are very numerous, and a considerable number of them are Hebrews, who, even in the old jealous times, exercised the noble art of medicine, and who now rank very highly among their professional brethren. These physicians haunt the neat and tasteful apothecary shops, where they sit upon the benching that passes round the interior, read the newspapers, and discuss the politics of Europe, Asia, Africa, and America, with all the zest that you may observe to characterize their discussions in Goldoni's plays. There they spend their evenings and many hours of every day, and thither the sick send to call them,—each physician resorting to a particular apothecary's, and keeping his name inscribed on a brass plate against the wall, above the head of the druggist, who presides over the reunions of the doctors, while his apprentice pestles away at their prescriptions.

In 1786 there were, what with priests, monks, and nuns, a multitude of persons of ecclesiastical profession in Venice; and though many convents and monasteries were abolished by Napoleon, the priests are still very numerous, and some monastic estblishments have been revived under Austrian rule. The high officers of the Church are, of course, well paid, but most of the priesthood live miserably enough. They receive from the government a daily stipend of about thirty-five soldi, and they celebrate mass, when they can get something to do in that way, for forty soldi. Unless, then, they have private income from their own family, or have pay for the education of some rich man's son or daughter, they must fare slenderly.

There is much said, in and out of Venice, about their influence in society; but this is greatly modified, and I think is chiefly exercised upon the women of the old-fashioned families.[4] I need hardly repeat the well-known fact that all the moral power of the

---

[4] It is no longer usual for girls to be educated in convents, and most young ladies of the better classes up to the age of thirteen or fourteen years, receive their schooling in secular establishments, whither they go every day for study, or where they sometimes live, as in our boarding schools, and where they are taught the usual accomplishments, greater attention being paid to French and music than to other things.

Roman Church over the younger men is gone; these seldom attend
mass, and almost never go to confession, and the priests are their
scorn and by-word. Their example, in some degree, must be much
followed also by women; and though women must everywhere
make more public professions of religion than men, in order to
retain social standing, I doubt if the priests have a very firm hold
upon the fears or reverence of the sisters and wives of liberal
Venetians.

If, however, they contribute in any wise to keep down the
people, they are themselves enslaved to their superiors and to each
other. No priest can leave the city of Venice without permission of
the Patriarch. He is cut off as much as possible from his own
kinspeople, and subjected to the constant surveillance of his class.
Obliged to maintain a respectable appearance on twenty cents a
day; hampered and hindered from all personal liberty and private
friendship, and hated by the great mass of the people, I hardly
think the Venetian priest is to be envied in his life. For my own
part, knowing these things, I was not able to cherish toward the
priests those feelings of scornful severity which swell many
Protestant bosoms; and so far as I made their acquaintance, I
found them kind and amiable. One ecclesiastic, at least, I may
describe as one of the most agreeable and cultivated gentlemen I
ever met.

Those who fare best among the priests are the Jesuits, who
returned from repeated banishment with the Austrians in this
century. Their influence is very extended, and the confessional is
their forte. Venetians say that with the old and the old-fashioned
these crafty priests suggest remorse and impose penances; that
with the young men and the latter-day thinkers they are men of
the world, and pass off pleasant sins as trifles. All the students of
the government schools are obliged by law to confess twice a
month, and are given printed certificates of confession, in blank,
which the confessor fills up and stamps with the seal of the
Church. Most of them go to confess at the church of the Jesuits,
who are glad to hear the cock-and-bull story invented by the
student, and to cultivate his friendship by an easy penance and a

liberal tone. This ingenuous young man of course despises the confessional. He goes to confess because the law obliges him to do so; but the law cannot dictate what he must confess. Therefore, he ventures as near downright burlesque as he dares, and (if the account he gives of the matter be true) puts off his confessor with some well-known fact, as that he has blasphemed. Of course he has blasphemed, blasphemy being as common as the forms of salutation in Venice. So the priest, who wishes him to come again, and to found some sort of influence over him, says, "Oh dear, dear! This is very bad. Blasphemy is deadly sin. If you *must* swear, swear by the heathen gods: say Body of Diana, instead of Body of God; Presence of the Devil, instead of Blood of Mary. Then there is no harm done." The students laugh over the pleasant absurdity together, and usually agree upon the matter of their semi-monthly confessions beforehand.

As I have hinted, the young men do not love the government or the Church; and though I account for the loss of much high hope and generous sympathy in growth from youth to middle age, I cannot see how, when they have replaced their fathers, the present religious and political discontent is to be modified. Nay, I believe it must become worse. The middle-aged men of Venice grew up in times of comparative quiet, when she did not so much care who ruled over her, and negatively, at least, they honored the Church. They may now hate the foreign rule, but there are many consid-erations of timidity and many effects of education to temper their hate. They may dislike the priests, but they revere the Church. The young men of to-day are bred in a different school, and all their thoughts are of opposition to the government and of war upon the Church, which they detest and ridicule. The fact that their education is still in the hands of the priests in some measure does not render them more tractable. They have no fears to be wrought upon by their clerical professors, who seldom have sought to act upon their nobler qualities. The influence of the priesthood is again limited by the fact that the teachers in the free schools of the city, to which the poor send their children, are generally not priests; and ecclesiastics are no longer so commonly the private tutors of the children of the rich as they once were, when they lived with the family, and exercised a direct and important influence on it. Express permission from the Pope is now necessary to the maintenance of a family chaplain, and the office is nearly disused.[5]

The Republic was extremely jealous of the political power of the priests, who could not hold secular office in its time. A curious punishment was inflicted upon the priest who proved false to his own vows of chastity, and there is a most amusing old ballad—by no means cleanly in its language—purporting to be the lament of a priest suspended in the iron cage, appointed for the purpose, from the belfry of the Campanile San Marco, and enduring the jeers and insults of the mob below. We may suppose that with advancing corruption (if corruption has indeed advanced from remote to later times) this punishment was disused for want of room to hang out the delinquents. In the last century, especially, the nuns and monks led a pleasant life. You may see in the old pictures of Pietro Longhi and his school how, at the aristocratic and fashionable convent of San Zaccaria, the lady nuns received their friends and acquaintances of this world in the ante-room where the dames and their cavaliers flirted and drank coffee, and the gentlemen coquetted with the brides of heaven through their grated windows.

Among other privileges of the Church, abolished in Venice long ago, was that ancient right of the monks of St. Anthony, Abbot, by which their herds of swine were made free of the whole city. These animals, enveloped in an odor of sanctity, wandered here and there, and were piously fed by devout people, until the year 1409, when, being found dangerous to children and inconvenient to everybody, they were made the subject of a special decree, which deprived them of their freedom of movement. The Republic was always limiting the privileges of the Church! It is known how,

---

[5] In early days every noble Venetian family had its chaplain, who, on the occasion of great dinners and suppers, remained in the kitchen, and received as one of his perquisites the fragments that came back from the table.

when the holy inquisition was established in its dominions in 1249, the State stipulated that great part of the process against heresy should be conducted by secular functionaries, and that the sentence should rest with the Doge and his councillors,—a kind of inquisition with claws clipped and teeth filed, as one may say, and the only sort ever permitted in Venice. At present there is no absolute disfavor shown to the clergy; but, as we have seen, many a pleasant island, which the monks of old reclaimed from the salty marshes, and planted with gardens and vineyards, now bears only the ruins of their convents, or else, converted into a fortress or government *dépôt,* is all thistly with bayonets. Anciently, moreover, there were many little groves in different parts of the city, where the pleasant clergy, of what Mr. Ruskin would have us believe the pure and religious days of Venice, met and made merry so riotously together by night that the higher officers of the Church were forced to prohibit their little *soirées.*

An old custom of rejoicing over the installation of a new parish priest is still to be seen in almost primitive quaintness. The people of each parish—nobles, citizens, and plebeians alike—formerly elected their own priest, and, till the year 1576, they used to perambulate the city to the sound of drums, with banners flying, after an election, and proclaim the name of their favorite. On the day of the *parroco's* induction his portrait was placed over the church door, and after the celebration of the morning mass a breakfast was given, which grew to be so splended in time that in the fifteenth century a statute limited its profusion. In the afternoon, the new *parroco,* preceded by a band of military music, visited all the streets and courts of his parish, and then, as now, all the windows of the parish were decorated with brilliant tapestries, and other gay-colored cloths and pictures. In those times, as in these, there was an illumination at night, throngs of people in the campo of the church and booths for traffic in cakes of flour and raisins,—fried in lard upon the spot, and sold smoking hot, with immense uproar on the part of the merchant; and for three days afterward the parish bells were sounded in concert.

The difficulty of ascertaining anything with certainty in Venice attends in a degree peculiarly great the effort to learn exactly the present influence and standing of the nobility as a class. One is tempted, on observing the free and unembarrassed bearing of all ranks of people toward each other, to say that no sense of difference exists, and I do not think there is ever shown, among Italians, either the aggressive pride or the abject meanness which marks the intercourse of people and nobles elsewhere in Europe; and I have not seen the distinction of rich and poor made so brutally in Italy as sometimes in our own *soi-disant* democratic society at home. There is, indeed, that equality in Italian fibre which I believe fits the nation for democratic institutions better than any other, and which is perhaps partly the result of their ancient civilization. At any rate, it fascinates a stranger to see people so mutually gentle and deferential, and must often be a matter of surprise to the Anglo-Saxon, in whose race, reclaimed from barbarism more recently, the native wild beast is still so strong as to sometimes inform the manner. The uneducated Anglo-Saxon is a savage; the Italian, though born to utter ignorance, poverty, and depravity, is a civilized man. I do not say that his civilization is of a high order, or that the civilization of the most cultivated Italian is at all comparable to that of a gentleman among ourselves. The Italian's education, however profound, has left his passions undisciplined while it has carefully polished his manner; he yields lightly to temptation, he loses his self-control, he blasphemes habitually; his gentleness is conventional, his civilization not individual. With us, the education of a gentleman (I do not mean a person born to wealth or station, but any man who has trained himself in morals or religion, in letters, and in the world) disciplines the impulses, and leaves the good manner to grow naturally out of habits of self-command and consequent habitual self-respect.

The natural equality of the Italians is visible in their community of good looks as well as good manners. They have never, perhaps, that high beauty of sensitive expression which is found among Englishmen and Americans (preferably among the latter), but it very rarely happens that they are brutally ugly; and the man of low rank and mean vocation has often a beauty of as fine sort as the man of education and refinement. If they changed clothes, and the poor man could be persuaded to wash himself, they might successfully masquerade, one for another. The plebeian Italian, inspired by the national vanity, bears himself as proudly as the noble, without at all aggressing in his manner. His beauty, like that of the women of his class, is world-old,—the beauty of the pictures and the statues: the ideal types of loveliness are realized in Italy; the saints and heroes, the madonnas and nymphs, come true to the stranger at every encounter with living faces. In Venice, particularly, the carriage of the women, of whatever rank, is very free and noble, and the servant is sometimes to be distinguished from the mistress only by her dress and by her labor-coarsened hands,—certainly not always by her dirty finger-nails and foul teeth; for though the clean shirt is now generally in Italy, some lesser virtues are still unknown: the nail-brush and tooth-brush are of but infrequent use; the four-pronged fork is still imperfectly understood, and as a nation the Italians may be said to eat with their knives.

The Venetian, then, seeing so little difference between himself and others, whatever his rank may be, has, as I said, little temptation to arrogance or servility. The effects of the old relationship of patron and client are amusingly noticeable in the superior as well as the inferior; a rich man's dependents are perfectly free with advice and comment, and it sometimes happens that he likes to hear their lively talk, and at home secretly consorts with his servants. The former social differences between common-ers and patricians (which, I think judging from the natural temper of the race, must have been greatly modified at all times by concession and exception) may be said to have quite disappeared in point of fact; the nobility is now almost as effete socially as it is politically. There is still a number of historic families, which are in a certain degree exclusive; but rich *parvenus* have admission to their friendship, and commoners in good circumstances are permitted their acquaintance; the ladies of this patrician society visit ladies of less rank, and receive them at their great parties, though not at more sacred assemblies, where they see only each other.

The Venetians have a habit of saying their best families are in exile, but this is not meant to be taken literally. Many of the best families are yet in the city, living in perfect retirement, or very often merged in the middle class, and become men of professions and active, useful lives. Of these nobles (they usually belong to the families which did not care to ask nobility of Austria, and are therefore untitled)[6] the citizens are affectionately proud, while I have heard from them nothing but contempt and ridicule of the patricians who, upon a wretched pension or meagre government office, attempt to maintain patrician distinction. Such nobles are usually Austriacanti in their politics, and behind the age in everything; while there are other descendants of patrician families mingled at last with the very populace, sharing their ignorance and degradation, and feeling with them. These sometimes exercise the most menial employments: I knew one noble lord who had been a *facchino*, and I heard of another who was a street-sweeper. *Conte che non conta, non conta niente,*[7] says the sneering Italian proverb; and it would be little less than miraculous if a nobility like that of modern Venice maintained superior state and regard in the eyes of the quick-witted, intelligent, sarcastic commonalty.

The few opulent patricians are by no means the most violent of Italianissimi. They own lands and houses, and as property is unsafe when revolutionary feeling is rife, their patriotism is tempered. The wealth amassed in early times by the vast and enterprising commerce of the country was, when not dissipated in riotous splendor, invested in real estate upon the main-land as the Republic grew in territory, and the income of the nobles is now

---

[6] The only title conferred on any patrician of Venice during the Republic was Cavaliere, and this was conferred by a legislative act in reward of distinguished service. The names of the nobility were written in the Golden Book of the Republic, and they were addressed as Illustrissimo or Eccellenza. They also signed themselves *nobile,* between the Christian name and surname, as it is still the habit of the untitled nobility to do.

[7] A count who does n't count (money) counts for nothing.

from the rents of these lands. They reside upon their estates during the season of the *villeggiatura,* which includes the months of September and October, when every one who can possibly leave the city goes into the country. Then the patricians betake themselves to their villas near Padua, Vicenza, Bassano, and Treviso, and people the sad-colored, weather-worn stucco hermitages, where the mutilated statues, swaggering above the gates, forlornly commemorate days when it was a far finer thing to be a noble than it is now. I say the villas look dreary and lonesome as places can be made to look in Italy, what with their high garden walls, their long, low piles of stabling, and the *passée* indecency of their nymphs and fauns, foolishly strutting in the attitudes of the silly and sinful old Past; and it must be but a dull life that the noble proprietors lead there.

It is better, no doubt, on the banks of the Brenta, where there are still so many villas as to form a street of these seats of luxury, almost the whole length of the canal, from Fusina to Padua. I am not certain that they have a right to the place which they hold in literature and sentiment, and yet there is something very charming about them with their gardens, and chapels, and statues, and shaded walks. We went to see them one day early in October, and found them every one, when habitable, inhabited, and wearing a cheerful look, that made their proximity to Venice incredible. As we returned home after dark, we saw the ladies from the villas walking unattended along the road, and giving the scene an air of home-like peace and trustfulness which I had not found before in Italy; while the windows of the houses were brilliantly lighted, as if people lived in them; whereas, you seldom see a light in Venetian palaces. I am not sure that I did not like better, however the villas that were empty and ruinous, and the gardens that had run wild, and the statues that had lost legs and arms. Some of the ingenious proprietors had enterprisingly whitewashed their statues, and there was a horrible primness about certain of the well-kept gardens which offended me. Most of the houses were not large, but there was here and there a palace as grand as any in the city. Such was the great villa of the Contarini of the Lions, which was in every way superb, with two great lions of stone guarding its portals, and a gravel walk, over-arched with stately trees, stretching a quarter of a mile before it. At the moment I was walking down this aisle I met a clean-shaven old canonico, with red legs and red-tasselled hat, and with a book under his arm, and a meditative look, whom I here thank for being so venerably picturesque. The palace itself was shut up, and I wish I had known, when I saw it, that it had a ghostly underground passage from its cellar to the chapel, wherein, when you get half way, your light goes out, and you consequently never reach the chapel.

This is at Mira; but the greatest of all the villas is the magnificent country-seat of the family Pisani at Stra, which now, with scarcely any addition to its splendor, serves for the residence of the abdicated Emperor of Austria. There is such pride in the vastness of this edifice and its gardens as impresses you with the material greatness which found expression in it, and never raises a regret that it has utterly passed away. You wander around through the aisles of trim-cut lime-trees, bullied and overborne by the insolent statues and expect at every turn to come upon intriguing spectres in bag-wigs, immense hoops and patches. How can you feel sympathy for those dull and wicked ghosts of eighteenth-century corruption? There is rottenness enough in the world without digging up old putridity and sentimentalizing on it; and I doubt if you will care to know much of the way in which the noble owner of such a villa ascended the Brenta at the season of the *villeggiatura* in his great gilded barge, all carven outside with the dumpling loves and loose nymphs of the period, with fruits, and flowers, and what not; and within, luxuriously cushioned and furnished, and stocked with good things for pleasure making in the gross old fashion.[8] King Cole was not a merrier old soul than Illustrissimo of that day; he outspent princes; and his agent, while he harried the tenants to supply his master's demands, plundered Illustrissimo frightfully. Illustrissimo never looked at accounts. He said to his steward, "*Caro veccio, fè vu. Mi remeto a quel che fè*

---

[8] Mutinelli, *Gli Ultimi Cinquant' Anni della Repubblica di Venezia.*

vu." (Old fellow, you attend to it. I shall be satisfied with what you do.) So the poor agent had no other course but to swindle him, which he did; and Illustrissimo, when he died, died poor, and left his lordly debts and vices to his sons.

In Venice, the noble still lives sometimes in his ancestral palace, dimly occupying the halls where his forefathers flourished in so much splendor. I can conceive, indeed, of no state of things more flattering to human pride than that which surrounded the patrician of the old aristocratic Republic. The house in which he dwelt was the palace of a king, in luxury of appointment and magnificence of size. Troops of servants that ministered to his state peopled its vast extent; and the gondolas that carried his grandeur abroad were moored in little fleets to the piles that rose before his palace, painted with the family arms and colors. The palace itself stood usually on the Grand Canal, and rose sheer from the water, giving the noble that haughty inaccessibility which the lord of the main-land achieved only by building lofty walls and multiplying gates. The architecture was as costly in its ornament as wild Gothic fancy, or Renaissance luxury of bad taste, could make it; and when the palace front was not of sculptured marble, the painter's pencil filled it with the delight of color. The main-land noble's house was half a fortress, and formed his stronghold in times of popular tumult or family fray; but at Venice the strong arm of St. Mark suppressed all turbulence in a city secure from foreign war; and the peaceful arts rejoiced in undisturbed possession of the palaces, which rose in the most delicate and fantastic beauty, and mirrored in the brine a dream of sea-deep strangeness and richness. You see much of the beauty yet, but the pride and opulence which called it into being are gone forever.

Most palaces, whether of the Gothic or classicistic period, have the same internal arrangement of halls and chambers, and are commonly built of two lofty and two low stories. On the ground floor, or water level, is a hall running back from the gate to a bit of garden at the other side of the palace; and on either side of this hall, which in old times was hung with the family trophies of the chase and war, are the porter's lodge and gondoliers' rooms. On the first and second stories are the family apartments, opening on either side from great halls, of the same extent as that below, but with loftier roofs, or heavy rafters gilded or painted. The fourth floor is of the same arrangement, but has a lower roof, and was devoted to the better class of servants. Of the two stories used by the family, the third is the loftier and airier, and was occupied in summer; the second was the winter apartment. On either hand the rooms open in suites.

We have seen something of the ceremonies, public and private, which gave peculiar gayety and brilliance to the life of the Venetians of former days; but in his political character the noble had yet greater consequence. He was part of the proudest, strongest, and securest system of his time. He was a king with the fellowship of kings, flattered with the equality of an aristocracy which was master of itself, and of its nominal head. During the earlier times it was his office to go daily to Rialto and instruct the people in their political rights and duties for four hours; and even when the duties became everything and the rights nothing (after the Serrar del Consiglio), the friendly habit of daily intercourse between patricians and citizens was still kept up at the same place. Once each week, and on every holiday, the noble took his seat in the Grand Council (the most august assembly in the world, without doubt), or the Ten, or the Three, according to his office in the State,—holding his place in the Council by right of birth, and in the other bodies by election of his peers.

Although the patricians were kept as one family apart from the people, and jealously guarded in their aristocratic purity by the State, they were only equals of the poorest before the laws of their own creation, and their condescension to the people was fequent and great. Indeed, the Venetians of all classes are social creatures, loving talk and gossip, and these constant habits of intercourse must have done much to produce that equality of manner now observable in them. Their amusements were for a long time the same, the nobles taking part in the public holidays, and in the popular exercises of rowing and swimming. In the earlier times, hunting in the lagoons was a favorite diversion; but as the decay of the Republic advanced, and the patrician blossomed into the fine gentleman of the last century, these hearty sports were relinquished, and everything was voted vulgar but masking in carnival, dancing and gaming at Ridotto, and intriguing everywhere.

The accounts which Venetian writers give of Republican society in the eighteenth century form a *chronique scandaleuse* which need not be minutely copied here. Much may be learned of Venetian manners of this time from the comedies of Goldoni; and the faithlessness of society may be argued from the fact that in these plays, which contain nothing salacious or indecent, there is scarcely a character of any rank who scruples to tell lies; and the truth is not to be found in works intended to school the public to virtue. The ingenious old playwright's memoirs are full of gossip concerning that poor old Venice which is now no more; and the worthy autobiographer, Casanova, also gives much information about things that had best not be known.

As the Republic drew near its fall, in 1797, there was little left in its dominant class worth saving, if we may believe the testimony of Venetians, which Mutinelli brings to bear upon the point in his Annali Urbani, and his History of the Last Fifty Years of the Republic. Long prosperity and prodigious opulence had done their worst, and the patricians, and the lowest orders of the people, their creatures and dependents, were thoroughly corrupt; while the men of professions began to assume that station which they now hold. The days of a fashionable patrician of those times began at a little before sunset, and ended with the following dawn. Rising from his bed, he dressed himself in dainty linen, and placed himself in the hands of the hair-dresser to be combed, oiled, perfumed, and powdered; and then sallied forth for a stroll through the Merceria, where this excellent husband and father made tasteful purchases to be carried to the lady he served. At dinner, which he took about seven or eight, his board was covered with the most tempting viands, and surrounded by needy parasites, who detailed the spicy scandals of the day in payment of their dinner, while the children of the host were confided to the care of the corrupt and negligent servants. After dinner, the father went to the theatre, or to the *casino,* and spent the night over cards and wine, in the society of dissolute women; and renewed on the morrow the routine of his useful existence. The education of the children of the man of fashion was confided to a priest, who lived in his family, and called himself an abbate, after the mode of the *abbés* of French society; he had winning manners with the ladies, indulgent habits with his pupils, and dressed his elegant person in silks of Lyons and English broadcloths. In the pleasant old days he flitted from palace to villa, dining and supping, and flattering the ladies, and tapping the lid of his jewelled snuff-box in all fashionable companies. He was the cadet of a patrician family (when not the ambitious son of a low family), with a polite taste for idleness and intrigue, for whom no secular sinecure could be found in the State, and who obliged the Church by accepting orders. Whether in the palace on the Grand Canal, or the villa on the Brenta, this gentle and engaging priest was surely the most agreeable person to be met, and the most dangerous to ladies' hearts, with his rich suit of black, and his smug, clean-shaven face, and his jewelled hands, and his sweet, seducing manners. Alas! the world is changed! The priests whom you see playing *tre-sette* now at the *conversazioni* are altogether different men, and the delightful abbate is as much out of fashion as the bag-wig or the queue. When in fashion he loved the theatre, and often showed himself there at the side of his noble patron's wife. Nay, in that time the theatre was so prized by the Church that a popular preacher thought it becoming to declare from his pulpit that to compose well his hearers should study the comedies of Goldoni, and his hearers were the posterity of that devout old aristocracy which never undertook a journey without first receiving the holy sacrament; which had built the churches and endowed them from private wealth!

Ignorance, as well as vice, was the mode in those elegant days, and it is related that a charming lady of good society once addressed a foreign *savant* at her *conversazione,* and begged him to favor the company with a little music, because, having heard that he was *virtuous,* she had no other association with the word than its technical use in Italy to indicate a professional singer as a *virtuoso*. A father of a family who kept no abbate for the education of his children ingeniously taught them himself. "Father," asked one of his children, "what are the stars?" "The stars are stars, and little things that shine as thou seest." "Then they are candles, perhaps?" "Make thy account that they are candles exactly." "Of wax or tallow?" pursues the boy. "What! tallow-candles in heaven? No, certainly—wax, wax!"

These, and many other scandalous stories, the Venetian writers recount of the last days of their Republic, and the picture they produce is one of the most shameless ignorance, the most polite corruption, the most unblushing baseness. I have no doubt that the picture is full of national exaggeration. Indeed, the method of Mutinelli (who I believe intends to tell the truth) in writing social history is altogether too credulous and incautious. It is well enough to study contemporary comedy for light upon past society, but satirical ballads and lampoons, and scurrilous letters cannot be accepted as historical authority. Still there is no question but Venice was very corrupt. As you read of her people in the last century, one by one the ideas of family faith and domestic purity fade away; one by one the beliefs in public virtue are dissipated; until at last you are glad to fly the study, close the filthy pages, and take refuge in doubt of the writers, who declare that they must needs disgrace Venice with facts since her children have dishonored her in their lives. "Such as we see them," they say, "were the patricians, such the people of Venice, after the middle of the eighteenth century. The Venetians might be considered as extinguished; the marvellous city, the pomp only of the Venetians, existed."

Shall we believe this? Let each choose for himself. At that very time the taste and wealth of a Venetian noble fostered the genius of Canova; and then, when their captains starved the ragged soldiers of the Republic to feed their own idleness and vice, when the soldiers dismantled her forts to sell the guns to the Turk, when her sailors rioted on shore and her ships rotted in her ports, she had still military virtue enough to produce that Emo, who beat back the Algerine corsairs from the commerce of Christendom, and attacked them in their stronghold, as of old her galleys beat back the Turks. Alas! there was not the virtue in her statesmen to respond to this greatness in the hero. One of their last public acts was to break his heart with insult and to crave peace of the pirates whom he had cowed. It remained for the helpless Doge and the abject patricians, terrified at a threat of war, to declare the Republic at an end, and San Marco was no more.

I love Republics too well to lament the fall of Venice. And yet, *Pax tibi, Marce!* If I have been slow to praise, I shall not hasten to condemn, a whole nation. Indeed, so much occurs to me to qualify with contrary sense what I have written concerning Venice, that I wonder if, after all, I have not been treating throughout less of the rule than of the exception. It is a doubt which must force itself upon every fair and temperate man who attempts to describe another people's life and character; and I confess that it troubles me so sorely now, at the end of my work, that I would fain pray the gentle reader to believe much more good and much less evil of the Venetians than I have said. I am glad that it remains for me to express a faith and hope in them for the future, founded upon their present political feeling, which, however tainted with self-interest in the case of many, is no doubt with the great majority a high and true feeling of patriotism. And it is impossible to believe that a people which can maintain the stern and unyielding attitude now maintained by the Venetians toward an alien government disposed to make them any concession short of freedom, in order to win them into voluntary submission, can be wanting in the great qualities which distinguish living peoples from those passed hopelessly into history and sentiment. In truth, glancing back over the whole career of the nation, I can discern in it nothing so admirable, so dignified, so steadfastly brave, as its present sacrifice of all that makes life easy and joyous, to the attainment of a good which shall make life noble.

The Venetians desire now, and first of all things, Liberty, knowing that in slavery men can learn no virtues; and I think them fit, with all their errors and defects, to be free now, because men are never fit to be slaves.

CHAPTER XXII

OUR LAST YEAR IN VENICE

(AS IT SEEMS SEVEN YEARS AFTER.)

THE last of four years which it was our fortune to live in
the city of Venice was passed under the roof of one of her
most beautiful and memorable palaces, namely, the Palazzo
Giustiniani, whither we went, as has been told in an earlier chapter of this book, to escape the encroaching nepotism of Giovanna,
the flower of serving women. The experience now, in Cambridge,

293

Mass., refuses to consort with ordinary remembrances, and has such a fantastic preference for the company of rather vivid and circumstantial dreams, that it is with no very strong hope of making it seem real that I shall venture to speak of it.

The Giustiniani were a family of patricians very famous during the times of a Republic that gave so many splendid names to history, and the race was preserved to the honor and service of St. Mark by one of the most romantic facts of his annals. During a war with the Greek Emperor, in the twelfth century, every known Giustiniani was slain, and the heroic strain seemed lost forever. But the State that mourned them bethought itself of a half-forgotten monk of their house, who was wasting his life in the Convent of San Nicolò; he was drawn forth from this seclusion, and, the permission of Rome being won, he was married to the daughter of the reigning Doge. From then descended the Giustiniani of aftertimes, who still exist; indeed, in the year 1865 there came one day a gentleman of the family, and tried to buy from our landlord that part of the palace which we so humbly and insufficiently inhabited. It is said that as the unfrocked friar and his wife declined in life, they separated, and, as if in doubt of what had been done for the State through them, retired each into a convent, Giustiniani going back to San Nicolò, and dying at last to the murmur of the Adriatic waves along the Lido's sands.

Next after this Giustiniani I like best to think of that latest hero of the family who had the sad fortune to live when the ancient Republic fell at a threat of Napoleon, and who alone among her nobles had the courage to meet with a manly spirit the insolent menaces of the conqueror. The Giustiniani governed Treviso for the Senate; he refused, when Napoleon ordered him from his presence, to quit Treviso without the command of the Senate; he flung back the taunts of bad faith cast upon the Venetians; and when Napoleon changed his tone from that of disdain to one of compliment, and promised that in the general disaster he was preparing for Venice Giustiniani should be spared, the latter generously replied that he had been a friend of the French only because the Senate was so; as to the immunity offered, all was lost to him in the loss of his country, and he should blush for his wealth if it remained intact amidst the ruin of his countrymen.

The family grew in riches and renown from age to age, and, some four centuries after the marriage of the monk, they reared the three beautiful Gothic palaces, in the noblest site on the Grand Canal, whence on one hand you can look down to the Rialto Bridge, and on the other far up towards the church of the Salute and the Basin of Saint Mark. The architects were those Buoni, father and son, who did some of the most beautiful work on the Ducal Palace, and who wrought in an equal inspiration upon these homes of the Giustiniani, building the delicate Gothic arches of the windows, with their slender columns and their graceful balconies, and crowning all with the airy battlements.

The largest of the three palaces became later the property of the Foscari family, and here dwelt with his father that unhappy Jacopo Foscari, who after thrice suffering torture by the State for a murder he never did, at last died in exile; hither came the old Doge Foscari, who had consented to this cruel error of the State, and who after a life spent in its service was deposed and disgraced before his death; and hither, when he lay dead, came remorseful Venice, and claimed for sumptuous obsequies the dust which his widow yielded with bitter reproaches. Here the family faded away generation by generation, till (according to the tale told us) early in this century, when the ultimate male survivor of the line had died, under a false name, in London, where he had been some sort of obscure actor, there were but two old maiden sisters left, who, lapsing into imbecility, were shown to strangers by the rascal servants as the last of the Foscari; and here in our time was quartered a regiment of Austrian troops, whose neatly pipe-clayed belts decorated the balconies on which the princely ladies of the house had rested their jewelled arms in other days.

The Foscari added a story to the palace to distinguish it from the two other palaces Giustiniani, but these remain to the present day as they were originally planned. That in which we lived was called Palazzo Giustiniani of the Bishops, because one of the family was the first Patriarch of Venice. After his death he was made a saint by the Pope; and it is related that he was not only a very pious, but a very good man. In his late hours he admitted his beloved people to his chamber, where he meekly lay upon a pallet of straw, and at the moment he expired, two monks in the solitude of their cloister heard an angelical harmony in the air: the clergy performed his obsequies not in black, funereal robes, but in white garments, and crowned with laurel, and bearing gilded torches, and although the Patriarch had died of a malignant fever, his body was miraculously preserved incorrupt during the sixty-five days that the obsequies lasted. The other branch of the family was called the Giustiniani of the Jewels, from the splendor of their dress; but neither palace now shelters any of their magnificent race. The edifice on our right was exclusively occupied by a noble Viennese lady, who, as we heard,—vaguely, in the right Venetian fashion,—had been a ballet-dancer in her youth, and who now in her matronly days dwelt apart from her husband, the Russian count, and had gondoliers in blue silk, and the finest gondola on the Grand Canal, but was a plump, florid lady, looking long past beauty, even as we saw her from our balcony.

Our own palace—as we absurdly grew to call it—was owned and inhabited in a manner much more proper to modern Venice, the proprietorship being about equally divided between our own landlord and a very well known Venetian painter, son of a painter still more famous. This artist was a very courteous old gentleman, who went with Italian and clock-like regularity every evening in summer to a certain *caffè*, where he seemed to make it a point of conscience to sip one sherbet, and to read the Journal des Débats. In his coming and going we met him so often that we became friends, and he asked us many times to visit him, and see his father's pictures, and some famous frescos with which his part of the palace was adorned. It was a characteristic trait of our life, that though we constantly meant to avail outselves of this kindness, we never did so. But we continued in the enjoyment of the beautiful garden which this gentleman owned at the rear of the palace and on which our chamber windows looked. It was full of oleanders and roses, and other bright and odorous blooms, which we could enjoy perfectly well without knowing their names; and I could hardly say whether the garden was more charming when it was in its summer glory, or when, on some rare winter day, a breath from the mountains had clothed its tender boughs and sprays with a light and evanescent flowering of snow. At any season the lofty palace walls rose over it, and shut it in a pensive seclusion which was loved by the old mother of the painter and by his elderly maiden sister. These often walked on its moss-grown paths, silent as the roses and oleanders to which one could have fancied the blossoms of their youth had flown; and sometimes there came to them there grave, black-gowned priests,—for the painter's was a devout family,—and talked with them in tones almost as tranquil as the silence was, save when one of the ecclesiastics placidly took snuff,—it is a dogma of the Church for priests to take snuff in Italy,—and thereafter, upon a prolonged search for his handkerchief, blew a resounding nose. So far as we knew, the garden walls circumscribed the whole life of these ladies; and I am afraid that such topics of this world as they touched upon with their priests must have been deplorably small.

Their kinsman owned part of the story under us, and both of the stories above us; he had the advantage of the garden over our landlord; but he had not so grand a gondola-gate as we, and in some other respects I incline to think that our part of the edifice was the finer. It is certain that no mention is made of any such beautiful hall in the property of the painter as is noted in that of our landlord, by the historian of a Hundred Palaces of Venice,—a work for which I subscribed, and then for my merit was honored by a visit from the author, who read aloud to me in a deep and sonorous voice the annals of our temporary home. This hall occupied half the space of the whole floor; but it was altogether surrounded by rooms of various shapes and sizes, except upon one side of its length, where it gave, through Gothic windows of vari-colored glass, upon a small court below,—a green-mouldy little court, further dampened by a cistern, which had the usual curb of a single carven block of marble. The roof of this stately *sala* was traversed by a long series of painted rafters, which in the halls of nearly all Venetian palaces are left exposed, and painted or carved and gilded. A suite of stately rooms closed the hall from the Grand Canal, and one of these formed our parlor; on the side opposite the Gothic windows was a vast aristocratic kitchen, which, with its rows of shining coppers, its great chimney-place well advanced toward the middle of the floor, and its tall gloomy windows, still affects my imagination as one of the most patrician rooms which I ever saw; at the back of the hall were those chambers of ours overlooking the garden of which I have already spoken, and another kitchen, less noble than the first, but still sufficiently grandiose to make most New World kitchens seem very meekly minute and unimpressive. Between the two kitchens was another court, with another cistern, from which the painter's family drew water with a bucket on a long rope, which, when let down from the fourth story, appeared to be dropped from the clouds, and descended with a noise little less alarming than thunder.

Altogether the most surprising object in the great *sala* was a sewing-machine, and we should have been inconsolably outraged by its presence there, amid so much that was merely venerable and beautiful, but for the fact that it was in a state of harmonious and hopeless disrepair, and, from its general contrivance, gave us the idea that it had never been of any use. It was, in fact, kept as a sort of curiosity by the landlord, who exhibited it to the admiration of his Venetian friends.

The reader will doubtless have imagined, from what I have been saying, that the Palazzo Giustiniani had not all that machinery which we know in our houses here as modern improvements. It had nothing of the kind, and life there was, as in most houses in Italy, a kind of permanent camping out. When I remember the small amount of carpeting, of furniture, and of upholstery we enjoyed, it appears to me pathetic; and yet, I am not sure that it was not the wisest way to live. I know that we had compensation in things not purchasable here for money. If the furniture of the principal bedroom was somewhat scanty, its dimensions were unstinted, the ceiling was fifteen feet high, and was divided into rich and heavy panels, adorned each with a mighty rosette of carved and gilded wood two feet across. The parlor had not its original decorations in our time, but it had once had so noble a carved ceiling that it was found worth while to take it down and sell it into England; and it still had two grand Venetian mirrors, a vast and very good painting of a miracle of St. Anthony, and imitation-antique tables and arm-chairs. The last were frolicked all over with carven nymphs and cupids; but they were of such frail construction that they were not meant to be sat in much less to be removed from the wall against which they stood; and more than one of our American visitors was dismayed at having these proud articles of furniture go to pieces upon his attempt to use them like mere arm-chairs of ordinary life. Scarcely less impressive or useless than these was a monumental plaster-stove, surmounted by a bust of Æsculapius; when this was broken by accident, we cheaply repaired the loss with a bust of Homer (the dealer in the next campo being out of Æsculapiuses) which no one could have told from the bust it replaced; and this and the other artistic glories of the room made us quite forget all possible blemishes and defects. And will the reader mention any house with modern improvements in America which has also windows, with pointed arches of marble, opening upon balconies that overhang the Grand Canal?

For our new apartment, which consisted of six rooms, furnished with every article necessary for Venetian housekeeping, we paid one dollar a day, which in the innocence of our hearts we thought rather dear, though we were somewhat consoled by reflecting that this extravagant outlay secured us the finest position on the Grand Canal. We did not mean to keep house as we had in Casa Falier, and perhaps a sketch of our easier *ménage* may not be out of place. Breakfast was prepared in the house, for in that blessed climate all you care for in the morning is a cup of coffee, with a little bread and butter, a musk-melon, and some clusters of white grapes, more or less. Then we had our dinners sent in warm from a cook's who had learned his noble art in France; he furnished a

dinner of five courses for three persons at a cost of about eighty
cents; and they were dinners so happily conceived and so justly
executed, that I cannot accuse myself of an excess of sentiment
when I confess that I sigh for them to this day. Then as for our
immaterial tea, we always took that at the Caffè Florian in the
Piazza of Saint Mark, where we drank a cup of black coffee and
ate an ice, while all the world promenaded by and the Austrian
bands made heavenly music.

Those bands no longer play in Venice, and I believe that they
are not the only charm which she has lost in exchanging Austrian
servitude for Italian freedom; though I should be sorry to think
that freedom was not worth all other charms. The poor Venetians
used to be very rigorous (as I have elsewhere related) about the
music of their oppressors, and would not come into the Piazza
until it had ceased and the Austrian promenaders had disappeared,
when they sat down at Florian's, and listened to such bands of
strolling singers and minstrels as chose to give them a concord of
sweet sounds, without foreign admixture. We, in our neutrality,
were wont to sit out both entertainments, and then go home well
toward midnight, through the sleepy little streets, and over the
bridges that spanned the narrow canals, dreaming in the shadows
of the palaces.

We moved with half-conscious steps till we came to the silver
expanse of the Grand Canal, where, at the ferry, darkled a little
brood of black gondolas, into one of which we got, and were
rowed noiselessly to the thither side, where we took our way
toward the land-gate of our palace through the narrow streets of
the parish of San Barnabà, and the campo before the ugly façade
of the church; or else we were rowed directly to the water-gate,
where we got out on the steps worn by the feet of the Giustiniani
of old, and wandered upward through the darkness of the
stairway, which gave them a far different welcome of servants and
lights when they returned from an evening's pleasure in the Piazza.
It seemed scarcely just; but then those Giustiniani were dead, and
we were alive, and that was one advantage; and, besides, the
loneliness and desolation of the palace had a peculiar charm, and

were at any rate cheaper than its former splendor could have been. I am afraid that people who live abroad in the palaces of extinct nobles do not keep this important fact sufficiently in mind; and as the Palazzo Giustiniani is still let in furnished lodgings, and it is quite possible that some of my readers may be going to spend next summer in it, I venture to remind them that if they have to draw somewhat upon their fancy for patrician accommodations there, it will cost them far less in money than it did the original proprietors, who contributed to our selfish pleasure by the very thought of their romantic absence and picturesque decay. In fact, the Past is everywhere like the cake of proverb: you cannot enjoy it and have it.

And here I am reminded of another pleasure of modern dwellers in Venetian palaces, which could hardly have been indulged by the patricians of old, and which is hardly imaginable by people of this day, whose front doors open upon dry land: I mean to say the privilege of sea-bathing from one's own threshold. From the beginning of June till far into September all the canals of Venice are populated by the amphibious boys, who clamor about in the brine, or poise themselves for a leap from the tops of bridges or show their fine, statuesque figures bronzed by the ardent sun, against the façades of empty palaces, where they hover among the marble sculptures, and meditate a headlong plunge. It is only the Venetian ladies, in fact, who do not share this healthful amusement. Fathers of families, like so many plump, domestic drakes, lead forth their aquatic broods, teaching the little ones to swim by the aid of various floats, and delighting in the gambols of the larger ducklings. When the tide comes in fresh and strong from the sea the water in the Grand Canal is pure and refreshing; and at these times it is a singular pleasure to leap from one's door-step into the swift current, and spend a half-hour, very informally, among one's neighbors there. The Venetian bathing-dress is a mere sketch of the pantaloons of ordinary life; and when I used to stand upon our balcony, and see some bearded head ducking me a polite salutation from a pair of broad, brown shoulders that showed above the water, I was not always able to recognize my acquaintance, deprived of his factitious identity of clothes. But I always knew a certain stately consul-general by a vast expanse of baldness upon the top of his head; and it must be owned, I think, that this form of social assembly was, with all its disadvantages, a novel and vivacious spectacle. The Venetian ladies, when they bathed, went to the Lido, or else to the bath-houses in front of the Ducal Palace, where they saturated themselves a good part of the day, and drank coffee, and, possibly, gossiped.

I think that our balconies at Palazzo Giustiniani were even better places to see the life of the Grand Canal from than the balcony of Casa Falier, which we had just left. Here at least we had a greater stretch of the Canal, looking, as we could, up either side of its angle. Here, too, we had more gondola stations in sight, and as we were nearer the Rialto, there was more picturesque passing of the market-boats. But if we saw more of ths life, we did not see it in greater variety, for I think we had already exhausted this. There was a movement all night long. If I woke at three or four o'clock, and offered myself the novel spectacle of the Canal at that hour, I saw the heavy-laden barges go by to the Rialto, with now and then also a good-sized coasting schooner making lazily for the lagoons, with its ruddy fire already kindled for cooking the morning's meal, and looking very enviably cosey. After our own breakfast we began to watch for the gondolas of the tourists of different nations, whom we came to distinguish at a glance. Then the boats of the various artisans went by, the carpenter's, the mason's, the plasterer's, with those that sold fuel, and vegetables, and fruit, and fish, to any household that arrested them. From noon till three or four o'clock the Canal was comparatively deserted; but before twilight it was thronged again by people riding out in their open gondolas to take the air after the day's fervor. After nightfall they ceased, till only at long intervals a solitary lamp, stealing over the dark surface gave token of the movement of some gondola bent upon an errand that could not fail to seem mysterious or fail to be matter of fact. We never wearied of this oft-repeated variety, nor of our balcony in any way; and when the moon shone in through the lovely arched window and sketched its exquisite outline on the floor, we were as happy as moonshine could make us.

Were we otherwise content? As concerns Venice, it is very hard to say, and I do not know that I shall ever be able to say with certainty. For all the entertainment it afforded us, it was a very lonely life, and we felt the sadness of the city in many fine and not instantly recognizable ways. Englishmen who lived there bade us beware of spending the whole year in Venice, which they declared apt to result in a morbid depression of the spirits. I believe they attributed this to the air of the place, but I think it was more than half owing to her mood, to her old, ghostly, aimless life. She was, indeed, a phantom of the past, haunting our modern world,— serene, inexpressibly beautiful, yet inscrutably and unspeakably sad. Remembering the charm that was in her, we often sigh for the renewal of our own vague life there,—a shadow within the shadow; but remembering also her deep melancholy, an involuntary shiver creeps over us, and we are glad not to be there. Perhaps some of you who have spent a summer day or a summer week in Venice do not recognize this feeling; but if you will remain there, not four years as we did, but a year of six months even, it will ever afterwards be only too plain. All changes, all events, were affected by the inevitable local melancholy; the day was as pensive amidst that populous silence as the night; the winter not more pathetic than the long, tranquil, lovely summer. We rarely sentimentalized consciously, and still more seldom openly, about the present state of Venice as contrasted with her past glory. I am glad to say that we despised the conventional poetastery about her; but I believe that we had so far lived into sympathy with her, that, whether we realized it or not, we took the tone of her dispiritedness, and assumed a part of the common experience of loss and of hopelessness. History, if you live where it was created, is a far subtler influence than you suspect; and I would not say how much Venetian history, amidst the monuments of her glory and the witnesses of her fall, had to do in secret and tacit ways with the prevailing sentiment of existence, which I now distinctly recognize to have been a melancholy one. No doubt this sentiment was deepened by every freshly added association with memorable places; and each fact, each great name and career, each strange tradition as it rose out of the past for us and shed its pale lustre upon the present, touched us with a pathos which we could neither trace nor analyze.

I do not know how much the modern Venetians had to do with this impression, but something I have no question. They were then under Austrian rule; and in spite of much that was puerile and theatrical in it, there was something very affecting in their attitude of what may best be described as passive defiance. This alone made them heroic, but it also made them tedious. They rarely talked of anything but politics; and as I have elsewhere said, they were very jealous to have every one declare himself of their opinion. Hemmed in by this jealousy on one side, and by a heavy and rebellious sense of the wrongful presence of the Austrian troops and the Austrian spies on the other, we forever felt dimly constrained by something, we could not say precisely what, and we only knew what, when we went sometimes on a journey into free Italy, and threw off the irksome caution we had maintained both as to patriotic and alien tyrants. This political misery circumscribed acquaintance very much, and reduced the circle of our friendship to three or four families, who were content to know our sympathies without exacting constant expression of them. So we learned to depend mainly upon passing Americans for our society; we hailed with rapture the arrival of a gondola distinguished by the easy hats of our countrymen and the pretty faces and pretty dresses of our countrywomen. It was in the days of our war; and talking together over its events, we felt a brotherhood with every other American.

Of course, in these circumstances, we made thorough acquaintance with the people about us in the palace. The landlord had come somehow into a profitable knowledge of Anglo-Saxon foibles and susceptibilities; but his lodgings were charming, and I recognize the principle that it is not for literature to make its prey of any possibly conscious object. For this reason, I am likewise mostly silent concerning a certain *attaché* of the palace, the right-hand man and intimate associate of the landlord. He was the descendant of one of the most ancient and noble families of Italy,—a family of popes and cardinals, of princes and ministers, which in him was diminished and tarnished in an almost inexplicable degree. He was not at all worldly-wise, but he was a man of great learning, and of a capacity for acquiring knowledge that I have never seen surpassed. He possessed, I think, not many shirts on earth; but he spoke three or four languages, and wrote very pretty sonnets in Italian and German. He was one of the friendliest and willingest souls living, and as generous as utter destitution can make a man; yet he had a proper spirit, and valued himself upon his name. Sometimes he brought his great-grandfather to the palace; a brisk old gentleman in his nineties, who had seen the fall of the Republic and three other revolutions in Venice, but had contrived to keep a government pension through it all, and now smiled with unabated cheerfulness upon a world which he seemed likely never to leave.

The palace-servants were two, the gondolier and a sort of housekeeper,—a handsome, swarthy woman, with beautiful white teeth and liquid black eyes. She was the mother of a pretty little boy, who was going to bring himself up for a priest, and whose chief amusement was saying mimic masses to an imaginary congregation. She was perfectly statuesque and obliging, and we had no right, as lovers of the beautiful or as lodgers, to complain of her, whatever her faults might have been. As to the gondolier, who was a very important personage in our palatial household, he was a handsome, bashful, well-mannered fellow, with a good-natured blue eye and a neatly waxed mustache. He had been ten years a soldier in the Austrian army, and was, from his own account and from all I saw of him, one of the least courageous men in the world; but then no part of the Austrian system tends to make men brave, and I could easily imagine that before it had done with one it might give him reasons enough to be timid all the rest of his life. Piero had not very much to do, and he spent the greater part of his leisure in a sort of lazy flirtation with the women about the kitchen fire, or in the gondola, in which he

sometimes gave them the air. We always liked him; I should have
trusted him in any sort of way, except one that involved danger.
It once happened that burglars attempted to enter our rooms, and
Piero declared to us that he knew the men; but before the police,
he swore that he knew nothing about them. Afterwards he
returned privately to his first assertion, and accounted for his
conduct by saying that if he had borne witness against the
burglars, he was afraid that their friends would jump on his back
(*saltarmi adosso*), as he phrased it, in the dark; for by this sort of
terrorism the poor and the wicked have long been bound together
in Italy. Piero was a humorist in his dry way, and made a jest of
his own caution; but his favorite joke was, when he dressed
himself with particular care, to tell the women that he was going
to pay a visit to the Princess Clary, then the star of Austrian
society. This mild pleasantry was repeated indefinitely with
never-failing effect.

More interesting to us than all the rest was our own servant,
Bettina, who came to us from a village on the main-land. She was
very dark, so dark and so Southern in appearance as almost to
verge upon the negro type; yet she bore the English-sounding
name of Scarbro, and how she ever came by it remains a puzzle to
this day, for she was one of the most pure and entire of Italians.
I mean this was her maiden name; she was married to a trumpeter
in the Austrian service, whose Bohemian name she was unable to
pronounce, and consequently never gave us She was a woman of
very few ideas indeed, but perfectly honest and good-hearted. She
was pious, in her peasant fashion, and in her walks about the city
did not fail to bless the baby before every picture of the Madonna.
She provided it with an engraved portrait of that Holy Nail which
was venerated in the neighboring church of San Pantaleon; and
she apparently aimed to supply it with playthings of a religious
and saving character, like tht piece of ivory which resembled a
small torso, and which Bettina described as "A bit of the Lord,
Signor," and it was, in fact, a fragment of an ivory crucifix, which
she had somewhere picked up. To Bettina's mind, mankind
broadly divided themselves into two races, Italians and Germans,

to which latter she held that we Americans in some sort belonged. She believed that America lay a little to the south of Vienna, and in her heart I think she was persuaded that the real national complexion was black, and that the innumerable white Americans she saw at our house were merely a multitude of exceptions. But with all her ignorance, she had no superstitions of a gloomy kind: the only ghost she seemed ever to have heard of was the spectre of an American ship captain which a friend of Piero's had seen at the Lido. She was perfectly kind and obedient, and was deeply attached in an inarticulate way to the baby, which was indeed the pet of the whole palace. This young lady ruled arbitrarily over them all, and was forever being kissed and adored. When Piero went out to the wine-shop for a little temperate dissipation, he took her with him on his shoulder, and exhibited her to the admiring gondoliers of his acquaintance; there was no puppet-show, no church festival, in that region to which she was not carried; and when Bettina, and Giulia, and all the idle women of the neighborhood assembled on a Saturday afternoon in the narrow alley behind the palace (where they dressed one another's thick black hair in fine braids soaked in milk, and built it up to last the whole of the next week), the baby was the cynosure of all hearts and eyes. But her supremacy was yet more distinguished when, late at night, the household gave itself a feast of snails stewed in oil and garlic in the vast kitchen. There her anxious parents have found her seated in the middle of the table with the bowl of snails before her, and armed with a great spoon, while her vassals sat round, and grinned their fondness and delight in her small tyrannies; and the immense room, dimly lit, with the mystical implements of cookery glimmering from the wall, showed like some witch's cavern, where a particularly small sorceress was presiding over the concoction of an evil potion or the weaving of a powerful spell.

From time to time we had fellow-lodgers, who were always more or less interesting and mysterious. Among the rest there was once a French lady, who languished, during her stay, under the disfavor of the police, and for whose sake there was a sentinel with a fixed bayonet stationed day and night at the palace gate. At last, one night, this French lady escaped by a rope-ladder from her chamber window, and thus no doubt satisfied alike the female instinct for intrigue and elopement and the political agitator's love of a mysterious disappearance. It was understood dimly that she was an author, and had written a book displeasing to the police.

Then there was the German baroness and her son and daughter, the last very beautiful and much courted by handsome Austrian officers; the son rather weak-minded, and a great care to his sister and mother, from his propensity to fall in love and marry below his station; the mother very red-faced and fat, a good-natured old creature who gambled the summer months away at Hombourg and Baden, and in the winter resorted to Venice to make a match for her pretty daughter.

Then, moreover, there was that English family, between whom and ourselves there was the reluctance and antipathy, personal and national, which exists between all right-minded Englishmen and Americans. No Italian can understand this just and natural condition, and it was the constant aim of our landlord to make us acquainted. So one day when he found a member of each of these unfriendly families on the neutral ground of the grand *sala*, he introduced them. They had, happily, the piano-forte between them, and I flatter myself that the insulting coldness and indifference with which they received each other's names carried to our landlord's bosom a dismay never before felt by a good-natured and well-meaning man.

The piano-forte which I have mentioned belonged to the landlord, who was fond of music and of all fine and beautiful things; and now and then he gave a musical *soirée,* which was attended, more or less surreptitiously, by the young people of his acquaintance. I do not think he was always quite candid in giving his invitations, for on one occasion a certain count, who had taken refuge from the glare of the *sala* in our parlor for the purpose of concealing the very loud-plaided pantaloons he wore, explained pathetically that he had been so long out of society, for patriotic reasons, that he had no longer a dress suit. But to us they were very delightful entertainments, no less from the great variety of character they afforded than from the really charming and excellent music which the different amateurs made; for we had airs from all the famous operas, and the instrumentation was by a gifted young composer. Besides, the gayety seemed to recall in some degree the old, brilliant life of the palace, and at least showed us how well it was adapted to social magnificence and display.

We enjoyed our whole year in Palazzo Giustiniani, though some of the days were too long and some too short, as everywhere. From heat we hardly suffered at all, so perfectly did the vast and lofty rooms answer to the purpose of their builders in this respect. A current of sea air drew through to the painter's garden by day, and by night there was scarcely a mosquito of the myriads that infested some parts of Venice. In winter it was not so well. Then we shuffled about in wadded gowns and boots lined with sheep-skin,—the woolly side in, as in the song. The passage of the *sala* was something to be dreaded, and we shivered as fleetly through it as we could, and were all the colder for the deceitful warmth of the colors which the sun cast upon the stone floor from the window opening on the court.

I do not remember any one event of our life more exciting than that attempted burglary of which I have spoken. In a city where the police gave their best attention to political offenders, there were naturally a great many rogues, and the Venetian rogues, if not distinguished for the more heroic crimes, were very skilful in what I may call the *genre* branch of robbing rooms through open windows, and committing all kinds of safe domestic depredations. It was judged best to acquaint Justice (as they call law in Latin countries) with the attempt upon our property, and I found her officers housed in a small room of the Doge's palace, clerkly men in velvet skull-caps driving loath quills over the rough official paper of those regions. After an exchange of diplomatic courtesies, the commissary took my statement of the affair down in writing, pertinent to which were my father's name, place, and business, with a full and satisfactory personal history of myself down to the period of the attempted burglary. This, I said, occurred one morning about daylight, when I saw the head of the burglar peering above the window-sill, and the hand of the burglar extended to prey upon my wardrobe.

"Excuse me, Signor Console," interrupted the commissary, "how could you see him?"

"Why, there was nothing in the world to prevent me. The window was open?"

"The window was open!" gasped the commissary. "Do you mean that you sleep with your windows open?"

"Most certainly!'

"Pardon!" said the commissary, suspiciously. "Do *all* Americans sleep with their windows open?"

"I may venture to say that they all do, in summer," I answered; "at least, it's the general custom."

Such a thing as this indulgence in fresh air seemed altogether foreign to the commissary's experience; and but for my official dignity, I am sure that I should have been effectually browbeaten by him. As it was, he threw himself back in his arm-chair and stared at me fixedly for some moments. Then he recovered himself with another "*Perdoni!*" and, turning to his clerk, said, "Write down that, *according to the American custom,* they were sleeping with their windows open." But I know that the commissary, for all his politeness, considered this habit a relic of the times when we Americans all abode in wigwams; and I suppose it paralyzed his energies in the effort to bring the burglars to justice, for I have never heard anything of them from that day to this.

The truth is, it was a very uneventful year; and I am the better satisfied with it as an average Venetian year on that account. We sometimes varied the pensive monotony by a short visit to the cities of the main-land; but we always came back to it willingly, and I think we unconsciously abhorred any interruption of it. The days, as they followed each other, were wonderfully alike, in every respect. For eight months of summer they were alike in their clear-skied, sweet-breathed loveliness; in the autumn, there where the melancholy of the falling leaf could not spread its contagion to the sculptured foliage of Gothic art, the days were alike in their sentiment of tranquil oblivion and resignation, which was as autumnal as any aspect of woods or fields could have been; in the winter they were alike in their dreariness and discomfort. As I remember, we spent by far the greater part of our time in going to the Piazza, and we were devoted Florianisti, as the Italians call those that lounge habitually at the Caffè Florian. We went every evening to the Piazza, as a matter of course; if the morning was long, we went to the Piazza; if we did not know what to do with the afternoon, we went to the Piazza; if we had friends with us, we went to the Piazza; if we were alone, we went to the Piazza; and there was no mood or circumstances in which it did not seem a natural and fitting thing to go to the Piazza. There were all the prettiest shops; there were all the finest *caffès;* there was the incomparable Church of St. Mark; there was the whole world of Venice.

Of course, we had other devices besides going to the Piazza; and sometimes we spent entire weeks in visiting the churches, one after another, and studying their artistic treasures, down to the smallest scrap of an old master in their darkest chapel; their history, their storied tombs, their fictitious associations. Very few churches escaped, I believe, except such as had been turned into barracks, and were guarded by an incorruptible Austrian sentinel. For such churches as did escape, we have a kind of envious longing to this day, and should find it hard to like anybody who had succeeded better in visiting them. There is, for example, the church of San Giobbe, the doors of which we haunted with more patience than that of the titulary saint: now the sacristan was out; now the church was shut up for repairs; now it was Holy Week and the pictures were veiled; we had to leave Venice at last without a sight of San Giobbe's three Saints by Bordone, and Madonna by Bellini, which, unseen, outvalue all the other Saints and Madonnas that we looked at; and I am sure that life can never become so aimless, but we shall still have the desire of some day going to see the church of San Giobbe. If we read some famous episode of Venetian history, we made it the immediate care of our lives to visit the scene of its occurrence; if Ruskin told us of some recondite beauty of sculpture hid away in some unthought-of palace court, we invaded that palace at once; if in entirely purposeless strolls through the city we came upon anything that touched the fancy or piqued curiosity, there was no gate or bar proof against our bribes. What strange old nests of ruin, what marvelous homes of solitude and dilapidation, did we not wander into! What boarded-up windows peer through, what gloomy recesses penetrate! I have lumber enough in my memory stored from such rambles to load the nightmares of a generation, and stuff for the dreams of a whole people. Does any gentleman or lady wish to write a romance? Sir or madam, I know just the mouldy and sunless alley for your villain to stab his victim in, the canal in which to plunge his body, the staircase and the hall for the subsequent wanderings of his ghost; and all these scenes and localities I will sell at half the cost price; as also, balconies for flirtation, gondolas for intrigue and elopement, confessionals for the betrayal of guilty secrets. I have an assortment of bad and beautiful faces and picturesque attitudes and effective tones of voice; and a large stock of sympathetic sculptures and furniture and dresses, with other articles too numerous to mention, all warranted Venetian, and suitable to every style of romance. Who bids? Nay, I cannot sell, nor you buy. Each memory, as I hold it up for inspection, loses its subtle beauty and value, and turns common and poor in my hawker's fingers.

Yet I must needs try to fix here the remembrance of two or three palaces, of which our fancy took the fondest hold, and to which it yet most fondly clings. It cannot locate them all, and least of all can it place that vast old palace, somewhere near Cannaregio, which faced upon a *campo*, with lofty windows blinded by rough boards, and empty from top to bottom. It was of the later Renaissance in style, and we imagined it built in the Republic's declining years by some ruinous noble, whose extravagance forbade his posterity to live in it, for it had that peculiarly forlorn air which belongs to a thing decayed without being worn out. We entered its coolness and dampness, and wandered up the wide marble staircase, past the vacant niches of departed statuary, and came on the third floor to a grand portal which was closed against us by a barrier of lumber. But this could not hinder us from looking within, and we were aware that we stood upon the threshold of our ruinous noble's great banqueting-hall, where he used to give his magnificent *feste da ballo*. Lustrissimo was long gone with all his guests; but there in the roof were the amazing frescos of Tiepolo's school, which had smiled down on them, as now they smiled on us; great piles of architecture, airy tops of palaces, swimming in summer sky, and wantoned over by a joyous populace of divinities of the lovelier sex that had nothing but their loveliness to clothe them and keep them afloat; the whole grandiose and superb beyond the effect of words, and luminous with delicious color. How it all rioted there with its inextinguishable beauty in the solitude and silence, from day to day, from year to year, while men died, and systems passed, and nothing remained unchanged but the instincts of youth and love that inspired it! It was music and wine and wit; it was so warm and glowing that it made the sunlight cold; and it seemed ever after a secret of gladness and beauty that the sad old palace was keeping in its heart against the time to which Venice looks forward when her splendor and opulence shall be indestructibly renewed.

There is a ball-room in the Palazzo Pisani, which some of my readers may have passed through on their way to the studio of the charming old Prussian painter, Nerlÿ; the frescos of this are dim and faded and dusty, and impress you with a sense of irreparable decay, but the noble proportions and the princely air of the place are inalienable, while the palace stands. Here might have danced that Contarini who, when his wife's necklace of pearls fell upon the floor in the way of her partner, the King of Denmark, advanced and ground it into powder with his foot, that the king might not be troubled to avoid treading on it; and here, doubtless, many a gorgeous masquerade had been in the long Venetian carnival; and what passion and intrigue and jealousy, who knows? Now the palace was let in apartments, and was otherwise a barrack, and in the great court, steadfast as any of the marble statues, stood the Austrian sentinel. One of the statues was a figure veiled from head to foot, at the base of which it was hard not to imagine lovers, masked and hooded, and forever hurriedly whispering their secrets in the shadow cast in perpetual moonlight.

Yet another ball-room in yet another palace opens to memory, but this is all bright and fresh with recent decoration. In the blue vaulted roof shine stars of gold; the walls are gay with dainty frescos; a gallery encircles the whole, and from this drops a light stairway, slim-railed, and guarded at the foot by torch-bearing statues of swarthy Eastern girls; through the glass doors at the other side glimmers the green and red of a garden. It was a place to be young in, to dance in, dream in, make love in; but it was no more a surprise than the whole palace to which it belonged, and which there in that tattered and poverty-stricken old Venice was a vision of untarnished splendor and prosperous fortune. It was richly furnished throughout all its vast extent, adorned with every caprice and delight of art, and appointed with every modern comfort. The foot was hushed by costly carpets, the eye was flattered by a thousand beauties and prettinesses. In the grates the fires were laid and ready to be lighted; the candles stood upon the mantels; the toilet-linen was arranged for instant use in the luxurious chambers; but from the basement to roof the palace was in solitude; no guest came there, no one dwelt there save the custodian; the eccentric lady of whose possessions it formed a part abode in a little house behind the palace, and on her door-plate had written her *vanitas vanitatum* in the sarcastic inscription, "John Humdrum, Esquire."

Of course she was Inglese; and that other lady, who was selling off the furniture of her palace, and was so amiable a guide to its wonder in her curious broken English was Hungarian. Her great pride and joy amidst the objects of *vertu* and the works of art, was a set of "Punch," which she made us admire, and which she prized the more because she had always been allowed to receive it when the government prohibited it to everybody else. But we were Americans, she said; and had we ever seen this book? She held up the "The Potiphar Papers," a volume which must have been inexpressibly amused and bewildered to find itself there, in that curious little old lady's hand.

Shall I go on and tell of the palace in which our strange friend Padre L—— dwelt, and the rooms of which he had filled up with the fruits of his passion for the arts and sciences; the ante-room he had frescoed to represent a grape-arbor with a multitude of clusters overhead; the parlor with his oil-paintings on the walls, and the piano and melodeon arranged so that Padre L—— could play upon them both at once; the oratory turned forge and harboring the most alchemic-looking apparatus of all kinds; the other rooms in which he had stored his inventions in portable furniture, steam-propulsion, rifled cannon, and perpetual motion; the attic with the camera by which one could photograph one's self,—shall I tell of this, and yet other palaces? I think there is enough already; and I have begun to doubt somewhat the truth of my reminiscences, as I advise the reader to do.

Besides, I feel tht the words fail to give all the truth that is in them; and if I cannot make them serve my purpose as to the palaces, how should I hope to impart through them my sense of the glory and loveliness of Venetian art? I could not give the imagination and the power of Tintoretto as we felt it, nor the serene beauty, the gracious luxury of Titian, nor the opulence, the worldly magnificence of Paolo Veronese. There hang their mighty works forever, high above the reach of any palaverer; they smile their stately welcome from the altars and palace-walls, upon whoever approaches them in the sincerity and love of beauty that produced them; and thither you must thus go if you would know them. Like fragments of dreams, like the fleeting

"Images of glimmering dawn,"

I am from time to time aware, amid the work-day world, of some happiness from them, some face or form, some drift of a princely robe or ethereal drapery, some august shape of painted architecture, some unnamable delight of color; but to describe them more strictly and explicitly, how should I undertake?

There was the exhaustion following every form of intense pleasure, in their contemplation, such a wear of vision and thought, that I could not call the life we led in looking at them an idle one, even if it had no result in after times; so I will not say that it was to severer occupation our minds turned more and more in our growing desire to return home. For my own part personally I felt keenly the fictitious and transitory character of official life. I knew that if I had become fit to serve the government by four years' residence in Venice, that was a good reason why the government, according to our admirable system, should dismiss me, and send some perfectly unqualified person to take my place; and in my heart also I knew that there was almost nothing for me to do where I was, and I dreaded the easily formed habit of receiving a salary for no service performed. I reminded myself that, soon or late, I must go back to the old fashion of earning money, and that it had better be sooner than later. Therefore, though for some reasons it was the saddest and strangest thing in the world to do, I was on the whole rejoiced when a leave of absence came, and we prepared to quit Venice.

Never had the city seemed so dream-like and unreal as in this light of farewell,—this tearful glimmer which our love and regret cast upon it. As in a maze, we haunted once more and for the last time the scenes we had known so long, and spent our final phantasmal evening in the Piazza; looked, through the moonlight, our mute adieu to islands and lagoons, to church and tower; and then returned to our own palace, and stood long upon the balconies that overhung the Grand Canal. There the future became as incredible and improbable as the past; and if we had often felt the incongruity of our coming to live in such a place, now, with tenfold force, we felt the cruel absurdity of proposing to live anywhere else. We had become part of Venice; and how could such atoms of her fantastic personality ever mingle with the alien and unsympathetic world?

The next morning the whole palace household bestirred itself to accompany us to the station; the landlord in his best hat and coat, our noble friend in phenomenal linen, Giulia and her little boy,

Bettina shedding bitter tears over the baby, and Piero, sad but firm, bending over the oar and driving us swiftly forward. The first turn of the Canal shut the Palazzo Giustiniani from our lingering gaze, a few more curves and windings brought us to the station. The tickets were bought, the baggage was registered; the little oddly assorted company drew itself up in a line, and received with tears our husky adieux. I feared there might be a remote purpose in the hearts of the landlord and his retainer to embrace and kiss me, after the Italian manner, but if there was, by a final inspiration they spared me the ordeal. Piero turned away to his gondola; the two other men moved aside; Bettina gave one long, hungering, devouring hug to the baby; and as we hurried into the waiting-room, we saw her, as upon a stage, standing without the barrier, supported and sobbing in the arms of Giulia.

It was well to be gone, but I cannot say we were glad to be going.

William Dean Howells was born in 1837 in an Ohio town where after hardly more than an introduction to formal studies he began, at the age of nine, to set type in his father's printing shop. When after a number of moves the family settled in Columbus Howells became a journalist. In 1860 he wrote a campaign biography of Lincoln, and Lincoln having won the election, he was rewarded with the job of consul at Venice. This led to *Venetian Life* (1866), his second published book, the first having been one of verse done conjointly with another poet.

In the final decades of his career — he was the editor of important reviews, he was interested in economic questions and had political involvements, he was the author of over twenty novels, six autobiographical volumes, eleven travel books, thirty-one plays for the stage — Howells came to be looked upon, in his own country and abroad, as America's foremost man of letters. He died in 1920.

This book was typeset by
American-Stratford Graphic Services
of Brattleboro, Vermont;
and printed and bound by
McNaughton & Gunn, Inc.,
of Ann Arbor, Michigan.